FIRST COMES
MARRIAGE

My Not-So-Typical
American Love Story

HUDA AL-MARASHI

Prometheus Books

59 John Glenn Drive
Amherst, New York 14228

Cover illustration by Missy Chimovitz
Cover design by Liz Mills
Cover design © Prometheus Books

Chapter 5: Beaten by Devotion adapted from Huda Al-Marashi, "Beaten by Devotion," in *Beyond Belief: The Secret Lives of Women in Extreme Religions*, ed. Susan Tive and Cami Ostman (Berkeley, CA: Seal Press, 2013).

Chapter 11: Lunch Company adapted from Huda Al-Marashi, "Is This a Date?" in *Hippocampus Magazine*, May 1, 2014.

Chapter 14: Say It Loud adapted from Huda Al-Marashi, "Otherwise Engaged," in *Love, InshAllah: The Secret Love Lives of American Muslim Women*, ed. Ayesha Mattu and Nura Maznavi (Berkeley, CA: Soft Skull Press, 2012).

Inquiries should be addressed to
Prometheus Books
59 John Glenn Drive
Amherst, New York 14228
VOICE: 716–691–0133 • FAX: 716–691–0137
WWW.PROMETHEUSBOOKS.COM

22 21 20 19 18   5 4 3 2 1

Library of Congress Cataloging-in-Publication Data

Identifiers: LCCN 2018019607 (print) |
ISBN 9781633884472 (ebook) | ISBN 9781633884465 (hardback)

Printed in the United States of America

To my husband

And among His Signs is this, that He created for you mates from among yourselves, that ye may dwell in tranquility with them, and He has put love and mercy between your (hearts): verily in that are Signs for those who reflect.
—Quran 30:21

CONTENTS

Author's Note   9

BOOK I

Chapter 1: Husband Potential   13
Chapter 2: Muslim Love   17
Chapter 3: A Girl Like That Won't Stay   25
Chapter 4: A Small Island of Unity   31
Chapter 5: Beaten by Devotion   41
Chapter 6: A Divine Crystal Ball   47
Chapter 7: This American Rite of Passage   55
Chapter 8: See Me at the Prom   59
Chapter 9: A Big Family Secret   63
Chapter 10: Marching Toward Marriage   73
Chapter 11: Lunch Company   81
Chapter 12: A Sudden Thrill of Control   87
Chapter 13: The Engagement of Our Children   93
Chapter 14: Say It Loud   103
Chapter 15: Sins for No Good Reason   115
Chapter 16: Every Choke, Sob, and Sniffle   127

CONTENTS

Chapter 17: The Sting of Regret   131

Chapter 18: Women in Islam   141

Chapter 19: A Day for Me and the Girls   145

Chapter 20: The Proof of Our Youth   153

Chapter 21: Crises A, B, and C   167

Chapter 22: A Bride Is with Us   173

Chapter 23: Love Her, Boy, Love Her   179

Chapter 24: Biology   187

BOOK II

Chapter 25: A Big, Fat Arab Stereotype   201

Chapter 26: Trying to Make a Life   209

Chapter 27: The Aspiring Doctor's Wife   215

Chapter 28: An Edible Identification Card   219

Chapter 29: I Love Huda.doc   223

Chapter 30: A Matter of Life and Death and God Himself   233

Chapter 31: Shia Heretic   245

Chapter 32: The Love I Missed   251

Chapter 33: A Family of Three   259

Chapter 34: How to Fix Hadi and Me   273

Chapter 35: Fictions of Love   281

Chapter 36: As If by Magic   287

Acknowledgments   295

AUTHOR'S NOTE

I pored over my old journals and emails in writing this memoir, but what follows on these pages is still its own kind of fiction. A memoirist must make countless trade-offs between what moments to include and exclude, and this very deliberate negotiation creates its own version of the truth. I think this is one of the many reasons why memoirs are so particularly prickly for the people we share our lives with—our stories on the page look so very different from the day in and day out we experience together.

My husband has his own memories of our early years together, and I am grateful not only that he carries around a considerably less angst-ridden version of these events but also that he encouraged me to share mine. At his request, I have changed his name and the names of those related to him. I also gave all other characters, with the exception of those I've lost touch with, the option of using their real names. However, for the sake of clarity, I created composite characters to represent my friends from college.

Last, I relied on the descriptor "American" in many places where it would have been more accurate to specify that I was referring to the dominant American culture or its Anglo-American and Western influences. While I recognize that it is problematic to set myself apart from the American experience in this way, I wanted to use language that most closely resembled how my family and I thought or spoke at the time, and immigrant communities in the United States commonly use the shorthand of "American" to describe their host

society. By extension, I also appreciate that no definable character-
istics apply to the labels "Arab," "Muslim," or "Iraqi," but so as not
to belabor the text with repeated reminders that these are general-
izations, I chose, once again, to mirror what would have been most
natural for me or one of my characters to have said or thought in
each scene.

BOOK I

CHAPTER 1

HUSBAND POTENTIAL

I cannot remember a time when I didn't think of Hadi Ridha as a potential husband. The day my family first met the Ridhas, Mrs. Ridha took one look at me—six years old and my hair in braids—and my baby sister, Lina, and said, "*Mashallah, mashallah*. We don't need to look anymore. We found our pretty girls."

At the time, I didn't know that my father and Dr. Ridha had gone to the same medical school in Baghdad. I didn't know that they'd found each other at an American Academy of Neurology meeting in San Diego and that Dr. Ridha had invited us to his home for dinner. I didn't know that the Ridhas were also Iraqi and Shia, because those were descriptors I still didn't know to apply to myself.

All I knew that day was that the Ridhas were different in the same way we were different. They spoke Arabic with "ch" sounds, replacing the "k" sounds; they ate rice with stews called *marga*; and they kept their five daily prayers, even though Mrs. Ridha, like Mama, did not cover her hair with the hijab. These were my signs that of the two types of boys in the world—those who were possible to marry and those who were impossible—the Ridha boys belonged to the former, the small population of boys from which I'd be allowed to choose a husband.

It was a remarkable discovery for the early 1980s. The only Arab community in our small, seaside Northern California town was a secular social group filled with a mix of Lebanese, Palestinians,

Syrians, and a few Iraqis who had immigrated so long ago they spoke more English than Arabic. No one in my parents' small band of friends was quite like the Ridhas, whose dialect was still so fresh on their tongues, who knew so many other Iraqi immigrant families in the United States, and who matched our family not only in religion and level of devotion but also in ages and interests. The fathers got along. The mothers got along. The Ridha boys played well with my brother, Ibrahim, and Lina and I played well with their daughter, Jamila.

In spite of the four-hundred-mile distance between our Northern and Southern California homes, our families clung to each other. When the Ridhas came to our house, we took day trips to Carmel Beach, Big Sur, and San Francisco. We came back dirty and tired, and waited in line for a turn in one of the two bathrooms in our small ranch home. When my family stayed with the Ridhas, they drove us to Los Angeles County, to their newly founded Islamic center or *masjid*, and to events with the other Iraqi families gradually moving into the area.

By the time my little sister, Lina, was four years old, she'd already intuited that the Ridha boys were the marriageable kind. After a picnic one sunny afternoon in Big Sur, she turned to Jamila Ridha, the oldest child among us, and said, "I'm full. Now can I have my wedding?"

Lina had been gripped by wedding fever ever since she'd fallen asleep and missed her chance to be a flower girl in Jamila's aunt's wedding. Jamila had promised Lina she could have a pretend wedding just as soon as everyone was done eating. At home, we'd baked Lina a cake, using a box mix, while she put on her favorite summer dress, the one with the ruffles and the hula-dancer print, and then she stuck a comb with a short tulle veil in her mess of curly blond hair.

Now Jamila brushed the potato-chip salt off her fingers, reached out for Lina's hand, and guided her off the bench of the picnic table.

Together we walked down the poison-oak-lined trail to the creek where our brothers were building a dam. Jamila climbed to the top of a flat rock, cupped her mouth, and called out, "Guys, come here."

I listened to her voice bellow and admired the ease with which she commanded our brothers. Jamila was thirteen years old, four years older than me, and I believed in her authority. The boys, however, were unimpressed. The three of them continued slapping down the rocks they'd chosen for their creek dam with a clank and a splash.

"Guys," Jamila repeated. "We promised."

My older brother, Ibrahim, waded out of the water, looking peeved. He hated it when Jamila tried to organize us.

Down from the rock, Jamila said, "Ibrahim, you'll do the ceremony."

Ibrahim shook his head. His eyes were green and his eyelashes so thick and bold that the girls at school teased that he wore mascara. "I'll do it for Lina," he said. "Not because you asked me to."

"Well," Jamila said, turning to her two brothers who were approaching in their swim trunks, "which one of you is going to be the groom?"

Without a word, the Ridha boys stepped into their sandals, which were left at the side of a nearby rock, and moved in behind Ibrahim. The sun had deepened the tone of the brothers' already dark skin. Amjad, the younger and shorter of the two, was wiry, pure flesh and bones, while Hadi was stockier with a small tummy and a waist that gave in on both sides to a slight crease.

I crouched down so that Lina and I were the same height and said, "You don't need a boy to have a wedding. How about if you get married by yourself?"

Lina dropped her chin so low it almost touched her chest, and pushed her lips into a frown. "But a bride has to have a husband," she said with such certainty it was clear that Lina already understood there were rules to getting married.

"Just play along," Jamila said to Amjad, but he folded his arms and gave a firm no. She then turned to twelve-year-old Hadi. "You'll marry Lina, won't you? She's little. She doesn't understand what being married means. You don't want her to be disappointed, do you?"

Hadi stood there with water dripping from his hair and listened to his sister's argument with his hands on his hips. He looked down and kicked the rock closest to his foot. He watched it scuttle across the ground.

"Okay," he said.

Surely Hadi knew there would be teasing—that our parents would laugh heartily at the memory of the little bride and her new husband for years to come—and yet he was willing to put up with this for my sister's happiness.

From the front of the campground firepit, where I stood as Lina's maid of honor, I watched Lina walk down the dusty aisle between a run of benches, clutching a bunch of artificial flowers with one hand, the other hand trying to suppress a giggle. Our mothers looked on from a bench off to the side, squealing in pure delight at Lina's irrepressible joy, the fluff of golden hair peeking out from behind her veil. Mrs. Ridha called out to her sons, "Pay attention, boys. One day you will dream to marry such pretty girls."

When Ibrahim opened his facetious wedding ceremony with, "Dearly beloved with the exception of Jamila," my gaze fell on Hadi standing at Lina's side, playing along with a sincerity I'd never seen in a boy. I took a snapshot of Hadi in my mind—still in his swim trunks and as tanned as a piece of overdone toast. I decided if I did, indeed, marry Hadi one day, this would be the moment I'd say I first fell in love with him.

CHAPTER 2

❁

MUSLIM LOVE

People can forgive you different food and customs; they can fall in love with your baklawa; and they can respect you for your long school uniform skirts and opaque tights, and for saying your daily prayers as fast as you can in a corner of your cabin during science camp. But saying you couldn't have a boyfriend or that you'd likely marry someone whom you had never gone on a date with, made you an alien. It made all the girls in your sixth-grade class circle around you during recess and ask why you couldn't just go with John; it wasn't as if he'd be your boyfriend or you had to kiss him or anything. It made the same girls corner you in the restroom at the spring social and ask why you couldn't just dance with Chris; you were making him so sad, and it was really so selfish and mean to keep saying no. It made the guy in the mall who just asked for your number tell you to go back to Kuwait where you came from.

Not being allowed to date was the issue that plucked me out of the realm of exotic and interesting and planted me firmly into a sad documentary about people from other cultures, the kind that makes its audience walk away grateful to be themselves. In my peers' insistent questions, their shakes of the head, I could almost see them reflecting on how lucky they were to be holding the keys to their own love lives, when there were girls like me whose mom and dad were going to drive them to the door of their future relationship and take a seat inside.

My peers' relief bothered me far more than the prohibition against dating itself. Deep down, I wanted to marry the Iraqi, Shia boy who would make my parents proud, someone who prayed and fasted, someone who knew as much Arabic as I did if not more, and someone who'd give our children Arabic names and take them to the masjid. I wasn't the trope of an immigrant's kid, prepared to reject her family's traditions in order to fit into mainstream culture. On the contrary, the contents of my mind deeply ashamed me. I could sing along to nearly every theme song on television, but my Arabic vocabulary was limited to words said around the house, my five daily prayers, and some of the shorter Quranic verses that I could recite but did not understand. I did not have a single memory of Iraq, not my mother's childhood home with the flat roof *satah* where she slept outside on balmy nights, not the creamy *gaymar* and freshly baked *samoun* she used to eat for breakfast, not the gilded shrines she made pilgrimages to every Ashura with their massive Persian carpets and crystal chandeliers.

I had been only two years old in 1979 when my family made their last trip to Iraq. An intense interrogation in the airport made Mama decide it wasn't worth going back anymore and that it was time to get the rest of her family out. There was no way I was going to sever what little ties I had to my culture and religion by marrying someone outside of it.

My entire extended family consisted of couples who had barely known each other when they wed, couples who had been introduced via photographs or paired together from within the same clan. Mama and Baba were themselves distant relatives, something I never told any of my friends for fear they'd recoil with disgust and forever brand me the child of an incestuous union. Baba was from a branch of the Marashis that left Iraq in the 1920s and settled in the tropical island of Zanzibar. He was studying abroad in Canada when his sister sent him Mama's picture, a wallet size he blew up to poster proportions and proudly toted back to Iraq to gift to my grandfather as a stand-in for the daughter he was taking with him. Whenever he came across the original wallet-size photograph, he'd show it to me and my siblings and tell us, "Look here. See how your mummy was so pretty," his Arab–East African accent thick, dragging out the o's and pushing hard on the t's.

Mama was, indeed, the quintessential pretty brunette—the kind who usually plays sidekick to a bombshell blond, the kind you wouldn't expect to find married to a short man, twenty years her senior, with thinning gray hair, a salt-and-pepper mustache, and the beginnings of a potbelly. People often mistook Mama for Baba's daughter, and Lina, Ibrahim, and me for his grandchildren, but Mama only wanted me to see the wisdom in her union and the folly in American dating.

"The problem with the women in this country is they expect too much," Mama would often say to me while getting ready for work. "They want love, they want passion, and they want it to last forever. Your father is a good man; he encouraged me to go back to school. Not every man would put up with his wife working and studying. If you want to start believing in this country's what-about-me garbage, there's no end to it."

When Mama arrived in the United States in 1972, she was eighteen years old. She didn't drive, speak English, or have a high school diploma. Baba urged her to go back to school right after my brother was born, and from then on, she'd always worked and studied, earning first her GED, then two different associate's degrees, then a bachelor's in nursing. Eventually she'd earn a master's and doctorate of nurse practice. She often said she would have gone to medical school had there been one in town.

For years, Mama worked the 3:00 to 11:00 p.m. shift on a pediatrics floor. We got home from school after she left for work, and most nights, we were in bed before she got back. Days often passed without us seeing her, and so when Mama was home, she expected us to be available for parenting. One afternoon, while getting ready for her shift, she told me of a coworker, "That little twit-twit Sandy has only been married for two months, and she already wants a divorce. She slept with her husband, kissed him, and now she says she doesn't even know him. How much more does she want to know?"

Standing in front of her dresser mirror, Mama swiped a padded applicator across a square of eye shadow and added, "People here tell me, 'You married a stranger.' What stranger? Someone your parents know and your family knows is a stranger? They think if they date someone and they kiss him and sleep with him, they know who they're marrying. What does that tell you about a person except for what they look like naked?"

"Mama!" I said, from where I sat on her bed, with the sharp tone of surprise I believed was expected of a twelve-year-old.

Mama ignored my theatrics. She'd always considered anything biological—pees and poops (Mama always referred to these in the plural), menstruation and sex—to be healthy topics of conversation. She unscrewed the cap from a tube of mascara and added, "That's how people think here. It's all about 'my feelings,' and 'do I love him?' But just because you don't love someone when you marry him, it doesn't mean you'll never love him. The important thing is to marry a good person, someone who shares your culture and religion, and then you'll fall in love with him later."

"Is that how it was for you with Baba?" I asked. "You didn't love him, but now you do."

"Things were different for me," Mama said, brushing the mascara wand along her top lashes. "I hadn't finished high school, and Jidu had just married Bibi."

Jidu and *Bibi* are the Iraqi words for "grandfather" and "grandmother," but in this case, Bibi was Mama's stepmother and Jidu's third wife. Jidu's first wife, Mama's mother, had died tragically and suddenly in her twenties. He remarried, only for his new wife to meet the same fate, this time as a result of a cooking fire. When Jidu found himself alone with seven kids between Mama's fifteen years and her youngest brother's eighteen months, his father pressured him to marry a distant cousin—a spinster in her forties, who lived in a palatial home with her brother, servants, and black cat.

Now Mama tossed the mascara back in her makeup box and continued, "Bibi didn't like having us all around the house, and she thought she was doing Jidu a great favor because she married off his daughters to doctors. So I just said okay because I always did what I was told, and I got lucky. Your father is a kind man, and I now have you beautiful kiddies to be grateful for."

Mama affixed her name tag to her collar and kissed me on the cheek on her way out the door. As always, Mama was too busy to waste a moment on regret. She could have easily blamed Bibi for marrying her off to a man who was not just twice her age but also her complete opposite, a sickly, nearly humorless man, far too serious and literal for Mama's mischievous sense of humor, her boundless energy for exercise, dancing, and projects of all kinds. But Mama did not blame Bibi. Rather she moved her and Jidu into our tiny ranch home, putting me and Ibrahim in the same room until she could afford to build a house with a granny unit above the garage. And not only did Mama never dwell on how different she was from my father, but she also told me time and again what a good man he was, how he took in her family, how he encouraged her to go back to school, and how devoted he was to us kids.

I believed this ability to embrace the relationship you were in was the upside to matchmade marriages. Muslim love was secure and uncomplicated, a decision entirely under a person's control, but American love was almost frighteningly fragile and mysterious. It had to be fallen into after a number of dates, and when couples on television and in movies finally uttered the L-word to each other, it was a grand moment, a surprise even to themselves. Maybe it was a frustrated, "Because I love you, all right," cried out in the midst of an argument. Or a tearful, "Now that I lost you, I know I love you." It was something that could befall them even when they were committed to other people. "We didn't mean for it to happen," the cheater might explain to his former beloved.

I feared the fickleness of American love—the notion that someone could love you and still fall in love with someone else, or like you but not be in love with you, or love you for a time and then lose that spark—but like all delicate things, there was something special about this kind of love. In a love marriage, you knew the couple at the altar were drawn together by more than their matching culture, religion, or family ties. They shared a connection to each other. The bride was someone wholly unique and irreplaceable, someone who made the groom misty-eyed watching her walk down the aisle, someone he'd describe as his best friend while holding her hand and reciting the vows that he'd written. These couples got married in weddings they planned for a year, and hired photographers to capture every moment, photographers who would later assemble their pictures into thick, bound photo albums and into framed portraits.

Mama, on the other hand, kept her wedding photographs in a manila envelope stuffed in the back of a half-empty photo album. The pictures weren't even taken at her wedding, but at a stopover in England at the request of my father's sister who lived in Newcastle and missed out on the actual wedding, which Mama had told me was really no more than a dinner with some family members at home and had ended with her washing the dishes. In these photos, Mama was wearing an A-line wedding gown made from white and silver lace thrown over an acetate lining. She wore a rhinestone crown out of which flew yards of tulle that pillowed at her feet. In her hands were a bunch of red carnations, and she looked uncomfortable, as if she was trying to suppress a giggle. Baba wore a navy blue suit, his hair and mustache a slightly darker gray. He looked at Mama with what my siblings and I call "Baba's proud face," lips forced closed as if to contain the beams of happiness shining inside him. In some of the pictures, Baba's four-year-old niece posed as the flower girl.

Mama's dress still hung at the back of her closet but without any attempt at preservation. We were welcome to wear it, play in it, or do whatever we wanted with it. Her tiara, minus several rhinestones, was in my bedroom, left over from all the Halloweens that I'd dressed up as a princess. I wanted Mama's wedding things to be too special for me to use, but every time I'd offer to return the tiara to her room, she'd shrug and say there was no need. Sometimes she'd add, "I never really liked the things from my wedding. My uncle bought everything, and they just told me to wear it."

Mama's wedding memorabilia told the story of resignation, loss, and acceptance that she didn't tell. Mama could have been the subject of one of those pity documentaries, albeit with an inspirational twist—the Story of How One Woman Overcame Her Heartbreaking Childhood and Arranged Marriage by Taking Pride in Her Children and Getting Lots of Education—but as remarkable as I knew Mama's example was, I didn't want to repeat it.

I wanted a love story with the Iraqi, Shia man of my dreams. I wanted to be a Wakefield sister who found her Tarek at Sweet Valley High, a Scarlett O'Hara who met her Raheem without the depravation of war, a Juliet who lived into old age with her Rumi. I didn't need a string of boyfriends or affairs—just one grand, sweeping love story so fantastic that it was worth a lifetime of romantic adventures.

Because, falling in love was a veritable jackpot. There was the bounty of the feelings themselves, the spiritual connection, the physical attraction, the thrill of having a handsome man devoted entirely to me, but it was also redemptive. It was life's way of saying, "Here, little Muslim girl, since you were so good and stayed away from boys before marriage, you will be rewarded with the perfect, Iraqi, Shia

husband who is so awesome you don't have to learn to love him."
And the story I had with this Mr. *Khair Inshallah*, Mr. Good God
Willing, would immediately banish all my American friends' pity and
fear that I was getting married for the wrong reasons. "I love him,"
I'd say, and it wouldn't matter if I only met the guy once in my living
room with my family all around me. Americans forgave everything
in the name of love, and so would I.

CHAPTER 3

A GIRL LIKE THAT WON'T STAY

Moment 1: Hadi was bouncing my Silly Putty around before it turned a corner and dropped into the hall bathroom's toilet. I was seven, and he was ten. He apologized with a quick, "I'm sorry," before running off. Four years later, I was sitting on the edge of the bed in Jamila's room. He came in, handed me a paper bag, and said, "Here. I owe you this." He left before I opened the bag and found a brand-new Silly Putty inside.

Moment 2: Hadi, Jamila, and Amjad had come to stay with us the summer before I started the eighth grade. They arrived with gifts in hand. We stood around, opening our presents, boys in one corner of the room, girls in another.

As I pulled back the plastic bag, Jamila said, "I don't know why, but Hadi insisted on paying for this with his own money."

Inside was an EZ Bake Oven, something I'd told Jamila I'd always wanted but never got.

I looked over at Hadi. Our eyes met, but he quickly looked down.

Moment 3: We were on a family trip to Disneyland later that same year. Hadi pulled a thick, veined leaf off a tree and said, "Keep this. It's a present for you."

With exaggerated drama, I took it in my hands and said, "I'll treasure it always."

For the remainder of the day, I kept the leaf in my pocket and then later guarded it in my wallet. If we became a couple, I'd want this leaf as a reminder that we'd been brought together by more than our families. Hadi had liked me all along.

I treated these memories as if they were in a savings account—there in case I needed them later—but I hoped I wouldn't have to make a withdrawal. As kind as Hadi was, I didn't feel those jumpy feelings that romance novels described when I was around him, no butterflies in my stomach, no inability to eat or sleep. He sported a messy mullet, and while this was a completely fashion-forward move in the 1990s, it did not work for Hadi. Because his hair was curly, the longer hair in the back bunched up into a wild, fuzzy ball reminiscent of an animal tail. He'd gone from chubby to last-notch-on-his-belt skinny, and he dressed like such a schoolboy with his shirt buttoned up all the way to the top and securely tucked into his pants.

I was only thirteen years old, but I understood that our family friendship afforded Hadi and me opportunities to get to know each other that I would not have with another suitor, someone who'd likely appear with his family as nothing more than an evening dinner guest. On some days, this was reason enough to like Hadi. Other days, I wished there was someone else out there for me, someone from within our small community who my parents approved of, who I didn't have to convince myself to like.

One evening Mama asked me to follow her into her walk-in closet while she got ready for bed. Right away, I knew she had something she wanted to discuss with me privately. In a hushed voice, she got straight to telling me that Um Sadek, a close family friend of the Ridhas, had asked Mrs. Ridha about me, and Mrs. Ridha had told her, "Don't even think about it. She is ours."

I stood there, holding the back of the chair that my mom usually tossed her clothes on, and tried not to show any reaction.

Mama stepped out of a pair of pants, her voice brimming with pride. "And then Um Sadek told her, 'Be careful. If you want her, do something about it now. A girl like that won't stay.'"

I gripped the chair harder.

"So," Mama asked and pulled a T-shirt and pair of pajama pants out of her dresser drawer, "do you like Hadi?"

My cheeks flushed with a mix of girlish flattery and a hot punch of frustration. Mama was asking me if I liked a boy when she'd always said feelings were irrelevant, that sensible girls put compatibility above all else. And I didn't know why she was telling me all this now. Had I just been spoken for as an eighth grader?

"I don't know," I said.

Mama pulled the shirt over her head and added, "Because if you don't like the idea, I should hint it to your Khala," referring to Mrs. Ridha as my aunt, a title of respect Iraqis applied liberally to any woman who was old enough to be their mother. "She is already worried that we will insist on somebody *seyyid*, and I told her that the Al-Marashis usually marry within the family and we always take an *istikhara* for this kind of thing."

I nodded at the unpleasant reminder. Even in the impossibly small world of boys I might be allowed to marry, there were obstacles to marrying an Iraqi, Shia like Hadi. My family belonged to a clan that claimed descent from the Prophet Muhammad, earning us the honorific title of seyyid. A man could marry a non-seyyid woman and still pass the title on to her children, but a woman could not. Since Hadi's family was not seyyid, our future children would lose their right to this distinction. Then, there was the custom of marrying cousins, both first and distant, or, at the very least, taking the permission of an aunt or an uncle before accepting a marriage offer from outside the family. And finally, there was the istikhara, the consultation of the Quran under the guidance of someone trained in the practice of interpreting its verses. According to my mother, no marriage in our family had taken place without one.

"His mom may say all that to you," I said, "but he actually has to like me, too."

"Hudie, the boy likes you. His eyes go wherever you go. And don't dismiss a mom liking you. A mom is more important than the boy."

It meant something to Mama that of all the girls Mrs. Ridha knew, she wanted me for her son. Mrs. Ridha was the closest thing the Southern California Iraqi community had to a matchmaker. She kept track of all the unmarried girls in our community, their ages, and what they were studying so she could make recommendations when asked.

Mrs. Ridha's approval didn't carry the same weight with me, but at the same time, I didn't want Mama to discourage Mrs. Ridha's interest. Hadi wasn't just another Iraqi Shia; he was someone born in America, someone raised on the same movies and television shows, someone who likely shared the same romantic notions about love.

"Do you have to tell them anything now?" I asked. "Can't we just wait and see what happens?"

"That's what I've been doing. I say, 'They're both young. Let's see how they feel when they get older.' You never know. The boy could change his mind about you, too."

Mama's words tugged at me. As much as I wanted the space to consider other people, I took comfort in the idea that Hadi would be there, liking me. For as long as I could remember, I'd heard stories about our community's risky marriage market where the freshest, sweetest girls never sat on the shelf. Mrs. Ridha always had a cautionary tale about a girl whose shelf life was expiring. "You know, it's nice to want to go to school and study," she'd say, "but a girl becomes twenty-four, twenty-five, and that's it. The only people who come for her are older, or they have been married before. Like this girl, I don't want to mention her name, but she was so pretty. Everyone asked about her, but she insisted she wanted to be a dentist. In the end, she became a dentist, but she married someone fifteen years older than her who had two kids from his first marriage. See how the *qisma* is."

Almost every marriage story I'd overheard Mrs. Ridha telling Mama ended with qisma, destiny. It never occurred to me to question how the poor girl in the story could be blamed for insisting on school if this relationship had been her fate, or to wonder if the girl might have actually liked the man with the two children. All I heard then was the tone of pity in which her story was retold, and that pity settled into my mind as a series of warnings—don't be too picky; our community is too small for you to hold out for the one; be the best girl so someone picks you first.

When Mama entered the conversation, it was often to add this much-repeated piece of wisdom: "School will always be there, but the time for marriage won't."

Coming from grade-obsessed Mama, a woman who fell asleep surrounded by her textbooks and piles of flash cards, a woman who made everything wait until after finals, this notion that a good suitor was a gift of fate carried the weight of an irrefutable truth.

"If you are motivated enough, you can do anything," Mama would say. "I used to bring you to class with me. Sit you down with a little coloring book. It was fun."

Mama made it seem like a challenge—if you worked hard enough, there was no reason why you couldn't get married young and have a family and go to school and have a career. "A woman should always have a way to support herself," she'd tell me. "You never know what can happen."

Our community of brain-drain Iraqis was filled with women just like Mama. Women who were doctors, dentists, pharmacists, and engineers: they got married young, had their children, and worked. Even the women who stayed at home with their children still whispered to their daughters, "Study. Study. Become something." In our Iraqi American community, mothers did not offer their daughters one path over the other—marriage, school, and careers were all tied together in a tight, little knot of what it meant to be successful. For the most part, this resonated with every definition of American success I'd grown up hearing, except for one important difference— love. In America, you had to fall in love.

CHAPTER 4

❁

A SMALL ISLAND OF UNITY

I went to an all-girls Catholic high school, settled in the middle of a neighboring agricultural town. My classmates were farmers' daughters, workers' daughters on scholarship, and commuters looking for a better alternative to the local public schools. For school events, the farming families would donate centerpieces made of colorful arrays of broccoli, cabbage, and cauliflower, and on free-dress days, many girls traded in their uniforms for their finest cowgirl gear—colorful denim pants without back pockets; plaid shirts with metal-tipped, pointy collars; and riding boots.

When people questioned Mama's decision to send her Muslim children to a parochial school, she'd say, "Some religion is better than no religion." That there were no boys at this particular school was a bonus. "Less distraction," she'd add.

At school, we began every class with a prayer and special intentions. With their hands folded on their desks, my classmates took turns praying for their sick dogs, dead grandmas, and fickle boyfriends. Praying for a boyfriend was something I never learned to accept. It sounded like praying for help with shoplifting or purchasing marijuana. For six periods a day, I listened to my peers ask God for variations of the following:

"I'd like to offer a prayer of thanks for Ricky."
"I wanna pray for Ricky because we're going through a really
     hard time right now."

"I wanna pray that God will help me forgive Ricky for being
such a big jerk."
"I wanna thank God for helping me and Ricky get back together."

Listening to my peers work through boyfriends and breakups,
I was convinced of another upside to being a Muslim woman. I'd
never waste valuable getting-into-a-good-college time on a pointless
relationship. I'd never worry about finding a date to the Winter Ball
or fret over wearing a bathing suit in public. Why a woman would
want to go anywhere in what was nothing more than a made-for-
water bra and underpants baffled me. I didn't want to introduce the
world to the stretch marks that my first and only growth spurt had
autographed on my thigh.

At school I defended these ideas to my friends. Every year I gave
talks to the world religions classes about Islam with the only other
Muslim girl in school, Nadia Khan. Nadia had Pakistani parents,
and she looked—and I say this while cursing Disney studios for
getting the stereotype right—just like Princess Jasmine. When our
classmates brought up the resemblance, we feigned great offense, but
Nadia did, indeed, have thick black hair that hung down her petite,
twig-thin body; full lips plumped up with Revlon's Toast of New
York; and kohl-lined cat eyes.

In those world religions classes, we repeated the same lines about
the five pillars of Islam; the hijab and how even if Nadia and I didn't
wear it, we still tried to be modest in our dress; and the differences
between Sunnis and Shias. I'd start by saying, "So there are the
two sects in Islam. The Shias believed that Imam Ali, the Prophet
Muhammad's son-in-law, should have taken over after the Prophet
died, and the Sunnis believed it should have been Abu Bakr. But the
split didn't even happen until years after, when Imam Husayn, the
Prophet's grandson, was killed. It was then that a group broke off
and decided to follow the descendants of the Prophet's line."

Nadia was my first Sunni Muslim friend. She folded her hands around her waist during certain parts of the five daily prayers while I kept my arms straight at my sides. She also recited her afternoon prayers separately instead of one after the other like I did. I used to feel as if those minor differences threatened our unity, the small island we inhabited in our sea of Catholic education. But whenever something came up about our dissimilarities, Nadia would say, "Oh, Hudie, like I care." It was enough for Nadia that we were both Muslims, and she was always quick to add this particular message to our classroom explanations.

"That's the only difference," she'd say, brandishing a polished fingernail, her sentences coming fast and without a full breath between them. "It's purely historical. It's the same religion, the same beliefs. We all pray, we all fast, and we all go on our Haj pilgrimage together. No one even really cares about it. See. Look at me and Huda. We're both from different sects, but it doesn't matter. We're still the best of friends."

Nadia was brilliant, but for some reason this made her less coherent rather than more. It was as if a genius creature lived inside her brain and made her speak as fast as it thought. But Nadia's genius had a big heart, and every time she made this last point, she put her arm around me for emphasis.

It was my favorite part of our talk because it filled me with such hope. Nadia and I belonged to a new generation of Muslims in America, and we were painting a picture of Islam on what was essentially a blank canvas. Those two smoking towers of black wouldn't appear until almost seven years later, in 2001. The Gulf War was newly behind us, and we had the luxury of thinking our biggest problem was the movie *Not without My Daughter*—which, judging by the number of girls in my school who had seen it, was the most important film of the entire decade.

During every talk we gave, someone would raise her hand and

ask how we could want to marry Muslim men when they were like the antagonist Moody, so overbearing and abusive. "Don't Muslim men beat their wives?" Rachel Lazar, the most outspoken girl in the class, once asked.

"No," Nadia said, "I have a whole family full of Muslim men, and my dad and all my uncles have never hit their wives."

Rachel was not satisfied with this answer, and her next question carried the tone of a challenge. "But what would you do if you fell in love with a guy who wasn't Muslim?"

"That's easy," I said, striding toward the middle of the classroom. "I wouldn't fall in love with a guy who wasn't Muslim. How could I fall in love with someone who doesn't share the things that are most important to me?"

My faith was the only security I had in what I'd already discovered to be a frightening and unpredictable world. Baba, a long-time sufferer from bronchiectasis, was often hospitalized for simple colds that turned into more stubborn infections or prolonged episodes of pneumonia. And then there was the arteriovenous malformation (AVM) found in Lina's mandible when she was eight years old and I was thirteen. For a year, my parents shuttled her back and forth to Stanford University and UCSF until her doctors settled on a treatment for the tangle of blood vessels lodged in her jaw, the location of her AVM so rare that her case was written up in medical journals. And through all that bone-rattling childhood fear, I carried prayer beads in my pocket and prayed until those prayers were answered. I wanted a future spouse who would help me hold up my world with his devotion—not draw punishment into my life for marrying someone outside of my religion.

"I don't see how you can say that," Rachel argued. "You can't control who you're going to fall in love with."

Here it was in real life—not spoken by some character in a book or in a film—that notion that you couldn't control who you love, that it was something that happened to you as accidentally as tripping. I wished Rachel could step into my world for just one moment and see the glaring contradiction in her reasoning. American culture extolled autonomy and personal power, but it accepted and even embraced complete helplessness when it came to love.

I replied, "Yes, you can, if you don't let yourself consider people outside your religion, and that makes sense because you're going to have kids and raise a family with this person."

In spite of the complete confidence I felt in my explanation, something in Rachel's face shook me. She looked over at her friends and rolled her eyes with such disdain that I almost heard her announcing that I was nothing to her, asexual and therefore unimportant.

My mind flashed to Hadi. I was tempted to offer up my list of moments as proof that a boy liked me and maybe I liked him, too. But I would never discuss this unnamed thing that Hadi and I shared so casually in front of my class. Mama talked to me about Hadi, in private, behind closed doors, but we never discussed this topic in front of my siblings or father. Mama had warned me time and again to admit to no crush, no interest in any boy in front of anyone ever—not my closest girlfriends and certainly never the boy. "You may change your mind," she warned, "but you cannot control what people will think. In their mind, they will always remember you tied to that one boy's name."

The snotty girl inside me wished I could walk over to Rachel and her friends, with my hands on my hips, and say, "You think you're so hot because you've been to every Winter Ball and prom with a different guy on your arm. Just watch. I'll be married before you've even had a steady boyfriend."

I sincerely believed getting married beat having a boyfriend. I repeatedly told myself that the girls around me could have all their temporary boyfriends because one day soon a boy would want to be with me forever. We'd host dinner parties with delicate china and gleaming flatware, and my life would soon be far more mature and sophisticated than Rachel and her friends and their petty concerns about boys and dates.

But every Friday, when my classmate Diana Marquez slept over, this built-up confidence got a thorough shaking. Diana and I would wrestle over our futures, this puzzle that did not have a single piece locked into place, and wonder how we were going to put together everything we wanted from life. We were the girls who had been plotting and planning our path to college since freshman year—running for student-body offices, joining clubs, studying for tests right through lunch, eyeing the valedictory crown, and grabbing every last possible point for our greedy above 4.0 GPAs. How were our degrees and careers going to fit with a boy loving us and marrying us and later with soft, chubby babies who chewed on our fingers with their smooth, toothless gums?

We made lists of careers that made you look smart, so even if we stopped working to take care of our families, people would know that we'd been bright enough to become something else first. Medicine was too long a career path not to use, but maybe law or physical therapy. "But isn't it a waste to go through that much schooling if we aren't going to use it?" Diana would ask.

"But we have to," I'd respond. "We can't have worked this hard to get all these As to be just moms."

Diana and I had no evidence to complicate this image of motherhood. We'd grown up in the age of the supermom, Murphy Brown, and "We girls can do anything. Right, Barbie?" We merely accepted that being a stay-at-home mom came with the word *just* firmly affixed to the front of it, and we moved on to creating scenarios for the perfect marriage proposal. I still remember one such daydream where Diana suggested, "Wouldn't it be great if your friends are like, 'Hey, can you drive us to the movies?' because they are in on it, too, and you go to open your car door and all these balloons fly out?"

"Yes," I added, "but there is this one balloon that doesn't come out, so you go and pull on it, and attached is this little box with a really big ring in it—"

"And then a limo pulls up," Diana said, "and you see him get out, wearing a tuxedo and holding flowers, and you say, 'Yes,' and you hug and cry—"

"And that's when you get into the limo," I said, "and there's a dress waiting for you because you are going to change and go out to dinner at a place with an amazing ocean view, and then when you get there, your favorite song is playing and you dance."

As Diana and I spun our fantasies, I admitted to no conflict. I rationalized that a surprise proposal just like this could indeed happen to me in spite of all my familial and cultural restrictions. Maybe a boy could ask my family for my hand without me knowing, and then he could arrange a proposal, if not as elaborate as this one then at least something similar. And after we were engaged, we could catch up on all the moments a Western couple may have had while they were dating. During the year that we were planning our wedding, my fiancé could whisk me away for a romantic birthday, Valentine's Day, and anniversary celebration of when we first became a couple.

Diana and I had an entire soundtrack for every romantic event we imagined, but no song captivated our imagination like Chris de Burgh's rendering of "The Lady in Red." Every time we got together, we belted out its lyrics and danced in rehearsal for the night when we would be the Lady in Red in our own lives. When the song ended, we'd take turns dipping each other with dramatic flourish. One night, while mid-dip, we caught sight of ourselves in my mirrored closet door. Diana was in my arms, with one leg kicked up high into the air, her head back, hair fanning out of a messy bun, wearing a sweatshirt and a pair of sweatpants and white socks, the latter stuffed into high heels. I wore the exact same ensemble.

"We look so beautiful, right now," I said in the deepest, most dramatic voice I could muster.

"It's the socks and the heels, isn't it?" Diana said in a flirty tone.

And that was all I needed to drop her on the floor where we both crumbled into a fit of giggles.

"Oh my God, I totally have to pee now," Diana said.

I laughed even harder, tears streaming down my face.

"If you don't stop laughing, I'm gonna pee on your head," Diana threatened while running out the door to the bathroom.

I stayed stretched out on the floor, catching my breath. The laughter that had coursed through me moments ago gave way to a melancholic stillness. Diana may have been Mexican American, but we always joked that we were essentially the same person. At some point, we had both lived in tiny three-bedroom ranch homes, overcrowded with immigrating relatives. Our parents had been making us sign the permission slips that came home from school for as long as we could read ("You know my signature," Mama would say). They allowed us to watch inordinate amounts of television—*Three's Company*, *Silver Spoons*, and *The Facts of Life*—and do our homework right in front of it. We'd eaten obscene amounts of candy and had the fillings to prove it. And we both understood that even though we talked to each other about marriage with age-inappropriate frequency, this was not a side of ourselves we wanted the outside world to see. Diana and I were far too driven; we were both the daughters of immigrants, and we had something to prove.

But dancing to "The Lady in Red" undid some of the commonality that bound us together. No matter how much our worries and desires matched, only Diana would be allowed to dance with a boy before she was married.

"Ready for another dance?" Diana asked as soon as she came back from the bathroom.

"Always," I said and extended my hands toward Diana, toward the bittersweet joy of wanting what you could not have.

In my junior year, I enrolled in Marriage and Parenting, a course required by our school's Religion Department. The first quarter was basically sexual education, complete with diagrams of genitals and a list of words we had to learn for a matching test. The words were familiar. Mama was the designated sex-talk giver in the family, and I'd already sat through at least three sex talks where I made a point of only half-listening (I believed in preserving the virginity of my mind). I'd gathered the basics: There were the penis and the testes and some business about hardening and shrinking and ejaculating sperm, but I thought it best to remain fuzzy on the specifics. If I had to guess, I would've said that the *belbool* (Iraqi slang for "penis" because God knows I would've never been able to use the appropriate term) got really, really small and then slipped in the woman.

I was equally befuddled by all the words for female parts. I'd heard about the vagina and clitoris, but I didn't know what word corresponded to what. Becoming-a-woman books always suggested studying yourself down there with a hand mirror, but that seemed a completely irrelevant exercise for a girl who grew up being warned that being too friendly with boys (i.e., casual chatting and laughing or, God forbid, flirtatious touching) was enough to ruin her reputation.

Not knowing anything about sex seemed the best way to prove this thing that was so important to the people in my community. It said, "Look at me. I am so naïve and innocent, I must be a virgin."

It wasn't a viewpoint Mama supported. Whenever I cried out, "Gross," or "Do we have to talk about this again?" she scolded, "It's not gross. It's beautiful, and it's science. This is one of Allah's great miracles. Now pay attention."

But as much as my mother tried to teach me that sex was important in Islam, that it was the foundation of a marriage, I believed the risks of knowing too much too soon outweighed the benefits. Islam's healthy and positive attitudes toward sex didn't matter when the people in our community were the ones gossiping, either choosing you or casting you aside, and the consistent message I got was that it was *ayb* or shameful for an unmarried girl to like a boy or to be excited about anything related to boys.

In the fifth grade, I had a sleepover for my birthday (my parents' rule was that I could have friends over, but I couldn't spend the night at anyone's house). When the conversation turned to my friends' on-screen crushes, I wanted to shush them. In my household, there was nothing cute or innocent about girls discussing boys. It wasn't long before Mama picked up on the topic and called me out of the living room and into the kitchen to ask, "Are your friends talking about boys?"

I nodded, mortified and ashamed, and then added, "But they're not real boys. Just actors."

She didn't meet my gaze. "Already?" she said as if she was addressing herself. "These are eleven-year-old girls. What's the matter with this country?"

That I could feel so much shame just being in the company of girls talking about boys made it clear—this was a taboo unlike any others.

A *hababa*, a good girl, was defined almost exclusively by what she didn't do. She didn't talk to boys. She didn't dance at parties. She didn't wear sleeveless dresses or wear short skirts. Show up at one party in the wrong dress, dance a little too long at a wedding, and that descriptor would be plucked from your name.

However, these strict guidelines oddly comforted me. "Huda hababa," I'd hear one of the aunties in our community say, and it was as if she had patted me on the back and said, "Don't worry. You have been such a good girl. You will be picked by the best guy." It was that implied guarantee that made all the self-denial, all the careful guarding of my reputation, worth it. The best guy would pick me— maybe it would be Hadi, or maybe it would be someone else—and in that small space between getting engaged and married, my love story would begin.

CHAPTER 5

BEATEN BY DEVOTION

Since my family lived a six-hour driving distance away from the greater Los Angeles area's Iraqi community, our appearances at social gatherings and at the masjid were infrequent but regular. Every year, without fail, on the anniversary of Imam Husayn's martyrdom, a day known as Ashura, my extended family of eight would don black mourning clothes and squeeze into our seven-seater minivan to make the journey to a run-down 1960s South Central Los Angeles church that had been converted to a masjid. On our way there, Mama, Jidu, and my uncle would listen to tape recordings of religious services that made them weep, their shoulders bobbing up and down with each sob.

My siblings and I did not cry. Not only was our Arabic vocabulary limited to the domestic, but also our family's tapes were garbled from use and full of words to which we'd had no exposure. Baba did not cry either. I'd only seen him cry once, when he found out one of his sisters had died, and that had been only a short, angry burst of tears. Bibi pulled her face behind her long, cloak-like *abaya* because sometimes she cried, but sometimes she didn't, and holding back tears at a time like this was not a sign of strength. Shia Muslims believe the tears they shed in the name of their ill-fated Imams, those spiritual leaders they regard as the rightful successors of the Prophet Muhammad, are blessed and rewarded. My family traveled to this mosque precisely because the speaker, referred to as the *Seyyid*, was a prominent religious scholar known for his ability to evoke the soul-cleansing cry my elders craved.

At the masjid, the Seyyid's voice, amplified by a tinny micro-phone, rang out into the parking lot. I watched my father, grandfather, uncle, and brother enter the door to the church's former nave where the pews now lined the walls and an enormous chandelier, donated by the Iraqi owners of a crystal shop, hung in the center. A curtain stretched across the area that had been the altar and divided the men's section and the women's section into drastically disproportionate parts.

Peering in from the door designated as the women's entrance, I balked at the space. The elders sat shoulder to shoulder on the pews pushed against the wall, and the floor was covered with women and children, sitting cross-legged, knee to knee. I pointed out the obvious. "There is no room for us." But Mama would not be swayed. We left our shoes at the growing mound by the door and waded through the sea of women and children, stopping to regain our footing in the spaces between their bodies.

"*Sallemi*," Mama said and prodded me to bend down and greet her friends with the traditional "assalamu alaikum," followed by a kiss on each cheek.

Mama's cousin Marwa had recently moved to the area and motioned for us to sit next to her. Space was made for Mama on the bench. Lina and I sat on the floor by her feet. Mama leaned in close and whispered translations of bits and pieces of the Seyyid's sermon, urging me to pay attention. "If you listen," she promised, "you'll understand."

But I didn't understand. I just looked around me at all the new faces, so recently arrived from Iraq you could still see it on their faces and in their clothes, and I wondered about their stories. When they cried for Imam Husayn, stranded in the desert with his family, his children and siblings brutally murdered before he was beheaded and the tents of his surviving family set on fire, did they remember themselves? Did they think of all the times when they had to say goodbye, as a mother to her son, a daughter to her father, a wife to her husband, a sister to her brother?

After the Gulf War, Southern California's Iraqi community doubled. With these new arrivals came customs that had long been forgotten. They reminded us of the different styles of black abayas, the open cloak and the pullover dress with trim of every color and design; of passing around trays heavy with saffron rice pudding and cups of cool, rose-water-sweetened sherbet; of the mourning ritual known as *lutmiyya*.

The first year the women attempted the lutmiyya, I watched my mother as I had never seen her before. Standing in a circle, she slapped her face in time with a poetic *nauha* about Imam Husayn's suffering that two women at the microphone took turns reciting. The women's hands on their cheeks made the sound of a unified clap. Their faces reddened, and their silky abayas flowed with their every movement, making their bodies appear as if they were dripping in sadness. When Mama motioned for me to join her, I shook my head. I couldn't stand there pretending that I understood, that I belonged.

The following year, Mama took my hand and brought me into the circle from the beginning. My heart pounding, I watched her for a hint as to what I should do. When she started to move, I copied her, bending so that my hair spilled forward while slapping my forehead with both hands. The movement of my hair brought a moment of reprieve from the summertime heat, a small breeze on my now sweaty neck. The muscles in my back warmed and loosened as we moved in circles around the room. Bend, slap, stand, and step.

On my third revolution around the room, something amazing happened. I understood. After years of attending services in an incomprehensible world, one line opened up my world. The speaker called out, "*Abd wallah, Ya Zahra. Ma ninsa Husayna.*" At first it was nothing more than a tight knot of language, but soon that knot unraveled into distinct, entirely intelligible words: "I swear to God, Oh Zahra, we will not forget Husayn."

Each time she said it, the cries of the group grew louder, and the women in the circle no longer stepped, but jumped, bringing their hands high up into the air and then pulling them right down on the top of their heads. I jumped with them, beating each side of my head with my hands, and before I knew it, I was crying with a mix of emotions. Relief to have understood, overwhelmed by the power of the words I was saying, the weight of their meaning. I was promising Fatima az-Zahra, Imam Husayn's mother, that I would not forget the death of her son.

I looked at the women in the circle around me, and fragments of stories I'd heard—of families rounded up in the middle of the night and deported to Iran in their pajamas, of sisters and brothers disappearing from their schools for not joining the government's party, of fathers accidentally run over on sidewalks in broad daylight—flooded my mind. Soon this ritual that had bewildered me, maybe even embarrassed me, made so much sense. All atrocities deserved this much, for people to bear witness and cry, to vow they would not forget.

I wished, with more regret than longing, that I was a little less American and a little more Iraqi. If only I spoke better Arabic, I could have understood the details of these stories rather than their outline. I could have told the world about the suffering contained within this room.

Each time I brought my hands up to my face, I slapped myself a little harder. The tender skin on my face stung, but it was a good hurt, a small burn to remind me how lucky I was to only know such inconsequential pain.

At times, I glanced at the women outside the circle, lightly beating their chests or sitting in the pews and crying quietly. Within our own tradition, these lamentation rituals were still the subject of some controversy, and I wondered if the women looking on thought the lutmiyya was too extreme. Suddenly I saw Diana and Nadia, and my teachers and classmates, in my mind. What would they think if they saw me here beating myself? And then Hadi appeared right next to them. It would be so much easier to marry a boy who understood this, who had stood on the other side of the curtain and beat his chest, too.

When the lutmiyya was over, we fanned our abayas to cool down and moved about the room, exchanging hugs and kisses with the wish, "May God accept your prayers."

I brought my hands to my lower back and stretched. This soreness was likely another reason why some of the women in the room did not participate.

Mama smiled at me and said, "I am proud of you, hababa."

One of the women who had stood in the circle next to Mama approached us and complimented Mama on her beautiful *lutm*, on raising the kind of daughter who would stand in memory of the Imam. Mama and her new friend's approval wrapped me in such warmth that the tug to be more Iraqi overwhelmed me. In that moment, I would have gladly given up my accent-free English to have our dialect of Arabic take root in my mind. I would have given up my American place of birth to at least have a clear, defining mark of being from somewhere else stamped into my passport. How refreshing to abandon all my expectations of a relationship that looked American but followed Iraqi rules. It would be so much easier, I imagined, to be a foreigner clearly from another place, the owner of one set of values, rather than this life within a single body constantly toggling between two minds.

CHAPTER 6

A DIVINE CRYSTAL BALL

As much as our mothers may have wanted Hadi Ridha and me to wind up together in the future, they didn't want to see us together until that appointed day. If Mama caught me talking to Hadi, she'd pull me aside and say it was unsuitable for a girl to talk to a boy. It made her look interested, and a girl should never appear interested in a boy. Mrs. Ridha would tell Hadi that it was inappropriate to approach a girl who was a guest in their home; it made him appear as if he was on the make. And neither one of us wanted our siblings to see us talking to each other either. Showing an interest in a member of the opposite sex was ayb, shameful. On the rare occasions we teased about an Al-Marashi kid being paired with a Ridha kid, it earned us a firm scolding, a lecture about how marriage was not a joking matter.

But every now and then, Hadi and I paused in the hallway and exchanged a few words or continued to carry on a conversation after our siblings had gotten up from the couch. Other times, Hadi would come into Jamila's room under the pretense of having something to say to her and then he'd stay, chatting with me. When we talked, it was always about banal things—my sophomore and junior years in high school, his first couple of years in college, our summer jobs, and, most recently, our favorite cars. Hadi's first car was an old BMW, and ever since I'd told him I wanted my first car to be a zippy red BMW convertible, it became *the* thing that we shared.

Once when crossing paths in the hallway of his parents' house, Hadi stopped and said, "So yesterday I saw a red BMW 325, and I have to agree with you. It is a really nice car."

"That's why it's my favorite," I said and leaned against the wall. I knew Hadi and I would talk until someone appeared, and we'd scatter like a pair of startled birds. But stealing these moments still felt like a necessary risk. Ever since Mama had asked me if I liked Hadi, I felt as if I were trying him on, as if he were a pair of shoes and I was wandering up and down the aisles of a store to see if he fit.

Hadi added, "I know. Like I have the Nissan now, and it's a great car, but it's just not the same. A BMW is different."

Hadi wore a pair of slightly shrunken white jeans and a denim shirt straight from the dryer. The top of his mullet was plastered down with mousse, its tail a black puff of frizzy hair that inspired me to self-pity. Of all the Iraqi families in California, my family had to grow close to the one whose son had a wild animal growing on his head.

With frustration and boredom creeping into my voice, I said, "Yeah, well. I wouldn't know. Never driven one."

"You could've driven mine," he said.

"Right," I answered.

"Hey, I offered."

"You offered, and you also know why that would've never happened."

Hadi was finally talking to me as if we did not belong to the kind of Muslim families who would've deemed my sitting in his car inappropriate, but I gave him no credit for the flirtatious hint.

"I'll have to buy you one," he said.

"You will?"

"Yes, I will."

"How would that work?" I asked. "I don't think your future wife would like you buying me a car."

"She'd understand."

"And why would she do that?"

He paused, and I wondered if I had been too forward. But Hadi didn't seem frustrated by my question—only surprised.

"She just would," he said with a smile.

Standing there, with all the wisdom of my sixteen years of age, I resented Hadi for trying to be respectful, for trying to say something without saying anything at all. In my mind, the one thing Hadi had going for him was that our families' friendship afforded us these stolen moments to write the opening of our relationship together, and I wanted him to say something daring, something that proved that in spite of his unkempt hair and wrinkly clothes, Hadi could deliver a story that I could not have had with anyone else.

Because although no one had come forward and officially asked for me yet, there'd been what I'd heard Mrs. Ridha call *haraka*, or activity. There was the boy who met me at a dinner at a family friend's house. My siblings and I had gone with my father since my mother was working, and in her absence, this boy had chatted with me all evening. He'd asked me if he could stay in touch, and when I couldn't find the words to say no, I told him he could write me a letter but that he'd have to put a girl's name in the return address. As soon as I said the words, I heard how this one little act of deception made me complicit in his attention. I heard the gossipy aunties in my community whispering to each other, "How did he get her address unless she gave it to him?" I heard my reputation crumbling.

As soon as I got home, I told my mother everything. She clucked her tongue and shook her head. "I knew I shouldn't have let you out of my sight," she said before calling our host and asking her to end things.

Then there was the family friend who came to visit. The mother caught me on my way out of the bathroom, my hair still dripping wet from the shower, and asked me right there in the hallway to my bedroom if I liked Sylvester Stallone because she had a son who looked just like Sylvester Stallone. The question itself stunned me. No self-respecting Muslim girl would admit to an adult in the community that she liked a man even if he was an actor. Weeks later, she returned with the Arab Sylvester, who must have been in his twenties, but at the time, with his car and his full-time job, he seemed decades older than me. Later my mother learned through the community grapevine that our family friend's desperation had been driven by her son's American girlfriend. I was her last-ditch effort to introduce him to someone from a shared religion and culture.

And months later, there would be the first boy I actually liked, from a family that matched ours in every way. His family had been visiting our seaside town for the weekend, and on the evening they joined us for dinner, the boy and I talked for hours about school and our classes. In that short visit, he was far more direct in suggesting that he liked me than Hadi ever was, but with email and cell phones years into the future and with letter-writing already having proven itself far too risky, there was no way we could stay in touch.

I was content to wonder if one day this new boy might be another potential, but Mama was concerned. This boy was not Hadi, and his mother was not Mrs. Ridha.

As soon as his family left our house, Mama appeared in my bedroom and sat down next to me on my bed. She told me Jidu had complained about our guests' son. "Is this the way people do things?" he'd said. "If they had wanted to come see Huda, they should have announced their intentions first." And Bibi had wanted to know, "Did they ask you for her, hah? Will you give her or not?" The only person who didn't think anything of our guests was Baba, and that was because he'd been too absorbed in his own socializing and storytelling to notice.

When Mama finished reporting the news from downstairs, I was in a state of disbelief. "Are you serious? They said that? How come people can't talk in this house without everybody assuming things?"

"What do you want me to tell you?" Mama said. "That's the way we do things."

"I know," I replied, leaning back onto my bed. "But it isn't always a good way."

"Maybe it isn't," Mama acknowledged. She ran her hand along my comforter for a moment and then asked, "So did he say anything to you?"

"No," I said. "What could he say?"

"I don't know. I'm just asking."

"Did his mom say anything to you?" I asked in a voice I hoped conveyed only curiosity, no interest.

"No."

After a pause, Mama asked, "Do you like him?"

I shrugged, trying to make it seem as if I didn't care either way. But I could tell by the jumpy way I felt inside that it was too late. I wanted Mama to like this boy better than she liked Hadi; I wanted to feel as if I had options. But just as that thought brightened in my mind, our friendship with the Ridhas clouded over it.

"Anyway, let's see," Mama said as she got up to leave, but apparently by *see* she meant, "Let's check in with you every few days to see if you are still interested in this new boy."

To each inquiry, I'd answer, "I don't know. I barely even know him," partly because it was true, partly because I thought it was wrong to admit I liked him.

One afternoon that conversation went in a direction that stunned me. She'd picked me up from school, and we were on our way home when she said, "I talked to Ibrahim about this situation, and he didn't like the idea. He thinks Hadi is a better person for you."

"What?" I said, my voice sharp. "There is no situation yet. Nobody's even asked for me."

"I know. We were just discussing things in general, and he said that Hadi's the kind of guy you'd want to marry your sister, and I thought you should know that."

"What makes him think that?"

"The same reasons I think that. He's kind, Hudie. He'd be good to you."

I pressed into the headrest, quiet, confused. It was one thing for my mother to like Hadi and another thing for Ibrahim to like him. Growing up, Ibrahim had been so indifferent to me, his annoying middle sister, that it made me desperate for his approval. When we were kids, he traded me his broken, tired old things not for my belongings (those he just took) but for days of servitude. One time, he offered me a purple mechanical pencil in return for a month of me being his servant. Then there was the promise that he'd tell me the one thing that I actually did well if I served him for another month. I agreed to both miserable offers as if they were great deals, but at the first month's end, I found myself crying over a nonworking pencil, and at the end of the other month, I was left with a laughing older brother who claimed to have forgotten my only talent. And now my mother was telling me that this brother who was a whole foot taller than me, who picked me up off the ground to get me out of his way, thought about whom I should marry, that he cared that my future husband be a certain kind of person.

Mama continued, "So after I talked to Ibrahim, I started praying, 'Dear God, you know best. My Hudie is the best girl, and she deserves the best person for her.' And then I started thinking maybe I should make an istikhara about whether I should encourage you to be with Hadi. Just for me to know if I'm doing the right thing."

My stomach tightened. In the Shia tradition, the Quran can be consulted under the guidance of someone trained in interpreting its verses. Although most people only seek this kind of direction in matters of the utmost importance (if at all), my family sought it out regularly. Relatives at home and abroad would call Jidu and ask him to undertake an istikhara on their behalf before accepting a job, traveling to a new destination, or buying a car or a house. Because the practice was so commonplace among our relatives, I wouldn't question it for years. I wouldn't even think to ask Mama why she'd made an istikhara about a boy who hadn't even proposed to me yet, because all I could feel then was burning curiosity. I wanted to know what God wanted for me; I wanted one piece of the puzzle that was my future to fall into place.

"Okay . . . ," I said, straightening my back and staring out at the stretch of highway in front of me.

With both hands on the steering wheel, she looked over at me and said, "It doesn't mean anything as far as you're concerned. I don't even have to tell you how it came out. I just wanted to know what I should do as a mother."

An istikhara can only be solicited by the person who holds the *niya* or intention. Since Mama couldn't request an istikhara on my behalf, she'd phrased the niya from her perspective. This, too, I did not question.

"Okay . . . ," I repeated uneasily.

"So do you want to know how it came out?" she asked, her eyes returning to the road.

I froze. Last night while I was doing my homework, God had been consulted about my future. I pictured Mama going up the stairs to Jidu and Bibi's room. She would've told Jidu she had a niya without divulging what it was about. Then Jidu would've said his evening prayers, and after checking to see if it was a favorable time of the day, he would've opened the Quran, read the verse he landed on, and interpreted whether its meaning fell under the category of good, very good, not so good, or not so bad. When Jidu advised her of the istikhara's outcome, certainly Mama would've told him what it was regarding. Now the two of them knew what God wanted for me, and I didn't.

"Tell me," I said. God Himself delivered an opinion about my future, and I wanted to know what He'd said.

"Are you sure?" she asked.

"Just tell me."

"It came out very good," she said, her voice ringing with a girlish squeal.

"Really," I said with a slow nod. My mind reeled, trying to think of every possible reason why my mother, my brother, and now God liked Hadi, too. "But what about the whole Hadi-not-being-seyyid thing? You don't care anymore?"

Mama quickly glanced over her shoulder as she merged onto the highway. "Of course I care," she said, "but we can't have everything. He's a good boy. We know his family. These are things you don't find every day."

Dr. and Mrs. Ridha appeared in my mind, along with memories of their kind and generous hospitality over the years. I couldn't imagine disappointing them. Maybe this was what Mama meant all those times she talked about learning to love someone. You found someone like Hadi who came from a good family, you found a way to make him cut his hair, and then you made a decision to love him.

I released a heavy sigh. Now that my curiosity had been satisfied, questions rushed into my mind about what this all meant: Was I supposed to marry Hadi now? Was my time on the marriage market already over at sixteen?

"Why do you like him so much?" I asked with an ache in my voice. "Why did you even make the istikhara?"

Mama shook her head as if she didn't know how to make me understand. "Hudie, every night I pray that God will bring you someone who sees your value. You don't see what I do. That boy loves you. He would treat you like a jewel."

Mama's words pointed me back to reality: girls like me married the right boy and fell in love later. I just didn't expect to become that girl now, for Mama to have glimpsed into a divine crystal ball and shown me my future while I was a junior in high school. I felt pressure building in my nose and at the back of my eyes. I turned to look out the window before I started to cry.

CHAPTER 7

THIS AMERICAN RITE OF PASSAGE

For months after the istikhara, I tried to think of reasons why God had picked Hadi. Maybe it was because we didn't know the other boy or his family as well as we knew the Ridhas. Or maybe it was because God knew the other boy had a girlfriend before me, and I believed I should only marry a guy who'd lived by the same strict code that I had (if I couldn't fight the double standard that let boys bend the rules before marriage without damage to their reputations, at least I wouldn't condone it).

I kept a list of things that confirmed the istikhara's wisdom.

1. If I married Hadi, I wouldn't have to be set up with anyone. Over the summer, Jamila got married to a man she met over one weekend. Hadi had cut his hair for the wedding and wore a tuxedo. These two things—the arranged marriage I didn't want and the haircut I did—felt like signs.

2. If I married Hadi, at least Baba would be there for my wedding. With Baba's most recent hospitalization, his time on earth felt like a fragile thing.

3. If I married Hadi, I'd have more freedom. Mama had always clung to a tight travel policy: "If we fly, we fly together, so if we die, we die together." She often followed up this morbid sentiment by saying, "You can do that after you get married.

Then it'll be your husband's job to worry about you." It made sense to get married and have more choices for school, for work, and for my future.

I didn't catch that there was nothing on the list particular to Hadi himself. I'd grown up listening to people describe marriage prospects as if they were commodities, labeled by profession, age, family name, country of origin, religious sect, and it never occurred to me that I didn't know much about Hadi as a person. It was my senior year. I had just spent the last few years moving through high school as if it were a giant checklist marked "Get into a Good College," and for the most part, I'd been able to tick off every goal I'd set for myself. I'd gone to Girl's State that summer. I was student-body president. I'd won several local speech competitions, and I'd been on the homecoming court. All this in spite of being the girl from the different religion who wore dark tights and the longest skirt in school and who was seventeen going on eighteen and had never been kissed. And somehow I felt strengthened by these recognitions, as if they proved definitively that it was possible to meld the rules of being Muslim with an American lifestyle. This list of reasons to marry Hadi was just another part of all the organizing and planning I was doing in the rest of my life—filling out college applications, writing essays, studying for the SATs, and picking a husband.

These thoughts were swirling around in my mind when Mama came to me in my bedroom and asked if I wanted my aunty Najma, who happened to live in Lebanon, to tailor me a dress. "You know, in case something should happen?" she added.

"Like what?" I asked because I suspected she meant something to do with an engagement, but I wanted to hear her say it.

"Are you going to go to your senior prom?" she asked. "You could always go with Hadi."

The question surprised me. Mama had learned about proms from Mrs. Ridha who'd sent Jamila with Hadi during her senior year.

I never thought Mama would care whether or not I attended this American rite of passage, but a part of me was relieved that she'd mentioned it. If I was going to be marrying Hadi in a matter of time, it didn't seem fair that I miss out on this last dance of my high school career, especially after spending years covering every shift at the student government's soda booth and listening to the parent chaperones cluck, "How come a pretty girl like you doesn't have a date?"

But at the same time, I knew the rules about going out with a boy before marriage—that it was basically forbidden unless the purpose was for marriage, and even then it was best to have a chaperone. Mama's suggestion seemed impossible.

"I don't see how that would work," I said, flipping the book in my lap shut. "What would you do? Pick up the phone and say to his mom, 'Will you please have your son take my daughter to her prom?'"

"His mom already called me and asked me if you wanted him to take you."

"And what did you tell her?"

"I said I had to ask you."

"Does it matter what I want? What would we say to Baba, Bibi, Jidu, the whole world?"

"We could figure something out."

I hugged my knees to my chest. "But what about it not being allowed?"

"Well, yes, but I don't want you to be disappointed. Would you be disappointed?"

"Maybe," I said, "but I'll get over it. I don't want to do something wrong just so I won't be disappointed."

"Do you want me to make an istikhara?"

I knew this suggestion was coming. Mama always looked to God for all her parenting decisions—camps, field trips, dances, parties—but in light of Mama's previous istikhara about Hadi, this question carried a different kind of charge. It was as if she was digging for confirmation from God, and this was something I needed, too. I wanted to hear again that Hadi was the one.

"Okay," I said. "Do it."

The next morning when Mama told me the istikhara came out good, she gushed, "And you know what else? I made another istikhara, about you and Hadi, to make sure I was doing the right thing to encourage you, and it came out good again."

This was the third sign from God that He wanted Hadi and me to be together, and I felt not just commanded to listen but blessed. It was as if God was pointing to a path and saying, "Take this boy and have a good life."

After dinner Mama, Lina, and I headed up to my room to flip through magazines and books to find pictures of dresses to fax to Aunty Najma. Lina knew why we were looking for dresses, and Mama didn't want her getting the wrong idea. Thumbing through a magazine, Mama said, "Now, just because Hudie is going to the prom, it doesn't mean that you can go to your prom too. If you have someone you'd consider marrying when you are in high school, that's a different story, but otherwise, it's a no."

Lina shot Mama an insulted look and said, "I know that. I just don't want Hudie to get married."

Something inside me sank. In all my eagerness to know this one thing that awaited me, I hadn't paused to consider all the ways in which marriage was tied to loss. My marriage would mean Lina and Baba having dinner alone while Mama was at work. It would mean Mama and Baba in their bedroom downstairs and Lina sleeping alone upstairs. It would mean that my bedroom would take on that same uninhabited feel that Ibrahim's had now that he'd gone off to college, except that I wouldn't return to my room the way he did on breaks. I'd have a husband, my own house. Marriage was a beginning, but it was also an end.

"I'm not getting married," I said for Lina's benefit and mine. Hadi had no idea these istikharas had been made. He didn't know that if he wanted to love me, I was prepared to love him back.

CHAPTER 8

❁

SEE ME AT THE PROM

My life's only love story was starting, and so far the only characters in the scene were our mothers. Our mothers had told our respective families that Hadi was coming up to stay with us so he could attend a car show at the racetrack right by our house. Mrs. Ridha would accompany him, and when it came time for me to go to my "mandatory school function," she'd suggest that Hadi drop me off on his way out.

I didn't take issue with the deceit as much as it bothered me that Hadi and I had never spoken to each other about going to my prom. I didn't want the first time we went out alone together to be awkward, for him to just show up at our house the night before and leave me to say, "So it looks like you're the lucky fella who gets to take me to my prom tomorrow."

But the only way I could talk to Hadi before the prom was to ask for help with my math homework. Hadi was now a junior in college, but he'd been taking college-level math since high school. He had coached me through a number of sticky equations in the past, and I knew if I complained long enough, Mama would pick up the phone and tell Mrs. Ridha to tell Hadi to expect a phone call. Then my mother would dial his number at the on-campus apartment he shared with his roommates, get him on the phone, and pass it to me. All this to avoid the impropriety of me calling a boy.

That night, after Hadi talked me through factoring a complicated equation, I brought up the prom, hoping to hear him say how much he wanted to go with me, how he'd longed his whole life for this opportunity. Stretched out on my bedroom floor, I prompted him with a series of negative statements that begged for correction, starting with, "I hope you don't feel like you have to go. It's just that I'm the student-body president, and it would be nice to finally go to an event instead of just setting it up and leaving."

"No, that's fine. I don't mind," he said.

"And, I have this red dress I've been wanting to wear that my aunt in Lebanon made for me. My friend Diana and I have this thing about being the Lady in Red."

The dress Aunty Najma sent me hung at the back of my closet, not only reproduced from the photograph I faxed her but improved according to Middle Eastern standards of formal wear. Aunty Najma had tiny red sequins stitched onto every curve of lace along the entire body of the dress. Although she had known nothing about the prom, she knew the dress symbolized the possibility that something could happen soon, something worthy of a celebration.

"I like that song too," Hadi said. "I have the tape."

"I only have it recorded off the radio, and it's missing the first part."

"I should make you a tape then. What other songs do you like?"

Right away, I knew I wouldn't tell Hadi which songs I wanted to hear. I wanted to believe he would go searching for lyrics that best communicated his feelings for me.

"Why don't you surprise me?" I said.

"I can do that."

"Well, I'm sure you're busy. I should let you get back to your work."

"That's okay. I don't really have that much to do."

"You're in college. How can you not have anything more important to do than talk to me?"

A few seconds passed without Hadi saying anything, and I wanted my question back. "You don't have to answer that," I said.

"No. It's fine."

"Okay, then."

"I guess I like talking to you."

"How come?"

Another long pause followed. I twirled my hair, sniffed the tip of one of my curls, flicked something out from under one of my fingernails, and then I couldn't take it any longer.

"If you don't have an answer, that's fine. It just seemed like you didn't want to get off the phone." I waited a moment, heard nothing, and then added, "So either you really don't like talking to me that much, or it's hard to say."

"It's that one," he said.

"Which one?"

"The last one."

"Do you ever think it might be easier to say?"

"Yeah."

"When?"

"I don't know. It's just hard over the phone."

"You're going to see me at my prom."

"Yeah."

"Maybe you should tell me then why you like talking to me, or . . . tell me what you want me to be to you. . . ."

He paused for so long I thought we were disconnected. "Hello?"

"Yeah, I'm here."

"Okay, never mind everything I said. You don't have to tell me anything."

"No. It's not that."

"It's just hard?" I asked.

"Yeah. It's hard."

"Well, I'll let you off the hook for now, but by my prom, I'm going to be expecting an answer," I said, half-joking, half-threatening. "Do you think you can come up with an answer by then?"

"Okay," he answered, but he sounded afraid.

When we finally hung up the phone, I went unsteady with worry. If I was ever going to experience a moment out of Diana and my daydreams, it had to be now, inside this space our mothers had built for us. I couldn't afford to make allowances for Hadi's shyness or for the culture we'd both grown up in, because this opportunity to be alone with a boy before I married him would not likely come again. But now if Hadi did say something to me at my prom, I would always wonder whether it was because he sincerely felt it or if it was because I had been shamelessly pushy. And Hadi's phone presence concerned me. He paused for far longer than the socially accepted standard in a conversation, so much so that I'd wished I had a buzzer to signal that the time for a response had expired. This phone call had been our longest conversation, the first on any topic of substance. How unfortunate to be discovering what Hadi was like on the phone now, now that the istikharas had been made, now that my future had been decided.

———————————— ✿ ————————————

CHAPTER 9

A BIG FAMILY SECRET

In the weeks leading up to the prom, I talked myself out of all my hesitations. There was no sense in missing out on yet another high school milestone if I was going to end up marrying Hadi anyway, and this was the perfect opportunity to start falling in love. Maybe Hadi would answer the questions I left him with at the end of our phone call as soon as we were alone in the car. Or maybe he would wait and ask the DJ to play "The Lady in Red" before he confessed how much he'd always loved me. Either way, by the end of the evening, we would be more than just a couple brought together by their families and shared religion.

That morning, I got my hair done at the mall. Back at home, I did my *wudhu* for my afternoon prayers, washing my face, arms, and feet while being careful not to disturb my updo at the second-to-the-last step, when a wet hand is run across the top of the head. After I prayed, I secured the hairs that had come loose under my head-covering, then put on nail polish and makeup. It wasn't until I came downstairs and discovered that Mrs. Ridha was occupying my grandparents in one room while Mama snuck me and Hadi out the door that the absurdity of going to the prom hit me. I was going through such an American rite of passage like such a Muslim, Arab girl. My prom was my first time out of the house with a boy, a boy who could be my future husband.

In the car, I reached for my seat belt and said, "I feel bad sneaking out like that."

"Sorry," Hadi said, and after an awkward pause added, "Your dress is nice."

Some of the evening's anticipation went flat at the tepid compliment. Just my dress was nice? I had hoped Hadi would tell me that I was beautiful.

"You look nice, too," I said, and I meant it. With a brand-new haircut, his face freshly shaven, and a crisp tuxedo, Hadi looked more handsome than I'd ever seen him before.

Another pause, and then Hadi said, "I have something for you. Open the glove compartment."

Already? I was sure it wasn't a ring, but maybe it was a piece of jewelry, something to promise us to each other.

I lifted the latch and found a miniature BMW convertible in a clear, plastic box—the model I had told him I wished my first car would be. And it was red.

"Thank you. That's really sweet," I said, my heart filling with warmth and a sudden jolt of nervousness. If Hadi had thought so far ahead as to buy me the toy car, then surely he had more planned. What if he answered my question from our phone conversation and asked me to marry him?

That year the prom was being held at my top choice of future wedding venues, a historic naval building that had once been a grand hotel situated less than a mile away from downtown and the beach. Hadi opened my car door, and we walked up the steps to the ballroom side by side with plenty of space between us. At the door, I took in the high ceilings and arched windows, the heavy draperies and wrought-iron candelabras affixed to the walls. To the side of the dance floor stood Diana and her date, a guy she'd met at one of her college campus tours. In the weeks leading up to the prom, I'd described the extent of my relationship with Hadi in teenage detail, but I had made Diana swear repeatedly not to give me away. Under no circumstances could she mention the name Hadi, not in front of him or my parents or my siblings. It was an all-around Never Ever. Now I led Hadi over to our table, our hands at our sides and a sizeable distance between us. Diana played the part of ignorance well, accepting introductions and handshakes without the "I've heard so much about you" I feared.

At our table, Nadia's place was unoccupied. We'd begged her to come with her brother, but she'd refused, saying a silly prom was not worth the sin. As I glanced around the room, Nadia's words returned to me along with a creeping sense of guilt. At neighboring tables, couples held hands, put their arms around each other, and leaned over in their chairs to kiss. Seeing Hadi in the chair next to me, his hands folded in his lap, I wondered why I had tried so hard to go to a dance. We didn't belong here.

I waited for Hadi to strike up a conversation with Diana or at least with her date, but Hadi was quiet. I tried to make conversation for everyone, and all the while, my mind prepared excuses for him. He was a college student. He was above the immaturity of a high school prom. But as I blabbered, a foundation of disappointment was being poured. Tomorrow Diana would not call to tell me that Hadi was a great guy, that he was cute, or funny, or a good catch. I wasn't shy. I didn't want to marry a shy guy.

We finished eating, the lights dimmed, and the music started. Diana got up to dance with her date. The other couples at our table followed. Soon Hadi and I were sitting alone. Over the thump of the music, I remarked about the food and the place, the people dancing around me, the songs being played, and then I gave up on conversation entirely. I realized Hadi wasn't going to break the rules and ask me to dance—that there would be no "Lady in Red" moment under a disco ball—and so instead, I suggested we go for a walk. First, we took the elevator upstairs to see the view of the city's lights and then downstairs to the tiled veranda.

With our elbows resting along the adobe wall that surrounded the length of the veranda, we looked out at the moonlit lawn and the silhouette of rose bushes that stood along its edges. The cool night air traveled through the holes of my unlined lace sleeves, making me shiver. Hadi offered me his jacket.

After an exchange of, "I'm fine" and "Please, take it," I took his jacket just to make the back-and-forth stop. He held it open for me while I slid in my arms, and right away, I blushed at the body heat we were sharing for the first time, the way the scent of his cologne now pressed upon my neck. I was pleased to discover Hadi's sleeves covered my hands. I'd always wished Hadi was more than three inches taller than me so that I'd feel small when I stood next to him. Now I knew that even if Hadi wasn't a big guy, he was big enough for me.

I looked down to my side at the terra-cotta pots filled with geraniums, and then I looked up at the moon in the cloudless sky, all the while hoping that my silence would force Hadi to speak.

It didn't.

I turned around so that my back rested against the wall, folded my arms, and said, "So, kind of boring, huh? Sorry I dragged you out here."

"I'm having fun."

"How could you be having fun? All we're doing is watching other people have fun," I said and then immediately regretted such a shameless attempt to get Hadi to talk.

"So is there anything you want to tell me?" I asked, trying to be more forthright. I waited a moment, expecting him to bring up our last phone conversation and tell me everything I'd been waiting to hear.

But Hadi stood there staring at me. No words. Just an awkward smile that I couldn't even read for confirmation that he'd understood me. An anxious itch overcame me. After all this effort to make a dress and sneak out here, was it possible that he wouldn't say anything?

I couldn't wait any longer. Without any attempt at subtlety, I asked, "Are you going to answer my question? The one from before, remember?"

"I remember," he said, his eyebrows rising slightly, his mouth twisting in a crooked half smile. He fidgeted, straightened his back, and shifted his weight from foot to foot.

I searched Hadi's face for a sign that he was about to speak, but his expression remained unchanged.

I shook my head. What was this guy's problem? I couldn't stay quiet for that long if I tried. Maybe he didn't really like me. But he came all the way here. He bought me that stupid toy BMW. What if I'd taken this risk, put my reputation on the line to go out with him, and these insipid smiles and a model car were the best he had to offer? What if he was just waiting for his mother to do everything for him? She'd arranged this prom. She'd arrange our marriage.

I looked down at the floor and at my shoes. Mama had used a hot-glue gun to attach a string of red sequins in a floral design along each shoe, but the sequins were not holding together. The loops that were meant to be petals flapped about, exposing white blobs of glue underneath.

"You know what," I said, forcing a chipper tone, "you can take me home now. I'm done."

"Are you sure?" Hadi asked, suddenly coming back to life.

"I'm sure. Here, why don't you take your jacket?"

"No, you keep it. I'm fine."

I was too busy ranting inside my head to say any more. I declared us over. I didn't know how to make sense of the istikharas' positive results, but on that quiet walk back to the car, I preferred the uncertainty of my future prospects to a lifetime with someone I did not like. Only an unlikeable person would leave another person to flounder in such an awkward moment. Only an unlikeable person wouldn't recognize the vulnerability in an unanswered question. Or a shy person, and shy was no better. This had been my chance to go out alone with a boy without being engaged or married to him, to write the opening to a love story that didn't have our parents on every page, and he ruined it.

At home I slipped on a T-shirt and a pair of sweat pants and yanked out the army of bobby pins that had been fortifying my hair since the morning. I ran a brush through the hair that was still stiff with hair spray and opened the door. Hadi was in the hallway upstairs, leaning against the banister.

"Getting ready for bed?" he asked.

Our culture had to make everything so damn familial. I could get over the fact that a boy didn't drive to my house to pick me up because he was already staying there. I could get over not having my proud parents snap my picture before I stepped out the door because my stupid prom was a big family secret. But what American girl had to bring her bad date home and make polite conversation with him in her pajamas? What American girl had to wake up and help her mother serve him and his mother tea and breakfast the next morning?

"Not yet," I said. "I'll probably do some of my homework. That's what every girl dreams of doing after her prom."

Hadi did not react to my sarcastic tone. "I could help if you want," he said.

I shrugged. "May as well."

We worked through a few problems on the floor of my bedroom, the door wide open. A short while later, Baba came upstairs to say good night. "Hah," he said, surprised to see Hadi in my room. Then he registered the book open in front of us. "Oh, you are doing your homework. Okay. Good for you."

He bent down and kissed my head, and I regretted sneaking out to go to the prom. The evening had not been worth the deceit. In the sweetest voice I could muster, I said, "I love you, Daddy."

I watched Baba descend the stairs in his plaid, flannel pajamas, so innocent, so naïve to the plots his wife and child had cooked up behind his back. I had betrayed such a naïve, unsuspecting man, a man whose pajama pants never seemed to reach past his ankles. I looked over at Hadi next to me, and I wanted to make him pay for not being worth the lie. I thought of a hundred different ways to say, "You screwed up," until I settled on, "You missed an opportunity, you know."

"If I did, I'm sorry."

"Well, you did," I said without looking up from my textbook.

"At least you got to be the Lady in Red."

"No, I didn't." I pushed the paper toward him. "Tell me what to do."

Step-by-step, Hadi walked me through the problem I'd copied out of my book. He never read the explanation, never flipped back to previous chapters to remind himself how to solve the equation. No matter what level of math I was in, ninth-grade algebra, tenth-grade geometry, eleventh-grade trigonometry, and now precalculus, Hadi knew the answers. I couldn't remember anything from one year to the next, but Hadi owned the math he knew. He could teach it, share it. This impressed me, but I didn't admit it. I worked by Hadi's side grumpily, and when he left the next day, I went up to my room and cried yesterday's tears.

A few nights later, the phone in my room rang. I expected to hear Diana's voice on the other line.

"Hi," Hadi said.

"Hi," I answered and waited. I tried to keep busy wrapping the cord around my finger, but after a few seconds of listening to air, I grew antsy. "So did you call just to say hi?"

"No. I wanted to call because I'm really sorry about everything that happened. I haven't been able to sleep or eat since. I wanted to call you earlier, but I didn't know what I would say if someone else answered the phone."

"I'm fine."

"I want to answer your question."

"You don't have to."

"I want to."

I waited again. After a minute, I added, "Listen, if you don't want to, then don't."

"No. I'm just not good with words. I need to think about what I'm going to say."

I heard him taking a deep breath. Then he paused again before saying, "Whenever I see myself in the future, the only person I imagine myself with is you."

I froze as if I were in a conversation with a deer on my lawn. If I moved, I feared he'd run away.

"I think about you all the time, and when I dream about you, I don't want to wake up. I wanted to answer your question, but I kept telling myself that's not the kind of thing you should say to someone who is going to be somebody else's wife."

A mix of tenderness and frustration overwhelmed me. "With all that talk about us, how could you assume I was going to marry someone else?"

"You don't know what it's like to hear about all the families that ask my mom about you," Hadi said. "Why would I think you would marry a guy like me? I'm not the tallest. I'm not the smartest. I'm not the best-looking. I figured one day I'd hear that you were engaged to someone else, and I'd move away and try not to ever see you again."

I pictured Hadi fretting over losing me to someone else, and I wanted to hear more. "But why would you plan on moving away? You would've met someone else and been happy with her."

"I couldn't bear to watch you married to somebody else, having kids that should've been mine."

I didn't know what to say. Diana and I had spent so much time picturing how we wanted a man to profess his love to us, but we never paused to consider what we'd say in return.

"That's funny," I said. "You assumed I'd marry someone else, and I always felt like I couldn't marry anyone else." And then hearing how that sounded, I added, "And that's great, because I like you, too. You've always been so sweet to me. It just bothered me to think you were waiting around for your mom to—you know—fix us up."

"I swear to you, I never thought that," Hadi said. "I just planned on spending the rest of my life dreaming about you."

My heart swelled, and my stomach filled with a kind of queasiness I'd never felt before. Maybe Mama was right, and you could learn to love someone. Maybe knowing a guy loved you was enough to flip the switch in your heart that made you love him back.

"But that's why I kept pushing you to say something to me," I said. "I gave you an opportunity to take matters into your own hands, and you didn't."

"I just kept thinking about how you were going to marry somebody better than me, somebody with a job and a house who can give you all the things you deserve, and I thought it would make things harder if I told you how I felt."

I liked the notion of Hadi being content to love me from afar. It was cinematic and tragic, and it filled me with a resolve to love him, too.

"I'm not going to marry anybody else," I said. "So if you want me to have what I deserve, you better become the best."

"I can do that if you'll help me."

"I will," I said, suddenly excited by the challenge of fixing him. Everything I didn't like about Hadi, I'd change. This was the premise of every romantic comedy I loved, coming to life. It would be just like the movie *Pretty Woman* except for the minor differences in the protagonist's gender and choice of profession.

Hadi and I talked for a total of three hours that night. An hour into our conversation, Mama came upstairs to see what was keeping me in my room, and when I mouthed that I was on the phone with Hadi, she nodded and whispered that she'd guard the phone line. Hadi and I reviewed our childhoods together, what we were really thinking at the moments we both remembered. Nothing about our conversation struck me as off—not Hadi's lack of confidence or my misguided determination to change him. On the contrary, I got off the phone with Hadi feeling as if I'd arrived into one of the scenes that Diana and I dreamt up. It was nothing like I'd pictured. There were no balloons, limousines, or music, but it was only the beginning. Hadi could always plan something amazing for our proposal.

CHAPTER 10

❁

MARCHING TOWARD MARRIAGE

The weekend of my high school graduation, houseguests occupied every corner of our home—Hadi and his entire family, his aunts, uncles, and cousins; and Mama's cousin Marwa and her children. Since there weren't enough bedrooms for individual families, we camped out according to gender. Women in the bedrooms, men on the floor in the living room and family room.

At the ceremony, my extended family and the Ridha clan took up the entire first two rows of the auditorium. From where I sat on stage, I saw Mama, Lina, and Baba, grinning, holding up signs with my name on them. Whenever I looked at Mama, she clapped and blew me kisses. Whenever I looked over at Hadi, our eyes locked until I turned away. He looked better at my prom. His hair was big today, bushy and wavy, and his sideburns were growing over his ears. I doubted he'd cut his hair since then. The shirt he wore was wrinkly too, and the denim blazer he wore over it struck me as unfashionable.

A train of self-pity chugged through me. This was my first time seeing Hadi since our phone conversation. I had expected that warmth I'd felt for Hadi on the phone to flood me as soon as I saw him, but here I was again picking on his clothes and his hair. And here I was, onstage at my high school graduation, struck by a shock of panic. If I didn't feel that kind of cinematic love for Hadi and we were marching toward marriage, then that meant I would never feel that kind of love for anyone, ever.

I stopped myself. No. That wasn't how Mama or my aunts felt about their husbands. That kind of love wasn't essential to a good marriage.

Our valedictorian took to the podium, and I writhed in my metal folding chair. In the end, I'd been denied the throne of academic excellence by the plague of every nerd's existence, physical education. In spite of four years of As and honor points, I could not undo the B plus that was caused by one measly skills test in volleyball when I did not serve the ball over the net—not even once.

I watched our speaker's cheeks quiver with nerves, and I told myself that she could have this speech because this was the only one she had in high school. I'd stood behind a microphone at more assemblies than I could count, and our classmates had already voted me Most Likely to Never Be Forgotten and Most Likely to be President of the United States. But this last thought filled me with more longing than comfort. I wanted that microphone in my hand more than I wanted the title of valedictorian. Behind a microphone, it didn't matter that I was only eighteen and already working my way into a marriage. When my voice carried strong and unwavering through an auditorium, nobody could box me into the Muslim woman stereotype. Not even myself.

After the ceremony, we stood outside the auditorium, taking pictures. When the fuss died down, Hadi wandered over to me and whispered, "You look cute." His words felt like their own kind of diploma, certifying that I was a grown woman with a man in her life now.

Later that night, I went to my school's grad night celebration, but I couldn't bring myself to play laser tag and jump around in a sumo wrestler's suit when I knew I had my entire future to plan with Hadi. I called Mama and told her I wanted to come home early. She told me exactly what I wanted to hear—that she'd send Hadi to pick me up.

This time when Hadi asked me if I wanted to go straight home, I said no. We drove to a restaurant across the street from school and slid into a booth covered in red vinyl.

"It felt weird to say 'two' to that hostess," Hadi said.

"It felt weird to hear it," I said, pressing my hand down on my stomach. The unsteady, queasy feeling I'd had when we were on the phone together had returned. I was alone in a restaurant with a boy for the first time in my life.

"How did my mom send you without it looking suspicious?"

"She made a point of announcing you needed to be picked up. Then my mom said to send me so that your mom wouldn't have to leave the house when she had so many guests, and then your mom said that if you weren't quite done, I should just wait for you in the car. And then at the door, she told me not to feel like we had to rush back."

"Wow. You'd think they had a script." Our mothers facilitated our coupling so naturally I had to wonder if matchmaking was a maternal instinct.

We didn't speak again until our food arrived. Hadi dipped a french fry in ketchup and said, "I'm so proud of you. You got so many awards today."

"Good. I want you to be proud of me," I said and pulled two napkins out of the dispenser. I passed one to Hadi and tucked the other under my plate. "Because then you'll understand why I don't have any intention of giving up on school."

I wanted an American love story so much, and yet I was the one who immediately slipped into the role of the Muslim woman being courted, secure in the presumption that the boy on the other side of the table was there for marriage, well versed in her rights and ready with demands. Although Mama had never sat me down and told me what to ask for as a woman in Islam, I'd prepared for the talks I'd given in those world religions classes. I knew my future spouse had to match if not improve the lifestyle I'd been accustomed to in my parents' home. I knew that I had a right to work and that my earnings belonged entirely to me and not to our household. I knew that I could request to be paid for childcare and housework. I knew that Hadi was the one who had to prove something to me.

"Of course. I wouldn't want you to."

"Because I have plans for myself," I said, still ignoring the plate of fries in front of me. "I don't know what I want to do yet, but I want to do something, and it's gonna be big. You only know the home-me, but the school-me is different."

"You don't have to tell me how special you are."

"I'm glad you think that because I plan on working like my mom," I said, now picking up a thick french fry and waving it at him. "I'm not the kind of girl who's going to stay home and make cakes. I'll make you cake, but only when I want to."

Hadi dug a spoon into his sundae. "Well, thank you. I'm sure it will be very good cake."

"Yes, it will," I said and bit into the fry that had been my pointer. "Now back to business. Since we both want to get advanced degrees, this should work out. My parents would never let me go to graduate school out of state, so we can apply together, and you can go to medical school, and I can go to whatever-I-decide school."

Back in March, I'd been wait-listed at Stanford. I moped and cried for about a day. I'd only been allowed to apply to colleges within driving distance, and at the time, I believed Stanford was the only university in our area with the kind of reputation that would prove to people that I was smart. As much as the people in our community stigmatized late marriage, they also made assumptions about the girls who married young, that they were less focused on school and only interested in starting a family. No matter when I got married, nobody would assume those things about me if I had been admitted to Stanford. But when I didn't get pulled off the wait list, I accepted my admission to Santa Clara University. They'd given me a small scholarship and a certificate to say I'd been accepted with honors. A certificate with gold edging. I told myself that was a university that knew how to treat a girl, but if I was married, I could go to school anywhere. I pictured Hadi getting into a prestigious medical school and us getting married after my second year. Then I could transfer and still have a name-dropping degree.

"You do want to go to medical school?" I added as an after-thought. It just occurred to me that I'd never asked Hadi myself. Hadi and I had known each other our entire lives, but the things we knew about each other were limited to what our mothers had told us and the few topics we'd discussed over the phone.

Hadi swallowed a spoonful of ice cream and said, "If I get in."

Hadi's lack of certainty was unexpected. "Why wouldn't you get in? You're smart," I said. I'd gone to his high school graduation; he'd been on the honor roll. He was probably like me, got upset over Bs.

"It's really hard to get in."

"But I'm sure if you do some research and get good letters of rec, you'll be fine."

Hadi raised his eyebrows and shrugged. I didn't like his noncom-mittal attitude. Whenever I wanted something, I made plans, plots, and lists. I feared that Hadi did not share the same ambition, and I wondered if I should press the issue or if he was just being humble. Humility, after all, was a good quality in a husband.

I went back to my fries, and I told Hadi we'd better hurry up and get home before our families wondered why we were gone so long. As we walked back to the car, I marveled at the foot of space we still left between us. I'd just spent a half hour discussing my future life with a boy whose hand I'd never held, a boy who had not even told me that he loved me. I thought of my classmates back at grad night, and I couldn't imagine telling anyone but Nadia and Diana about this. For the rest of the world, I'd need a different opening to this relationship; I'd need a better story.

When we got back home at a little past midnight, the family room was still full of our pajama-clad relatives drinking tea, watching television, joking, and laughing. After changing into our pajamas, Hadi and I sat among them, at opposite ends of the bench seating surrounding the breakfast-nook table. One by one, those around us got up to get ready for bed, but we stayed seated. When we were the only ones left at the table, Hadi scooted around the bench until he was sitting so close to me that our legs touched. It was the closest I'd ever been to him since we were children, squeezed in next to each other in the back row of the family car or peering over the pages of a comic book we were all trying to read. I looked up at Hadi, wanting to feel some certainty that this warmth coursing through me was love. But his eyebrows were so full. One end seemed to be reaching out in an effort to join the other. I hoped it was okay for a guy to pluck, but even if it was, how would I suggest it?

Hadi leaned in closer and smelled my hair. His chest pressed against the length of my arm, and I felt him breathe. I forbade myself any further study of his eyebrows, but Hadi was staring at me so intently and lovingly that I had to look down and fix my gaze on my hands folded in my lap.

From the corner of my eye, I saw Hadi reaching for the curly piece of string, attached to a sheet of wrapping paper discarded on the table. He twirled it between two of his fingers, and then, without saying anything, he took my hand out of my lap and tied the string around my ring finger.

I held my breath. *Please don't ask me to marry you now. It can't happen like this, with me in my pajamas, my hair a mess, no diamond ring, no audience.*

"I want to spend the rest of my life with you," he said, placing his palm against mine, his way of holding my hand without holding it at all.

"Is that supposed to be a question?" I asked and withdrew my hand back into my lap before anyone wandered into the kitchen.

"I'm asking you if you'll spend the rest of your life with me."

I stared down at my still-warm hand. Hadi's touch had been more remarkable than the question I'd spent night after night imagining. Those words did not slow time or cause music to erupt from the walls. They did not make fireworks burst from the sky or conjure up a crowd hooting congratulatory cheer.

I didn't want to accept that such life-changing words could feel so ordinary, that this moment I'd been waiting for my entire life could already be over with such little ceremony.

"Yes," I said and then added, "But this doesn't count, okay? You still have to ask me for real."

Hadi nodded, and I was relieved. The string was a tender gesture without a doubt, but I needed a grander memory for the official proposal in my life's only love story.

CHAPTER 11

LUNCH COMPANY

That fall, as soon as I moved into my dorm room, Hadi started calling me from his on-campus apartment at UC San Diego. These were secret phone calls—between Hadi, me, and my mother. I'd told Mama that Hadi had expressed his intention to marry me and that he wished to call, but in return, she'd given me only tacit consent. She did not want to be complicit in our conversing before Hadi's family officially approached us. These conversations could only be the behind-the-scenes work, the orchestrating of a relationship. If Hadi and I wanted to officially become a couple, all our parents would have to become involved, permission granted and hard, precious metal rings placed on our fingers.

In the meantime, I took notes in a journal while we talked.

> Hadi: It would be nice to actually touch you.
> Huda: It may be a disappointment.
> Hadi: I haven't been disappointed so far. You would be about as disappointing as an ice-cold glass of water on a hot day.
> Hadi: Whatever you are, I like. If you were to tell me you had three arms, I'd think that was great. You could carry more stuff. I'd think that's the way everyone should be.

I never scribbled down my feelings for Hadi or my thoughts about our impending engagement or marriage. All I wanted was a log of compliments that proved Hadi had said the kind of things to me that any Western woman might have fallen for, that we'd been brought together by more than family friendship and istikharas. I couldn't imagine a day when the omissions in those journals would speak more to my mind-set than the words they captured. At the time, I only wanted my flattery of the day recorded so I could get back to studying. I'd set a goal to graduate with a 4.0 GPA, and after an hour of talking, I looked for excuses to get off the phone. Sometimes I picked a fight.

On one such occasion, Hadi asked me if any of the people in my study groups were guys. I said that none of them were, and he said that he preferred it that way, adding, "I can't imagine how anyone could spend time with you and not fall in love with you."

I balked at the suggestion, called it ridiculous. Not only did Hadi sound jealous, but he was also making his feelings for me far too undiscriminating. "If I need to study with a guy to do well in a course," I added, "I will."

It was a silly declaration because I didn't mean it. Ever since a boy in my dormitory asked me if I wanted to join him at dinner and I had to tell him that I was Muslim and not allowed to socialize with boys, I'd made up my own set of rules to avoid being put in that awkward position again. Never sit next to a boy in class. Never speak to a boy unless he speaks to you first. Give an excuse if a boy asks you to study.

But three weeks into the quarter, I found myself struggling with my ethics class. Not only did Dr. Farber announce that she'd be giving us a multiple-choice midterm the following week (I preferred courses that required papers—I'd start them early, get feedback during office hours, and write and rewrite until I could almost guarantee myself an A), but the content of our class had also taken an uncomfortable turn. On the day we discussed sexual philosophy, Dr. Farber came to class bouncing a coiled black leather whip in her palm. She said we'd be exploring different cultural attitudes toward sex and that the ladies in the classroom would find Taoist sexual philosophy especially interesting. Taoist men, she explained, trained themselves to last. "That's why a Taoist man is *hard* to find," she added as if delivering a punch line.

The class had erupted in laughter, but I didn't get it. Last at what?

After class the curly-haired, blond guy who sat two rows over motioned me to his desk. He introduced himself as Matt and the woman standing next to him as Jen and said, "We're getting a study group together. Interested?"

"Sure," I said. I could use the help of what I figured to be a senior and a thirty-something on her second career.

"Do you wanna grab some lunch?"

I didn't. Matt and his mature friend seemed like boring lunch company, but it struck me as impolite to refuse now that they'd invited me to join their study group.

"Okay," I said.

We were headed for the cafeteria when Jen turned and walked away with a wave, and Matt started walking toward the parking lot.

I stopped. "Isn't Jen coming with us?"

"No, she always leaves right after class."

"Then aren't we going to the cafeteria?"

"I make it a policy not to eat there. I'll take you somewhere off campus."

I had to say something. But what? I'd already said I'd go to lunch. Maybe I was making this too complicated. In college, boys and girls had lunch together, and it didn't mean anything.

Matt opened the door of his run-down Datsun for me, and I sat down dizzy with regret. I remembered something Nadia had said: "When an unmarried boy and girl are alone together, the third person is the devil."

Matt parked outside a diner that looked like a barn, its name printed in capital letters that appeared to be dripping paint. Inside, a sign asked us to wait to be seated, and my stomach turned. I wanted to stand in line for fast food, eat, and get out.

At our table, I ordered a salad, and Matt frowned. "Don't tell me you're one of those girls who doesn't eat."

I didn't feel like explaining this restaurant's menu was a festival of meat and I only ate halal—a term that referred to anything permissible under Islamic law. Given the circumstances, my concerns were a tad ironic. Meat or no meat, this lunch was certainly not halal.

"I'm not that hungry," I said, which was true. I was so nervous and remorseful I'd lost my appetite.

After an awkward pause, I brought up our ethics class. "It's hard to get through all the reading," I said, hoping Matt might impart some upperclassman advice that would justify this outing.

"So don't read it," Matt said with a nonchalance that annoyed me. Why would I want to study with someone who didn't even do the reading?

When the check came, Matt paid for lunch despite my protests. I didn't know much about guys, but I knew that paying for meals implied things. He drove me back to my dormitory and idled in the loading zone.

"We should do that again sometime."

"We really should get together with Jen and study."

"Have you ever been to that amusement park around here? One of these weekends, we should go."

I panicked. "This has nothing to do with you, but I can only study with a guy, and even that can't be one-on-one. In my religion, guys and girls don't really go out together."

"What kind of a religion is that?"

"I'm Muslim."

Matt let his head fall back on the headrest with a thud. "You've got to be kidding me."

"I'm so sorry," I said, suddenly certain that this entire exchange was my fault. He'd just wasted twenty bucks on lunch.

"I've heard a lot of excuses from girls, but this is a first."

"No. It's not like that. I'm really not allowed."

Matt nodded dismissively. I apologized, got out of the car, and then sank into the bench at the front door of my dorm room. Mama had always said there was no such thing as a guy friend. I shuddered at the thought of what she and Hadi would think if they found out I'd gone out with a boy, and then I cursed the vagaries of American male-female relationships. At least in Islamic culture, a man secured a woman's consent to be pursued. For the first time, I saw a benefit to the directness I'd spent so many nights lamenting.

Back in my dorm room, I pulled my course catalog off my shelf and ran my finger along the list of phone numbers printed on the inside cover. I probably couldn't yank an A out of that professor, and I never wanted to see Matt again. What was the number to dial to drop a class?

CHAPTER 12

A SUDDEN THRILL OF CONTROL

Nadia called from UC Berkeley and told me of a girl in her Muslim Students' Association (MSA) who wore the niqab, a veil drawn across her face so that only her eyes showed. She was so attractive that covering her hair with a hijab was not enough to contain her beauty. Men would follow her home, relentless in their marriage proposals.

Thoughts of this girl occupied my mind for days. I'd joined the MSA at the start of the school year, and for the first time in my life, I had a social circle made entirely of people who not only shared my religion but who were also more conservative. In our meetings, the women sat on one side of the room, the men on the other. We averted our gazes before addressing one of the guys with the title "brother" before his first name. And one of the girls was already engaged, the rest screening suitors. This meant that Mama and Mrs. Ridha were right. Your early twenties really was the time to get married.

In my MSA friends' company, I felt remiss for being one of the three girls who didn't wear the hijab. "Inshallah, you will," my friend Amina had said to me in the library one afternoon. "You just have to be ready. When your *iman* is strong enough, you'll do it."

For Amina, the decision to wear the hijab was a sign that her faith could withstand the challenges of wearing a scarf in a Western country. She dealt with the stares, assumptions, and stereotypes because she cared more about earning the favor of Allah than she did about the opinion of others. And now there was this Super Muslima in my backyard, covering not just her hair but her face, too.

Although I had no desire to cover my face, I pictured this girl, her life made rich by rituals, and felt as if I'd fallen behind in my faith. As one of two Muslim girls in my high school, I had considered myself observant. I fasted during Ramadan, I said my five daily prayers and kept up a steady stream of personal supplications for Baba and Lina, I only ate halal meat, and I wore thick tights to school under my uniform skirt. But in college, I feared I was losing a piety contest that I didn't know existed. I may have been getting As in school, but these girls were excelling in our religion. The very least I could do was stop talking with a boy to whom I was not officially engaged.

The next time Hadi and I spoke, I confessed my concern. From my dorm room phone, I said, "After all these years of being told how it's wrong to talk to a boy you aren't engaged to, I feel bad that we're talking. I know I told my mom, but it's not my mom I'm worried about. It's more of a religious question."

"I can understand that," Hadi answered as if he'd already given the matter some thought.

"It's not that I don't want to talk to you. It's just that I don't know what you are to me for me to tell myself this is okay."

"I know what I'd like to be to you."

"You do?" I asked.

"I do, and in order for me to become that person, we're going to have to get our parents involved."

I sat up straighter in my desk chair. This would happen, and I felt a sudden thrill—not of love but of control. My life would follow the script I'd always imagined—engaged and married and with kids before the ripe, old age of twenty-five.

Hadi waited for Mrs. Ridha to leave on a trip to Iran to visit an important Shia shrine with Mama and Lina, and then he talked to his father. Hadi knew that his father was far too religious to resist an appeal to his Islamic duty to get married. Nearly all Muslim scholars encourage parents to help their children marry. This, they teach, is the best way to keep them on a straight path.

After a weekend with his father, Hadi called me in my dorm room and told me that his father planned to ask my father for my hand when they came to visit for the Thanksgiving holiday coinciding with Mama, Lina, and Mrs. Ridha's return. As much as I wanted to share this news with Mama, I couldn't imagine shouting that kind of information into a crackly overseas telephone line, and so I spent the next few weeks holding onto this information with the pride of newfound adulthood instead. I walked around campus thinking how very grown-up of me it was to be getting engaged, how very mature of me it was to be so ready for marriage five months after graduating from high school.

On the day of Mama, Lina, and Mrs. Ridha's arrival, Baba picked me up from school on his way to the airport. My weekend visits had felt haunted by Mama and Lina's absence, and I couldn't wait to see them. But during the car ride home, I found myself regarding them all, with the exception of Lina, warily and with a pounding sense of guilt. I was not accustomed to knowing more about future events than the adults in the room, and this knowledge felt like some sort of betrayal.

Dr. Ridha, Hadi, and his brother, Amjad, drove through the night and arrived at my parents' house before dawn on Thanksgiving morning. When I woke up, Dr. Ridha was leaning against the upstairs banister, waiting for his wife to finish up in the bathroom. He perked up when he saw me leaving my bedroom, as if I was what he had been waiting for all this time. With his head, he motioned for me to join him in Lina's bedroom, where he and Mrs. Ridha were staying.

Even though Dr. Ridha was of slightly less than average height and build, he was an imposing man. When he spoke, it was as if he were a judge issuing a verdict. He cleared his throat, paused to think, and then gave his ruling on the matter at hand. Now the thought of being alone to receive one of his declarations made me nervous.

Closing the door behind him, Dr. Ridha said, "You know why we are here today." His voice still rumbled with sleep, and his tone was too serious for his tousled hair and plaid pajamas.

I nodded.

"Do you have any objections?"

A volcano of nerves erupted within me. Whenever I pictured how I'd become engaged, I imagined two steps: one, when the parents talked to each other, and two, when the boy asked me. I didn't expect Dr. Ridha to speak to me directly. I'd known Dr. Ridha my entire life, but as Hadi's sometimes stern, sometimes playful father. I had no idea how to act like an adult around him when the only person I'd ever been in his presence was a child.

"No," I answered.

"You know we love you," he said and kissed me on both of my cheeks, his bristly mustache brushing against my face. This token of affection reassured me. *See*, I thought to myself, *the Ridhas are happy. I'm happy. It's good to marry family friends.*

Shortly after Dr. Ridha and I spoke, I sought out my mother in the kitchen. I found her measuring rice into a bowl. A bubbling pot of lamb and eggplant stew simmered on the stove, and a pallid turkey thawed in the sink. I hovered close by, telling her about my conversation with Dr. Ridha. She didn't even have a chance to comment before Baba burst into the kitchen and hurried over to where we stood.

"Come with me. I want to talk to both of you," he said, his face flushed.

Mama and I exchanged a knowing glance. On the inside, I shook like a hit piñata.

On the ground floor, the only unoccupied room was the master bedroom. As soon as Mama and I entered, Baba closed the door so forcefully it sounded as if he'd slammed it.

I sat on my parents' pushed-together, adjustable twin beds and drew my knees up to my chest. What had I done? Baba was going to be sick. The color in his face had given way to a cloudy gray.

"Are you all right, dear?" Mama asked. "Maybe you should sit down."

"Huh?" he said, momentarily disoriented, and then, snapping back into the moment, he added, "No, I don't want to sit down. You see, Dr. Ridha asked us for Hudie, and I don't know what to tell him."

Still holding my knees, I began to rock. I dreamt of rocking myself straight through the mattress and into the ground. I knew! I knew all along that this was going to happen, and I did not warn the poor man. But what could I have said? As much as our religion extolled marriage, in my father's presence, I felt as if saying you wanted to get married was equal to saying you wanted to live with a man and have sex. The very prospect chilled me with shame. I would never say those words to him. Never.

"So how did you answer?" Mama asked Baba, a hand on her hip.

"I said I would have to ask Huda. Let me ask you something, Hudie, do you want to marry this boy?"

I squirmed. With so much shame suddenly called up to the surface of my skin, I could only lament that I was being asked directly for my opinion, again. Why weren't our fathers behaving like the trope of an Arab dad, making arrangements for my future without consulting me? My mother never told me that in order to get married, I'd have to give my consent to my father and future father-in-law. *Dear God*, I prayed, *spare me this awkwardness. Let me close my eyes and wake up with a diamond the size of a grape on my finger.*

"I don't know," I said.

"You see, she's too young. She doesn't want to get married now. You don't want to get married, do you, Hudie?"

But I did want to get married. I wanted the satisfaction of having been plucked out of the marriage market before I'd even arrived. I wanted to tell my MSA friends that I was engaged and discuss weddings with them in the library. I wanted the love story I had been waiting for all these years to finally start—to have the flowers and plush toys I had watched girls get from their boyfriends all through high school, to have my first date, maybe my first kiss. I just didn't want to say any of those things to Baba.

Mama shot me a look as if to say, "You're not helping," but with my eyes, I pleaded, "You do something."

"Okay, dear, let's think about this. I already had Ibrahim by the time I was her age, and it isn't like they'd be getting married tomorrow. He's a nice boy, and we know his family. I don't think we'll ever know another family this well."

"Huh? But what about her cousin—"

"No, Baba," I said, suddenly finding my voice. In the Arab world, marriage among cousins was common if not expected, but this was a custom I had no intention of honoring. It was enough to deal with being the non-dating Muslim girl whose parents were distant cousins. I didn't want to spend the rest of my married life embarrassed by my relationship.

"Why not?" Baba asked, surprised.

"No, Baba," I repeated.

"How about if I tell him to give us more time?" he asked.

"For what?" Mama said. "People ask for more time when they want to get to know more about the family. There is nothing more to know about these people. We've slept in their home. They've slept in ours."

"So what do you want me to tell them?"

"Why don't you say, '*Inshallah bihal khair*,'" Mama said.

God willing, it will be blessed. There was an ambiguity to this reply that eased Baba's tense shoulders, his furrowed brow.

"Really, Hudie? Do you want me to tell them that?"

Baba's eyes begged me for a definitive no, but I nodded. As much as I wanted to be Baba's little girl forever, I wanted to grow up, to finally be a woman with a man in my life, more.

CHAPTER 13

THE ENGAGEMENT
OF OUR CHILDREN

Before Baba could start carving the turkey, Dr. Ridha stood at the head of a dining table full of steaming dishes: eggplant stew; basmati rice topped with saffron; sweaty, stuffed grape leaves; hummus; baba ghanoush; glistening *kibbeh*; golden turkey; and mashed potatoes. He cleared his throat and said, "We've been friends with the Al-Marashi family for many years now, and we are so happy to announce the engagement of our children, Huda and Hadi."

Over our guests' communal gasp of surprise, Dr. Ridha called Hadi and me up to the front of the room. There were pictures taken and a chorus of *Mabrook* all around. All this, just as Baba's head was replaced by a tomato bearing his exact features. Even the bald spot on top of his head turned red. His jaw dropped open, and his face twisted as if he was in enough pain to cry. One by one, our guests tried to congratulate him, but his only response was, "Okay, all right. Do you want this turkey?"

That night turned into an impromptu engagement party, and Baba turned into an impromptu madman. I was sitting at the breakfast nook table, catching up my friends on the details of the day, but my gaze was on Baba. Instead of sitting with the rest of the men in the living room, he repeatedly barged into the kitchen. He'd carry in a single plate filled with tangerine peels and set it in the sink, only to return moments later with a half-full, steaming teacup that looked as if it had been yanked from someone's hand.

When I saw Baba pull Mama toward the laundry closet, I picked up a few abandoned glasses off the table and made my way into the kitchen. As I maneuvered the glasses into the overcrowded dishwasher, I listened to Baba's unintentionally loud whisper.

"I don't know why Dr. Ridha had to make an announcement. I told him, 'Inshallah bihal khair.' That is not yes."

"Shh," Mama said. "People can hear you. Inshallah bihal khair is the way people say yes."

"Then why did you tell me to say that? I could've told them something else."

"And what's the problem now that he told them? Eventually people were going to find out."

"I thought we would at least wait for some time."

"Dear, it's done. Your daughter just got engaged. Now go sit with the men."

With Baba finally out of the room, Mrs. Ridha closed the door and slipped an Arabic music CD into the stereo. The women seated about the room clapped along to the rhythmic sounds of drums and tambourines. Mama tied a scarf around my hips and pulled me to the center of the room where I followed her every movement. Mama's hip-drops were delightfully subtle while mine were painfully deliberate, but dancing at Mama's side had convinced me—even if I was not ready to be a wife, I was ready to be a bride.

The next morning, Hadi and I, our two mothers, and Lina piled into the Ridhas' minivan to go ring shopping. I'd been officially engaged for less than twenty-four hours, and there were already so few components of the storybook American proposal left. I still hoped that

Hadi would get down on one knee and propose to me with a ring, but now he would not shout out a surprised and triumphant, "She said yes!" That answer was already known, first when he gave me the string and then again at last night's dinner. Soon we'd pick out a ring together, and my ring would not be a surprise either.

Our one-day-old relationship was already looking so Arab, so Muslim, and as we drove to the jewelry shop, I couldn't help but sympathize with Baba's hesitation, that regret of having given up your one chance to have something done the way you want. The only way I knew to make those bitter feelings disappear was to believe that if I picked a ring today, then maybe Hadi would whisk me away before he left on Sunday and propose to me properly, the way I'd seen it done countless times on television and in movies, down on one knee, without any parents involved.

When we arrived, Shireen Ahmadi, jeweler and family friend, was standing at the door of her boutique. She greeted us with a round of hugs and kisses, and another round of congratulatory ones when Mama told her my news. After ushering us into the store, Shireen led us to the display case of bridal sets. I took a quick scan of the gold and glitter enclosed and panicked. There was nothing there that I liked.

The white gold and platinum craze had yet to take off, so I was hoping for something set in gold and tastefully gaudy. A huge diamond in the center and maybe two other slightly less huge diamonds at the side. But there was nothing similar to that in the case. If I was going to have a hand in picking my own ring, I wanted to buy it from Shireen. Years ago, I'd admired a ring in Shireen's shop, and she'd whispered into my ear, "When the time comes, we'll find you something even better." That time was now, and I had to find something I liked. I slipped on a solitaire. Too boring. A tension mount. Too modern.

Courtesy of De Beers's commercials, I understood how serious a problem this was. A diamond was forever.

Shireen walked over to another case and came back with a ruby ring with two small trillion-cut diamonds on either side and slipped it on my finger. She offered to swap out the ruby with a diamond and brought out two rounds for me to pick from, a half carat of excellent clarity and a three-quarter carat that was not quite as good. It seemed almost a moral dilemma. Deep down, I wanted the biggest diamond I could possibly get—a hunk of sparkly light brilliant enough to blind and heavy enough to require wearing a sling. But choosing a diamond because of its size reeked of a grubbiness I did not want my new fiancé or his mother to smell.

Using tweezers, Shireen took turns holding each diamond over the ring's ruby center stone. I nodded as if I was carefully considering each option, but there was no question in my mind as to which I would choose. This was no longer an issue of aesthetics but of whether I was a quantity or a quality kind of girl.

Hadi took my hand in his as if to examine the ring. Shireen followed my hand's movements with the tweezer-held diamond.

"Which one do you like better?" he asked.

"I think I like the half."

"Yeah, me too," he answered. "It is a really nice diamond."

Our mothers stood on either side of us, wordlessly waiting for us to come to a decision on our own.

"So is this the one you want?"

"I think so."

I had wanted something with a center stone and two smaller diamonds on the side, and this was close enough. If I wanted something custom-made, I would have to give up the hope of a special proposal before Hadi left and I'd have to show up to school on Monday engaged but ringless.

Mrs. Ridha wanted to be sure I was happy with my decision. Speaking in Arabic so our Persian jeweler would not understand, she said, "Are you sure, *habibti*? Don't feel like you have to buy something because this is your friend. The most important thing is that you choose something you like. We can look at other places. You don't have to pick something today."

"No, I'm sure," I said. And it was true. I was sure I wanted to buy a ring that day, sure I wanted it from Shireen, and sure I wanted something I could start wearing right away.

Shireen started preparing the invoice and said the ring would be ready in a few weeks. A few weeks! What good was buying a ring from a family friend if she couldn't get the guy with the rectangular binoculars and the flaming torch, working in the back, to pop in the stinking diamond right now?

"You can't do it any sooner?" Mama asked. I wanted to kiss her for asking the question for me.

"No, these prongs are for an oval-shaped stone. We have to make new prongs to hold a round."

A wave of remorse washed over me. What was the point of rushing if I couldn't have the ring on Monday? But how could I change my mind after all this? But how ridiculous was it to buy a ring you didn't want because you didn't want to say that you didn't want it anymore? I had to say something. I had to tell Shireen I wanted to think about it. I had to do something besides nodding when Mama asked me, "Do you still want it?"

While Shireen and our mothers discussed the details of the purchase, I convinced myself I had made the right choice. It would have been rude to tell her I didn't want the ring now, and the ring was going to look like a blur of sparkles anyway. Its style wasn't that important.

We moved on to picking out a ring for Hadi. As customary, we'd both wear rings on our right hand and then switch it to the left when we got married. Since Muslim men do not wear gold, Hadi's ring would have to be custom-made in platinum. All we had to do was pick the style from the tray Shireen placed in front of us.

I wanted Hadi to choose a classic band, but he kept looking at the rings that had small diamonds in the center. This bothered me. Diamonds were for girls. Hadi was supposed to want something bold and manly and cheap. My family would buy his ring, and he was supposed to want the most inexpensive thing to prove his humility.

"You know I like these classic rings here. Maybe the one with a beveled edge?" I said.

"That's nice, but I wanted something different. Something that nobody else would have."

I nodded as if I got it, but on the inside, I clucked. Different? Guys aren't supposed to care about having something different.

With her head, Mama gestured me over to the chairs in the corner of the shop where she and Lina had taken a seat.

"Let him get what he wants," she said.

"But he's looking at the more expensive rings."

"So what? They're spending a lot more on you. It's not fair that they buy you a three-thousand-dollar ring, and we buy him something for five hundred dollars."

"Why not? I'm the girl. He's the guy."

Men were supposed to want the short end of the stick on everything. As self-sacrificing heads of households, they were supposed to be like Baba, rummaging around in the refrigerator for leftovers even when there was a hot, fresh dinner on the table. They were supposed to shave mold off bread and fruit and insist, "There's nothing wrong with it. I'll eat it."

"Hudie, this has nothing to do with that. Go and help him pick something he likes."

In the end, we settled on something with three small diamond chips in the center.

"Do you like it?" Hadi asked.

"Yeah," I said and smiled as if I truly did like it. "It's a nice ring."

"You know what makes it so nice?" Hadi whispered. "What it symbolizes. That I get to spend the rest of my life with you."

I smiled again, suppressing the urge to groan. After all this time waiting to hear someone say romantic things to me, I hated the way those loving words sounded coming from Hadi's mouth, so cloying, so confident when I was filled with so much doubt. I had just talked myself into buying a ring that I didn't really like for a proposal that wasn't even going to happen this weekend. I had just gotten engaged to a boy who wanted diamonds in the center of his ring as a way to make precious this symbol that he planned on treasuring for the rest of his life, while I was already wondering how soon I could change mine.

And although I did not know it at the time, I was jealous of Hadi, jealous of his joy and his trust in his choices—me, our engagement, his ring.

"Let's get it then," I said, pushing aside my regrets with a series of wishes. I wished that when Hadi did, indeed, get his hands on my ring, he would present it to me in a way so fantastic that it would destroy my every misgiving. I wished for Hadi to make me love what I did not love yet.

Back at home that night, Hadi asked me if we could go out for a drive together. I brightened at the prospect of sharing a romantic moment to hold onto after he left, but when I asked Mama for permission, she shook her head uneasily. "Ayb," she said. "You just got engaged yesterday. It would look like you were waiting all this time just so you could run out with a boy."

Our engagement announcement was nothing more than a verbal agreement between our two families, and even though this was not explicitly stated in the Quran, Islamic tradition still held that an unmarried man and woman could not spend time alone together.

They could not touch each other or even look at one another. Only an *aqid*, the Arabic word for a contract and also the Iraqi term for the Islamic marriage ceremony, could make our relationship halal or permissible, but when to perform the aqid ceremony was a delicate issue. Some families did the aqid right after the engagement so that the couple had permission to get to know one another before their wedding reception without the fear of sin, but other families believed the aqid granted far too much permission to tangle with before the wedding. As the actual marriage binding a man and woman together, the aqid removed the prohibition against premarital sex. If for some reason, things did not work out, the couple would be divorced and the girl's honor called into question.

After dinner that evening, Hadi and I lingered at the breakfast nook table that opened up onto the living room. Mama and Mrs. Ridha, along with Mama's cousin Marwa and Marwa's mother, settled into sofas and chairs, teacups in hand. They went back and forth over when to hold our engagement party, and settled on a month from now, at Marwa's house during Christmas break. Next their conversation ventured onto when to perform our aqid.

"Do it right away," Marwa's mother said. She sat in front of the fireplace, wrapped in a cotton chador, her hands resting on the curve of her cane. "Don't let them accumulate sins so early in their life."

"*La.*" Mrs. Ridha said no as if the suggestion itself was preposterous. "The beauty of a wedding is in watching a couple get married."

"Beauty? What good is beauty when every time the boy wants to look at her or touch her hand, it is a sin?" Marwa's mother said.

Mrs. Ridha gave the comment no regard. "Really, we live so far apart. When they see each other, we are with them. They aren't going to be alone enough for it to be an issue."

I knew Mrs. Ridha's position before she even said it. I'd overheard Mrs. Ridha and Mama having this conversation in the context of other engaged couples, strangers who gave them the freedom to speak their minds. Over the years, I'd gathered that Mrs. Ridha saw the aqid as a green light for a couple to do whatever they wanted before their wedding, and in her mind, there was no point of spending so much money on a party to wrap up a bride and present her to a groom who'd already opened his gift.

Although Mama shared Mrs. Ridha's reluctance to perform the aqid right after an engagement, it was not for the same reasons. Mama did worry about the sins I'd accumulate from looking at or touching my fiancé and the sins she'd accumulate as my accomplice, but she worried about the aqid's religious significance more. This was the only date of marriage God recognized; if things didn't work out between me and Hadi, she didn't want me to be an eighteen-year-old divorcée.

But if those issues were on Mama's mind that night, she did not mention them. As the mother of the bride-to-be, Mama had to be careful how she voiced her opinions. Pushing for the aqid could be taken as an eagerness to have me married off. Not pushing for it could as easily be interpreted as a lack of concern for my honor. Instead, she simply nodded in Mrs. Ridha's direction with the words, "You are right. They aren't going to see each other for some time. We can discuss this later."

Hadi and I watched the entire back-and-forth as spectators. No one asked for our opinion, nor did we attempt to offer one. My feelings on the aqid issue were just as mixed. I believed wedding ceremonies belonged on the same day as wedding receptions; television and movies were unanimous on this. That was where you got the best moments, the father walking the bride down the aisle, the groom waiting to receive his soon-to-be wife with tears in his eyes. However, without the permission to go out alone that the aqid granted, I didn't know how I'd be allowed the moments I'd been dreaming of, the kind of dates and outings that would make me fall in love.

CHAPTER 14

SAY IT LOUD

Even though I was living in the dorms, my parents expected me to come home every weekend. Since I didn't have my own car, Baba would make the seventy-mile trek to pick me up in his late 1980s Mercedes. If motor vehicles had rights, that poor car would have had Baba reported to Automobile Protective Services. The back seat and trunk were covered with papers and books. The cup holders were filled with coffee thermoses, Ziploc bags of mixed nuts, and gummy candies he called "sours." Sours, Baba claimed, helped keep him awake on long drives. Since Baba had been known to fall asleep behind the wheel, sours were probably as important to his safety as seat belts.

Given Baba's record, I never let him drive me home. I'd throw my duffle bag on the paper mountain behind the driver's seat and slide in behind the wheel. I spoke little during our rides together. Baba was a storyteller, and he filled our time together with anecdotes—memories from his childhood in Zanzibar and tales from the life of the Prophet Yusuf. But that changed after my engagement to Hadi.

"You know, Hudie," he'd say. "I never got a chance to ask you if you really like this boy."

Baba always worded his question the exact same way, his voice never exceeding the volume of a loud whisper. It was almost as if he felt shy to ask, and he may have been. Baba wasn't in the habit of questioning our choices. He usually waited until my siblings and

I had made our own decisions, and then he invariably voiced his support. It was a surprisingly effective parenting strategy. Because we knew Baba rarely opposed our choices, we only allowed ourselves things he would have approved of.

"He's a nice boy," I'd answer. "I like him."

In spite of the qualms niggling me, I knew better than to admit to any of them in front of Baba. I still hoped Hadi would make things right at our engagement party, but Baba had been looking for an excuse to back out of our commitment to the Ridhas ever since Thanksgiving. If he got a hold of any concern or worry on my part, he'd waste no time calling off my engagement.

When Baba picked me up at the end of the semester, less than a week before my party, he added a more explicit statement to his list of questions: "You know, you don't have to marry this boy."

"I know."

"We could just tell them we changed our mind."

"I don't want to do that."

"What about your cousin Fa—"

"No, Baba."

"Why not? He is a seyyid."

Mama loved Hadi too much to bring up that his family did not descend from the Prophet Muhammad. Baba loved being a seyyid too much not to mention it.

"That's not so important to me, Baba," I said. "It's more important for me to marry someone I know."

"Well, it will be a great honor to the Ridhas if you marry their son," he said with a pleased smile. "Now their grandchildren will be *mirza*. This is the name they give people whose mother is an *alwiya*. You know this is the word they use for the lady who is a seyyid?"

I nodded.

"You know our friend Abu Hassan is not seyyid, but he always calls his wife 'alwiya.' It is so nice." Baba dragged the "o" in *so*, and I perceived a hint there, a tiny suggestion that it would be equally nice if Hadi called me alwiya. It was as if Hadi could make up for not being a seyyid by being overly appreciative that I was.

I nodded again because that was what my siblings and I did around Baba. We listened and nodded regardless of what we were thinking.

Now Baba looked out the window and sighed, a small, disappointed cluck escaping his lips. "It's just that I don't like to see you go. I know your mummy was the same age when she got married, but now I am feeling so sorry for what I did to your Jidu."

My heart went to shreds. I wondered how a separation so painful—this rite of passage that took children from the homes they knew and loved and placed them in another—had become something so common, such a basic fact of life that the grief it inspired had no place in the midst of all the celebration.

As soon as I heard the Arabic music blaring from the tape deck inside cousin Marwa's house, I knew its heavy, rhythmic beat was preparing our guests for our grand entrance. I felt a shot of nervous energy, and before I could calm my nerves, Mama opened the double front doors and gave us the signal to enter. Hadi and I walked through the foyer and into the living room with a generous amount of space between us, our hands deliberately unlinked. The women in our families sent their tongues to the roof of their mouths to welcome us with their ululating cry.

Amid the joyful noise, I took in Hadi in his new double-breasted, pin-striped suit, me in my custom-made prom dress, now making its debut at our engagement party, and my mind bounced with hope and anxiety, with the questions of if, when, and how.

I was still holding out for a charming pop-the-question story, one that looked as if it could have been scripted in Hollywood. I had been prodding Hadi over the phone with a series of "You know, you haven't really asked me yet," to which he'd immediately reply, "Will you marry me?" Each time I told him that asking me over the phone did not count, he followed by sending me that four-word question over email, fax, and greeting card. Not wanting Hadi to think these anticlimactic attempts had satisfied me, I picked up the phone after every effort to inform him that, although cute and flattering, these proposals still did not cut it. They were only making the official, with-a-ring moment less special.

We sat on the loveseat parked in front of the fireplace, underneath a small balloon arch. Our families and guests had crowded in on the sofas and chairs around the living room, and from among them, Hadi's grandmother appeared to shower us in a mix of coins and colorfully wrapped hard candies.

Dr. Ridha took the microphone plugged into the stereo, welcomed our guests, and announced that we'd be exchanging our rings. The decision to wait on our aqid had held, and this party was about nothing more than this moment, these rings, and—I hoped—a proposal.

I took a deep breath. It had to be now. Oh my God. Yes. It was now.

Hadi took the ring box off the gold tray his mother carried over to him, and he turned toward me. Wait a minute. Why wasn't he kneeling?

Get down on the floor, man. Please.

Hadi leaned in and whispered something about spending the rest of his life with me. Something I couldn't pay attention to, because I was suddenly so angry. Why was he whispering?

"Say it loud," Baba called out from across the room.

I smiled awkwardly and prayed. *Please, God, make him say it out loud.*

"Say it loud," Baba called out again.

"*Yella*," everybody chimed in.

I shook with embarrassment. I needed Hadi to profess his undying devotion to me right here in front of our families so that I'd always have this proof that we'd had a love marriage. Then my aunts and uncles would understand why it didn't matter that Hadi wasn't seyyid or fair-skinned: his love for me was so beautiful and pure that it surpassed all other status-bolstering criteria.

"Will you marry me?" he whispered.

It was over. The words were spoken, and they could not be taken back. What now? Was I supposed to whisper too?

"Yes," I said because there was no other answer to give at that point. I smiled so no one would suspect that I was unhappy, but I felt a burning in my nose that meant I was dangerously vulnerable to tears.

Stop, I spoke to myself firmly. *Your chance for a beautiful proposal may be gone, but your chance to have fun at your only engagement party is not. Smile and be happy now. You can be sad about the proposal later.*

Hadi opened the velvet ring box. My ring. Yes. Everything would be fine as soon as I started wearing my ring.

I watched Hadi slip the ring on my finger, and then I studied my hand, waiting for it to transform into the adorned hand of an engaged woman. But the ring was awful. I grinned like a beauty queen so no one would see my disappointment, but my mind raced. *No, no.* The two-trillion-cut diamonds sandwiching the dazzling round center stone had all the shine of dirty glass.

Stop it, I commanded myself. *You have to love it. Okay, I love it. Who am I trying to kid? I hate it! Try a different angle. A side view is better. Just look at it from the side, always the side.*

I pushed Hadi's ring past the joint on his right ring finger, and the ladies in the room gave another ululating cry. Hadi's grandmother returned to shower us with an additional handful of coins and candy.

Mama ushered us into the family room, bringing along the tape deck. As the music grew louder, the guests migrated about the house. Those who thought it was okay to listen to music and dance in mixed groups of men and women stood up and formed a circle around Hadi and me, clapping as if to cheer us on. Those who had no objection to music but frowned upon dancing in mixed groups stayed in the living room or mingled around the appetizer table set up in the hallway. Those who thought music was *haram*, or forbidden, stepped outside, far away from the grasp of its sinful notes.

Since we'd announced our engagement last month, Mama, Lina, and I had danced together on the weekends. There was an *aroosa*, a bride, in our house now, and so there was a reason to play music and celebrate. Mama would tie a scarf tightly around my hips and coach me.

Hadi had not received similar instruction. On the phone, Hadi had told me that he did not like dancing nor did he care to learn. I'd insisted it was because he didn't know how. I'd teach him, and he'd like it. Now, for my sake, he stood in front of me. I told him to extend his arms, but instead of picking up on the classic Arab male shoulder shimmy, he moved his arms up and down like a bird trying to take off in flight.

But at least Hadi was trying, and so I danced on, believing that his dance moves would improve, pushing aside my proposal disappointment with a list of all the wonderful things about the day. I loved being the guest of honor, knowing that family had flown out just for me. I loved anticipating all the parties that were still to come, the bridal showers and the wedding, the joys of being the first to walk through the buffet line, the first to cut the cake, the person for whom the big stack of gifts was intended.

After the party, Hadi drove Baba, Lina, and me back to our hotel. He dropped them off in front of the lobby so that we could be alone while he escorted me back to my family's room.

Hadi opened the car door for me, then offered me his coat—a long, forest green leather overcoat that someone led him to believe was acceptable for a five feet seven inches twenty-one-year-old. I took it even though it made me look like a Christmas tree. We walked in silence until we stepped into the glass elevator on the face of the building. Hadi reached out for my hand, leaned over, and whispered, "I love you so much." This time his whispering didn't bother me. His voice was too sincere to judge and so heartfelt that I thought I detected the slightest hint of a crack.

I put my head on his shoulder and said, "I love you, too."

I meant it in the only way I was capable of meaning it then. I knew I didn't love him completely or unconditionally. I was too young to love anyone in that way. But I loved him for loving me, for playing the part of the groom while I played the role of the bride.

"It's about time," I said to lighten a moment that suddenly felt heavy with emotion.

"I've always felt it. For as long as I can remember, I've loved you. I was just waiting for us to be official before I said it out loud."

The elevator doors opened, and we stepped into the open hall overlooking the parking lot. I paused and took in a breath. I'd been so preoccupied with how Hadi asked me to marry him and what my family thought of him that I'd paid little attention to what Hadi had said when he'd offered me my ring. Only now did it occur to me that I'd underestimated the sentiment behind his words, the time he must have spent considering them.

"Why did you wait so long to tell me? It's not against the rules to love someone."

Our hands still linked, Hadi answered, "Because that's the kind of thing that you should only say to your wife, so I wanted us to be officially together before I said it."

I nudged Hadi forward with a slight swing of our hands. "So, if we didn't get engaged, you wouldn't love me."

"No. I'd love you. I just wouldn't have ever told you."

"I see," I said, stopping outside the hotel room door.

"What? You think it's silly?"

"No, I guess I'm surprised. I didn't know you had such strong feelings about this."

"You know what else I have strong feelings about?"

I wasn't ready to hear Hadi's answer. I had no idea how I'd reciprocate.

"What?" I finally asked.

When Hadi answered with the anticipated, "You," I smiled demurely and opened the door.

The next day, my entire family was invited to join Hadi and his extended family for dinner at his parents' house, but only my parents came with me. The rest of our clan had gone to Universal Studios instead. After dinner, Hadi asked me if I wanted to watch the video of yesterday's party. I followed him out of the living room, waiting for one of our mothers or Hadi's aunts to stop us, to say that we should bring the video out for everyone to see, but no one said anything. We sat on the floor, the door to Hadi's room wide open, and huddled around the camera's small viewfinder.

We appeared on the screen, walking in through Marwa's front door, our hands at our sides. "Cute couple," Hadi said and kissed me.

Warm, wet lips upon mine.

A lip's soft touch was so surprising, so tender, so natural—so not disgusting. I'd confided in Diana that kissing looked beautiful on television, but the exchange of saliva it involved struck me as terribly gross. It was like spitting inside another person's mouth. She shook her head at me with pitying eyes and said, "No, Hudie. It's nothing like that at all." It was this I then remembered, this my body now understood. What a complete form of communication kissing was. All this time I'd wanted some declaration of love from Hadi, but this kiss had made me feel it.

Hadi pulled away and said, "I've wanted to do that for a long time."

"What were you waiting for?" I asked.

He touched the diamond on my ring. "For you to be officially mine," he said.

Hadi's comment reminded me of him waiting to answer my question at the prom, then waiting to tell me he loved me, and now waiting to kiss me. It wasn't our religion's rules Hadi had been following, but they were his own.

Neither one of us brought up that we had technically committed a sin. Nor did we close the door because that would have drawn attention to the fact that we were in his room alone. We just relied upon the entry's short hallway to obstruct our view, and we kissed again. And again.

From deep within me, I felt a stirring, a pleasant but unsettling push of desire. Yesterday's disappointments seemed a distant memory. I wanted Hadi. Maybe that was all that had been missing from our relationship all along. This kiss that filled my mouth and my nose with his scent.

With one hand I touched Hadi's cheek, and with the other I ran my fingers through his hair. Hadi's hands moved along the length of my hair, his fingers massaging the back of my head, my neck.

I was kissing a boy. I was happy and nervous. Nervous that someone would walk in and see us kissing. Nervous that the moms, dads, aunts, and uncles outside assumed we were kissing. Nervous to face them when we left the room. They'd know. It would show on me.

But these kisses were worth the risk. For the first time, Hadi Ridha was more than just a name in my life. For the first time, since I was a six-year-old girl, standing at the doorway of this house, our relationship didn't feel like the hope of wishful parents. It felt natural. It felt like my choice. I wanted these soft, warm lips on me, this skin under my hand.

The sound of clapping, music, and conversation that had been playing in the background of our video cut off abruptly, and so did our embrace.

"That's the best video I've ever seen," Hadi said.

I smiled and said, "Good because I'm afraid to leave the room now. Curly hair expands on contact. One look at my hair and my mother will know we've been up to something."

Hadi got up and passed me a baseball cap from his closet. "Anyone asks, say it was a gift from me to you."

I pulled my hair into a ponytail that I slid through the slot in the back of the cap and wondered if it would be enough of a disguise. I could smell Hadi's cologne on me. I could still taste his fragrance on my lips.

We decided I would exit Hadi's room first, as if by leaving his room as individuals we'd put to rest the suspicion that we'd been doing anything as a couple. Fortunately, I found my family distracted with getting ready for our own departure. We all gathered in the foyer, in front of the Ridhas' stained-glass double doors, for a classic Arab goodbye—another twenty minutes of chatter at the door; an exchange of thank-yous; apologies for any trouble from the guests; apologies for shortcomings in hospitality from the hosts; and finally, a round of kisses on both cheeks, exchanged only between women and women, men and men.

One of Hadi's aunts said, "You look nice in Hadi's hat," and I couldn't tell if she was imagining us innocently watching our engagement video and trying on hats or if this was a hint that she knew.

When Mrs. Ridha leaned in to kiss me goodbye, one of Hadi's aunts joked, "Somebody's jealous." Then as I kissed each of his aunts goodbye, they teased, "We'll hug her longer for you," "Hadi wishes he was me right now," "Let your eyes take their fill of her now. Soon she'll be gone, and you'll be crying." This banter struck the adults around us as terribly funny. Making light of unmarried couples' sexual frustrations was practically a pastime in itself. (Not too long ago, Mrs. Ridha was sitting next to Mama on a bumpy car ride. Leaning into Mama, she'd joked, "If we were an engaged couple, this would make us so happy.")

I expected the teasing, but I didn't know my role in this. Was I supposed to look shocked and offended, or was I supposed to smile and joke along?

I stood by the door with the plainest face I could summon, but Hadi had struck a particularly joyless pose. His mother offered, "You can at least shake Huda's hand."

"No," Hadi said, his arms folded, the weight of his body shifted to one side.

"Why?" Mrs. Ridha asked. "This is a chance for you."

Hadi was adamant. "No. I will not shake my fiancée's hand. That's for people who are strangers, who don't mean anything to each other."

Hadi wore the face of a sullen teen, and I felt as if I was witnessing an exchange I shouldn't have been.

Get it over with, I pleaded in my mind. *Shake my hand and make them happy.*

"It's up to you," his mother surrendered with two hands in the air.

Hadi offered nothing in return but the same pout, his arms still folded. Our families were waiting for our farewell, and it was clear that it wasn't going to come from Hadi. I waved and said, "Bye," like a sixth grader, leaving her crush at the end of a school day. Hadi waved back, then followed us out the door to our car.

The disconnect between who we'd been in his room only minutes ago and who we were now, in front of our families, bewildered me. We'd gone from kisses and an embrace to one wave and a sulk. Into the cool night air, the closeness between us evaporated, the warmth of our kisses carried away by the chimney smoke seasoning the night sky.

From inside the car, I waved at Hadi one last time, the cold leather seats pushing through the thin barrier of my long, satin skirt. A shiver went through me and with it the weight of my transgression. A man's lips had touched mine. There was no going back no matter how much Hadi's behavior unsettled me. Never again could I claim my pure, untouched innocence.

CHAPTER 15

SINS FOR NO GOOD REASON

After I got back on campus, at the start of winter quarter, the reactions to my engagement ring were mixed.

1. What? Let me see that ring!

I'd expected my American dormmates to be shocked, to question how I got engaged and whether or not my marriage was arranged, but most of the girls on my floor ogled my ring and regarded me with a puzzled look that seemed to say, "Wait. Are we old enough to do this now?" A number of them even said, "You're so lucky. I wish I could marry my boyfriend, too."

2. You don't have to do this.

I was discussing *Madame Bovary* with my professor during office hours when I told her I was engaged and added, "Almost every woman in my family married her Charles. Maybe Emma expected too much from her 1850s world."

She pulled out her calendar and said, "Let's find a time to have dinner and talk." Later that week, over soup and sandwiches, I told her how I was engaged to the son of our closest family friends. She told me about her young marriage, how difficult it had been, and then added, "You do know you don't have to do this?" as if she was just making sure I'd been informed.

3. Whoa! Okay!

A handsome, blond guy approached me on my way out of the

library. He said he'd been watching me in the library for weeks and had been trying to work up the nerve to ask me out.

I held up my hand apologetically. "Sorry. I'm engaged."

"Whoa," he said, "I never thought to look for a ring at our age."

4. Mashallah! Now let's talk about the wedding.

My Muslim Students' Association (MSA) friends were the only ones I told every detail about my engagement party. I made light of all my disappointments, my ring with the cloudy diamonds, Hadi's commitment to whispering, and Baba's requests to "Say it loud." They comforted me with not just their laughter but also with their shared understanding of Muslim couples, of the way our families celebrate. However, it was precisely because of that shared knowledge that I didn't dare tell anyone about my unauthorized kiss. I couldn't risk my friends casting me off as the bad girl among them.

As a group, we were almost all first generation, born in America to immigrant parents, and the majority of us were the oldest daughters in our families. We had no older cousins or sisters to look to for tales of their engagements or wedding nights—no generation before us to shine light on the gap between what parents say and what young people do, no internet to bring us the news of Muslims in other parts of the United States, let alone the rest of the world. All we had was our shared questions, our collective wedding-night innocence. Together we tried to imagine how one went about the business of commencing sex:

Are you supposed to wear something sexy underneath your wedding dress and let him undress you, or do you go to the bathroom and change into one of those flowy gowns?

What about your evening prayers? Do you say, "Wait, let's pray," and then take each other's clothes off?

And then what about the manicure you spent all that money on? Do you believe your wudhu doesn't count if you're wearing nail polish? Maybe it's okay to make an exception for your wedding night, because how silly would it be to sit there taking off your nail polish before you prayed?

How bad do you think it hurts? It doesn't seem like there's enough room to stick anything up there. Has anyone ever worn a tampon?

Do you think it's really bloody? How embarrassing would it be to make such a mess on a guy? And then if you're in a hotel, do you leave it there on the sheet or do you wash it?

What about the hair down there? Will you wax it? Ouch.

These conversations with all their unknown answers lingered in my mind. Maybe it made for a more magical wedding night for it also to be the moment of your first kiss. And, if I had done too much and ruined our wedding night, then what was left to look forward to after we'd already had such a disappointing proposal? Were these memories good enough for the only love story I'd ever have? What if I rushed into committing myself to Hadi, and I could have had everything I wanted with someone else?

I had a guy in my life who I'd kissed but I never saw. We had nightly phone conversations, but after a long day poring over my books in the library, this sometimes felt like another thing on my to-do list. Many nights we argued over why I was always the one who wanted to get off the phone. How come Hadi never said he had to study? How was he going to get into medical school if he had so much time to spend on the phone talking to me?

The only way I could think to remedy this angst was to see Hadi again, to arrange for the moments that would make me fall for him. But planning for Hadi to visit felt like applying for an international travel visa. Before Hadi's metaphorical passport could be stamped, both sets of parents had to agree to the necessity and length of the journey and the itinerary (namely, how long we'd be alone together). I first planned a Valentine's Day visit, complete with an appointment for engagement pictures, dinner out, and tickets to the symphony. But a few days prior to his departure, Hadi called to tell me he'd come down with mononucleosis and had to cancel his trip. We made all the requisite jokes about who he'd been kissing. Then I hung up the phone and cried; our first Valentine's Day in our engaged lives was only adding to the list of disappointments I was trying to defeat.

After another week of phone conversations, our families agreed to a fresh attempt at engagement photographs. On the first weekend in March, Hadi would take a cab from the airport to my campus. He'd wait for me until I finished school for the day, and then we'd take the bus to the mall to take our photographs. Mama would pick us up from the mall and take us back to my house where we'd spend the rest of the weekend. Sunday, she'd drop Hadi off at the airport and me back at school.

Hadi knocked on the door to my dorm room early on Friday. Since our engagement party, we'd bickered so much over the phone that I wondered if we'd kiss again, wondered if we should. Maybe that first kiss was a passionate fluke, a transgression that now that we'd had more time to think about it, we wouldn't repeat.

But as soon as I opened the door, Hadi's arms circled my waist and his lips met mine, and the only thought that occurred to me was a single "oh" of recognition. In that moment, I understood that kissing was going to be something we did now, and maybe it took away from our wedding-night mysteries but never mind. There would be other things to discover that night, and this—this was too good to delay. These kisses proved that when we saw each other, things were different, better.

That morning, with the door to my room closed and locked, we kissed each other's lips, necks, ears. Because there was nowhere else to sit in my tiny dorm room, we sat on the edge of my bed. And then after a moment, we weren't sitting anymore. It was entirely functional—this movement from vertical to horizontal—and it never crossed my mind to worry that Hadi's hands would stray from where they rested on my waist. We'd already bent so many rules: I couldn't imagine we'd do more than kiss until we were married.

When I left for class an hour later, I felt that our kisses had fixed everything. All of those labored phone conversations were a by-product of distance, and if we had to bend the rules a little to bring us closer together, so be it. By American standards, kissing was innocent, and maybe Americans had the right idea on this. These kisses were the only things that made me feel as if I was in love. For the first time, I walked across campus, with my makeup faded away, my hair a mess, my body warm. I passed the same adobe buildings, manicured lawns, and blooming rose bushes that marked my daily path, but everything seemed changed, as if my entire being and the buildings themselves throbbed with the knowledge of my secret. I had been kissing a boy. A boy was waiting for me in my room.

When I returned an hour and a half later, Hadi was asleep in my room, his hands resting on his chest. I sat on the edge of the bed, watching his hands rise and fall with each breath. Hadi's fingers were long and thin but thick at the knuckles. The band he wore on his right hand had turned, the tapered bottom facing up. His lips were sealed with the weight of sleep, and in that instant, I knew I would kiss this boy in my room and wake him up.

Hadi's eyes opened as soon as my lips left his. He smiled and said, "That's nice."

"I know," I said to suppress the warm blush rising to my cheeks.

We kissed again, our kisses taking on a force of their own, a power to draw our hands under our shirts and onto the marvel of skin. I wondered if I should resist, and then I did not wonder anymore. Wondering ruined everything.

Hadi brought my head to his chest and held me there for a moment. "I have something for you," he said.

"You do?" I asked and sat up.

Hadi got up and bent down in front of the duffel bag, lying slump at the foot of my closet. When he turned around, he was holding a tiny velvet box. "Happy Valentine's Day," he said.

I wasted no time with polite you-shouldn't-haves and went straight to lifting the box's lid. Inside were pearl stud earrings. Delicate, small, and exactly what I'd coveted. Finally I was getting all the little things that I believed proved love in a relationship: visits, kisses, hugs, and tiny trinkets.

"I love them," I said, walking to the mirror over my wardrobe. I slid the gold hoops I was wearing into my jewelry box and put on the new earrings.

Hadi stood behind me and looked at my reflection. "They look beautiful on you," he said before sliding his hands around my waist and kissing my neck. I turned around and kissed him deeper now, our hands on each other's backs. I could see myself slipping my hands up his shirt; I could imagine him doing the same to me. The desire shocked me. I'd always wondered how teenage girls wound up pregnant, why they couldn't just resist sex, but in a flash, I understood how getting too close made it far too easy to take too much.

"We should get ready," I said to myself as much as to Hadi. He pretended not to hear me, and I liked that he wanted me too much to listen. I pushed him a hand's length away from me and said, "You know we'll be in big trouble if we don't take those pictures."

I gathered my things and told Hadi he could use my room. I crossed the hall into the bathroom, where I dug into my makeup case, the taste of men's cologne still on my lips, and marveled at this sweet but dangerous problem we now had. We had not set our

120

wedding date. In one day, I'd gone from thinking that kissing would be the only contact we'd have during our engagement to reaching under Hadi's shirt. I felt awash in shame and wondered what had come over me. A good Muslim girl was supposed to resist the boy, to be a reserved, proper lady until her wedding night. I thought of my MSA friends. I imagined them saving every act of intimacy until they were married. What did these kisses make me? Easy? Horny? The very thought made me cringe, but those kisses were the only time when all those noisy doubts about Hadi—his hair, eyebrows, clothes, and studies—finally went quiet.

Back at my parents' house, I changed out of my dress and noticed something in my reflection in my mirrored closet doors. A tiny purplish spot above my collarbone. I leaned in closer and found a similarly colored spot on my earlobe, and then a tiny purple burst at the tip of the arch of one lip.

I didn't feel unwell. Was it some kind of rash? No, it seemed more like a darkening of vessels, a bruise.

Oh my God. Was this a hickey?

No. It couldn't be. These marks were no bigger than the imprint of an infant's teeth, and hickeys were bigger, more welt-like. Or was that bruise-like?

I couldn't bear the possibility. Hickeys were the stuff of juvenile romances, of the back seat of cars, and of television sitcoms. It was Samantha in *Who's the Boss?*, hiding her love bite from Tony. Such an adolescent mark was unbefitting a woman involved in a mature and sophisticated relationship with her future husband. And the word itself was so disgusting. Pleasant words that described beautiful things never rhymed with *icky*.

I leaned in closer and ran my finger over the mark on my neck, relieved it was too small to show up in the pictures, pressing down to see if it hurt like a bruise. No pain, but I took no comfort in this. Too many terms to describe intimacy were coming together with their meanings today, each one an unwelcome revelation. It was one thing to have shared a series of individual kisses, but quite another to have made out, to be marked by hickeys. The words made everything we'd done feel more sinful.

When I came downstairs the next morning, the door to our guest room was closed with Hadi still asleep inside. The door to my parents' room was open, and there I found Mama in front of her desk, stuffing unwanted papers into the recycling bag she'd propped up on her chair.

She turned around as soon as I'd entered. "Good. You're up."

I stretched and plopped down on her unmade bed.

"You never told me how your day went yesterday," she said, without looking up from the stack of medical journals in her hand.

"It was fine," I said.

"What did you do?"

I shrugged. "He came, and I took him to class with me. Then we walked around campus, and I introduced him to my friends, and then it was time to go to the mall."

Mama raised her eyebrows mischievously and asked, "Did he kiss you?"

"No," I said with as much offense as I could muster, and then I searched her face to see if she knew I was lying. Maybe she'd seen the hickey. Maybe I had a kissed look.

If Mama didn't believe me, she didn't say so. She stuffed a nursing journal in with the recycling and sat down on the bed next to me. Her expression practical and sober, Mama said, "At some point he's going to get tired of looking at you."

"Mom," I said sharply, as if I'd never been more exasperated.

Mama's face now seemed to say, "Grow up." "Hudie, if he hasn't kissed you yet, he's going to. And you kids are so good I'd hate to see you building up sins for no good reason."

I hated it too, but there was nothing I could do about it now. The sin had been committed. I just wished I knew how bad of a sin this was. Was this one of the rules everybody broke, like listening to music and dancing, or was this a serious, day-of-judgment offense—the kind of thing where my hands and lips would awaken to confess against me?

"I don't want that either," I said.

"I know we haven't decided when to do your aqid, but I talked to Jidu, and if you want, he can do a little ceremony between the two of you, so you know, if the boy did decide to kiss you, at least, it wouldn't be a sin."

I didn't know exactly what Mama meant by "a little ceremony." In the Shia tradition, there is the permanent marriage established with the aqid contract, and then there is the more controversial *mutah*, a temporary marriage to render various kinds of liaisons between men and women halal or permissible. Engaged couples will sometimes undertake a mutah so that they can be alone together without a chaperone. Sometimes this comes with a caveat that the marriage will not be consummated until the permanent marriage ceremony is performed; sometimes it doesn't.

I didn't know what Jidu intended to read for us, nor did I care to know. Mutah was on the fringe of acceptable religious practice. Not only was it an issue Sunnis often criticized us for, but there were also many Shias, Mrs. Ridha among them, who found the institution distasteful. They argued that it was an outdated custom that had outlived its historic purpose. During times of war and extended travel, when men were forced to spend long periods away from their wives, mutah protected women from love-'em-and-leave-'em type affairs. It entitled a woman to a dowry and guaranteed that all children born from said relationships would be legitimate, the financial responsibility of their fathers. But contemporary mutah was often seen as a misappropriation, a way for men to get away with fooling around before marriage, guilt-free.

Mama knew this, probably even agreed with it, but in her mind, the religious necessity of sanctioning the time Hadi and I spent together trumped those concerns. When it came to sin, Mama believed it was better to be safe than sorry, and at the time, so did I. I could've clapped with relief. This was an out. A rescue from damnation.

"O-kay," I said with feigned reluctance. I couldn't have Mama thinking I was eager to kiss my fiancé sin-free.

Mama nodded as if she understood exactly the game I was playing. She stood up and placed a hand on her hip. "So you talk to Hadi first and see what he thinks because you didn't hear this from me. This is between you, Hadi, and your grandfather. I never suggested anything to you."

Although Mama believed she had a moral responsibility to make me aware of my options, she didn't want to be involved in whatever we chose past that point. Advising me was one thing, but going against Mrs. Ridha's wishes was another.

I nodded, and Mama placed her hands on my shoulders. "Now this doesn't mean you can have sex and come home pregnant."

I rolled my eyes. "That's gross, Mom."

"You say that now—"

"All right. All right," I interrupted. "Let's not go there."

As soon as Hadi woke up, I told him what was on my mind, as if the thought had come to me overnight, born of the events of the previous day. And then for good measure, I added, "I don't think either one of us got engaged so that we could sin."

Hadi agreed to a ceremony immediately. The choice to simply not kiss again until we were married never occurred to either one of us. We'd been offered a morsel of divine permission, and we were taking it.

Later that afternoon, without my having said anything to him, Jidu came downstairs, the Quran in his hands held open to a particular page with his index finger. We stood as was our custom when Jidu entered a room. He kissed us both on the cheek and inquired as to whether we were done eating our lunch. We said we were, and he gestured for us to follow him with his free hand. He led us into the downstairs guest room and closed the door behind him.

We all knew exactly why we had gathered, but we did not acknowledge it directly. Jidu merely looked us both in the eye and asked, "You want this?"

We nodded, and Jidu sat down on the edge of the bed. He opened the Quran to the marked page and read verses I didn't understand or recognize. I felt a flash of disappointment. I was supposed to teach myself to understand the Quran's classical Arabic before my wedding so that I wouldn't feel as I did now—like a child who needed her mother to translate her own marriage ceremony to her.

Jidu asked Hadi to present me with something to symbolize my *maher* or dowry. Hadi dug into his wallet and unearthed a collector's coin he'd picked up as a souvenir somewhere. Jidu looked at it curiously and then asked if I accepted this token. I did. I accepted both the token and, a moment later, the boy.

My consent now given, Jidu motioned for us to bend down. He kissed us both on the forehead and said, "May Allah fulfill all your desires in this life and the next. May Allah keep you for each other and for your children."

I bent down again and kissed Jidu's hand, grateful to be marrying someone my grandfather approved of, someone who spoke the same language, who shared the same religion and understood exactly why he had to *marry* me before he married me. But still I walked out of the room feeling no more married to Hadi than when I'd entered it. Hadi and I had merely filed spiritual paperwork with our Lord. It may have exempted us from the sin of the lustful glance or the occasional touch, but it did little to ease the shame of having already kissed, the sense that we had betrayed Baba and Hadi's parents.

CHAPTER 16

❀

EVERY CHOKE, SOB,
AND SNIFFLE

At the end of spring quarter, one of my history professors scrawled at the bottom of my paper, underneath a big red A, "You should be considering a career in academics."

It was as if he'd illuminated the obvious path for my future. Ibrahim was already in graduate school, pursuing a doctorate in Middle Eastern studies. He'd done the hard work of convincing my parents that there were legitimate careers outside of science and medicine, and after a childhood of sharing so little, I liked discussing my courses with Ibrahim over the phone, exchanging book titles and research topics. I could see myself following in my brother's footsteps.

I enjoyed spending my days in the library, annotating assigned readings, researching term papers, and perusing the book stacks when I needed a break. The scholarly perspective on history had cast a spell on me. Historians handpicked the events we remembered; they penned the stories that lived on in our memories. As a Shia, I felt this pulling me right back to Ashura, to the lamentation rituals I performed with my mother. I wondered if I could bring a breath of that empathic spirit to other atrocities the world had forgotten. The only thing that struck me as more tragic than all the suffering humanity had endured was that people rarely remembered it, rarely talked about it, and rarely had any reservations about repeating it.

The more direction I had in school, the more I wanted to talk to Hadi about his coursework. He planned on taking an extra year to complete a double major in psychology, and this concerned me. Taking more time in college spoke to a privileged, find-yourself view of education that the children of immigrants were not supposed to abide. Hadi's lost year was something to be lamented and mourned, but it frustrated me how little he seemed bothered by it.

I wanted to know exactly when we were going to get married and what was going to happen to my undergraduate degree, if I would transfer to somewhere closer to his medical school or if I would finish here. I wanted to know where to research graduate schools, where to make connections with professors. That summer, every time we talked on the phone, I worked in questions about where he planned to apply, where he thought he was going to get in, if he had professors to write letters of recommendation, if he had started his essay. Hadi's answers were vague and indirect, and this too infuriated me. He had done well on his Medical College Admission Tests that spring. I couldn't understand why he wanted to delay graduating.

And then one July afternoon, while staying at my parents' house for the summer, I pushed and Hadi relented. He confessed that his GPA was somewhere in the high 2.0s, and I responded with a shocked, "God no." I brought a hand up to my heart and held it there as if steadying myself. Tears spilled onto my face, and I was grateful for this proof of my hurt. I wanted Hadi to hear every choke, sob, and sniffle. I wanted him to crumble with regret for putting our academic futures in jeopardy.

"See, that's why I didn't tell you. And that's why I have to do the double major. So I can bring up my GPA."

"Do your parents know?"

"No. That's why I need some time to fix this."

I said nothing and reached for a tissue. Then I blew my nose into the phone and added, "But with those MCAT scores, I never imagined you were dealing with those kinds of grades."

"It's all the bio classes. They're designed to weed people out."

"But you're supposed to study so hard that you don't become one of those people."

"I study."

"No. I study. You go to class and poke around in your textbooks for what interests you, but that's not enough. You have to hustle to get good grades."

This engagement was supposed to be about me marrying the right guy by our culture's standards, about him wooing me, and about me falling in love. Now I doubted our basic compatibility. I was a list-maker and a goal-setter, but Hadi was approaching his future with a passivity that repelled me. If Hadi were my friend, I would've been able to hear him out. I might've encouraged him to share what was holding him back, but I didn't have the luxury of emotional distance. His ship was sinking, and I was on it.

After we hung up, I ran downstairs in search of Mama who I found cleaning her bathroom. As soon as I saw her, another round of tears choked me, and I fanned my face, trying to get enough air to talk.

"Oh my God," she said, abandoning the toilet brush to the bowl. "What happened?"

I took a deep breath but could not manage any words.

"There's been a car accident. Is it Hadi? Is he okay?"

"No. No car accident. It's just . . . It's just . . ." I covered my mouth and tried to suck back the tears. I knew in the grand scheme of life Hadi's GPA was a gnat-sized concern, but in the scheme of our relationship it changed everything.

"It's his grades," I said. "He gets Cs."

Mama uttered a pitying tsk. "Hababa, I thought somebody died the way you're crying. Cs aren't the best, but they aren't the worst."

She put an arm around me, pulled my head down to her shoulder, and said, "It will be okay. Remember all the istikharas we made. Every one of them came out good."

I let Mama's words comfort me. Who I married was the single most important decision of my life; there had to be a reason why God had guided me to this match.

CHAPTER 17

※

THE STING OF REGRET

Now that Mama had seen me so upset, we had an official situation. Relatives at home and abroad were consulted. Aunty Najma told Mama not to worry. "Are you marrying the boy or his degree? His marks don't change the fact that he's a good boy." Mama then called Mrs. Ridha and told her about my concerns. Mrs. Ridha then talked to Dr. Ridha who spoke to Hadi, and then the cycle repeated in reverse, ending with Mama's report on Mrs. Ridha's latest phone call, her hope that her son's grades would improve by next year.

I had no better alternative than to share this hope. Although religiously there was nothing preventing me from breaking off my engagement, the social consequences terrified me—the gossip, the tarnished reputation, the fact that we'd kissed. I turned to romantic comedies for comfort. They proved obstacles were a given in any relationship. We had merely arrived at the juncture in our relationship where the man takes drastic measures to prove he has become worthy of the woman's love.

When Hadi called a few days later, I expected him to announce his strategy to win me back, but he said, "I'm sorry I hurt you," like a man who'd lost a fight. "You deserve better."

Now Hadi told me his parents had taken away his car, his prized T-Top Nissan Z with the custom license plate frame that said, "All I want in life is my car and Huda."

There was no going back from this. I was the one who'd ratted out my fiancé. Now Hadi's parents had to prove to my family that efforts were being made to bring everything back up to code.

One part of me wanted to apologize. Another part of me was so mystified I couldn't resist saying, "You're kidding, right? What's taking away your car supposed to achieve?"

"Yeah, well," Hadi said in a voice so flat I could almost see him throwing up his hands in the air.

This problem was suddenly more disconcerting than grades. Dr. and Mrs. Ridha were punishing and rewarding Hadi as if he were a small child—get bad grades and lose your car. And Hadi took it, as if this was a state of affairs he was powerless to fight. This surprised me. I thought all children of immigrants reversed the parent-child relationship to some degree. In our household, my siblings and I navigated our educational careers entirely on our own. Ibrahim, Lina, and I got through homework and term papers, college and financial aid applications all by filling in our parents of our progress on a need-to-know basis. And because of this, our parents may have had every aspect of cultural and religious control over us but nothing disciplinary. The handful of times Mama or Baba declared us grounded, it sounded so foreign, so imitative of American television parents, we'd laughed until our sides ached and Mama stormed out of the room saying, "Go fly," or Baba gave up with a frustrated, "Okay, all right. Never mind."

In all these years of friendship with the Ridhas, I never realized that Hadi did not have the same kind of relationship with his parents. I wondered if it was because Dr. Ridha had none of the helplessness that drove us to protect Baba. Nor was he a cutesy immigrant dad with a heavy accent. Dr. Ridha spoke American English like an actor performing a voice; he knew exactly which sounds to manipulate to erase all traces of an accent. Nobody looked to Hadi to explain what his father was saying, but it happened to me, Lina, and Ibrahim all the time.

After a month of tense phone calls between Hadi and me, a community event brought my immediate family (including Ibrahim, home for summer break) to the Ridhas' house for a weekend. The day after we arrived, Dr. Ridha called Mrs. Ridha, my parents, Hadi, and me into the dining room. Closing the French doors behind him, he told us to take a seat at the table. My stomach lurched. I would never be able to speak honestly in front of Dr. and Mrs. Ridha; I didn't want to risk jeopardizing their opinions of me.

Hadi sat next to me on one side of the table without once looking in my direction. Mama, Baba, and Mrs. Ridha sat opposite us without uttering a word. At the head of the table, Dr. Ridha cleared his throat and invoked the name of God: "*Bismillah ar-rahman ar-raheem.*" He took a preparatory breath and said, "We are very happy and proud our son is engaged to such a good girl from such a good family. But I also understand that Huda has some concerns, and I think she should share those with us now so we can discuss them."

Everyone in the room turned toward me. From across the table, Mrs. Ridha's lips stiffened with nervous anticipation. Mama gave me the go-ahead with a single, encouraging nod. Baba looked bewildered. He had no idea why we had gathered. Neither Mama nor I had told him. Not only because Baba would've gladly called off my engagement but also because he was the kind to hold a grudge, especially on behalf of his children. Baba still had not forgiven one of my cousins for pushing me and pulling my hair when we were both toddlers.

My heart raced, and my breath thinned. I never thought I would be asked to speak for myself. I liked things better the way they were before, with me complaining to Mama and Mama repackaging those concerns into polite and acceptable terms. A childhood urge to whisper everything I wanted said into Mama's ear overwhelmed me.

I was being asked to stab Hadi with my words, and he had never seemed more defenseless. It was past noon, and Hadi had just rolled out of bed. His hair was rumpled, his face unshaven, and he still wore last night's T-shirt and shorts. This was not a guy ready to fight for the love of his life, but a guy who didn't know what hit him.

A guy who I did not want.

Those words flashed in a dim corner of my mind like a glaring, neon sign. This was my chance to return Hadi to his family, to tell them, "My mom bought this guy for me, but he doesn't fit."

But I'd been seized by a shot of inhibition that I would've required the assistance of narcotics to release. The thought was too radical, too dangerous to contemplate. The only thing I could do now was invest Dr. and Mrs. Ridha in my education. Then regardless of what happened with Hadi's schooling, nobody would expect me to sacrifice mine.

I exhaled a breath I didn't know I'd been holding and pretended I was at school, talking to a professor. With all the confidence I could muster, I said, "I'm doing really well in school, and it's really important to me that I continue. But I understand that Hadi may not have the grades to get into medical school. If he has other interests, I'm willing to support him in that. But I think he should figure out what that is soon so that we're both able to continue with our educations."

I searched Hadi's face for his reaction, but he didn't meet my gaze. He stared at the mirror hanging above the buffet table and said nothing to defend himself. Disgust now stained the sympathy I'd felt for him a few moments ago. Hadi had no fight in him, no plan. It was tragic, really. I knew plenty of girls who didn't care about school. Another woman might have taken Hadi's love and run with it, and another guy might've appreciated my ambition. We both might've been happier with other people.

Dr. Ridha cleared his throat again and asked me exactly what I wanted to study. This worried me. My current interests in history and academics had no currency in our community. People were always telling Mama what a shame it was that Ibrahim wanted a PhD instead of an MD, and I feared Hadi's parents wouldn't find my educational goals worth protecting. The only thing I had going for me was that I planned to study Islamic societies, and anything related to Islam carried weight with Dr. Ridha.

But beyond a nod, Dr. Ridha didn't respond to my answer. He merely turned to Hadi and asked if he had anything he wanted to say. Hadi shook his head, but his tense brow and buttoned lips gave me the impression that he was too frustrated to speak.

Baba, on the other hand, was never one to stay quiet in a situation. Irrespective of circumstance or audience, Baba had an anecdote to share. Now he looked to Hadi and said, "In my opinion, there are many other things one can do. I know many chiropractors and physical therapists myself, and they are doing quite well. This fellow, who is the physical therapist, he is a Pakistani Muslim. He has a very nice office, close to mine. I can give you his number if you like to talk to him, but the important thing is one should never give up on their studies. In medical school, I had to repeat several classes myself. My father had died, and I was so sad, but somehow, I got through it. This is the life."

No one commented on Baba's musings, and I was grateful that Baba had chosen to view Hadi's academic struggles with sympathy rather than recording it in memory as his first official complaint. Dr. Ridha turned to Mama for her input and caught her off guard. She tried to suppress an awkward smile and said, "It's important to me that Huda finishes her education, but I also think Hadi is a wonderful boy. I've always loved him like he was my own son, and I want to see him happy and doing well in whatever he chooses to do." Mrs. Ridha said the same of me.

Now it was Dr. Ridha's turn to weigh in. After a contemplative pause, he said, "Hadi has to improve. Of course, we do not accept his grades, and we are very, very disappointed in him. I do not know about him doing other things, but I know he has to do better. Now, we would like nothing more than to see you and Hadi married and happy together, but I think you and your family should think about whether you want to continue with this engagement and we will discuss this again after dinner."

Everything that came out of Dr. Ridha's mouth took me by surprise—his harsh disapproval of Hadi's grades, the ticking bomb of an option he'd dropped on the table, the detonator he'd placed in my hands. I had to get out of the room. The consequences of a broken engagement were dizzying, and I couldn't consider them—not now, not with everyone watching.

I went looking for Ibrahim in Hadi's room. I closed the door behind me, settled down on the floor in front of him, and burst into tears.

Ibrahim closed the Arabic grammar book he'd been toting around all summer and asked me what had happened; I summarized the conversation I'd just had.

"So break it off," he said. It was a plea more than a suggestion.

Ibrahim rarely gave me advice on anything outside of academics. Besides that brief moment on the phone where I told him about my engagement, we respected the boundaries of our sibling roles—his job was to tease me, and my job was to act exasperated. For Ibrahim to think the problems looming in my future were worth breaking the engagement that he'd believed in with such confidence, that said something. That said a lot.

But even if my family supported my decision to break my engagement, I was far too worried about what people would think to do anything. I imagined the Iraqi mothers and grandmothers clucking and whispering about me in the corners of our masjids and dinner parties. I didn't want to accept that all the years I'd spent guarding my reputation had earned me nothing more than a broken engagement and a future filled with second-rate suitors.

"I can't," I said with conviction.

"Why?" Ibrahim asked. "Because of what a bunch of dumb, old Iraqi ladies think? Then you wouldn't have to worry about what you'll do about school. You could apply wherever I go to do my PhD and at least do your master's with me."

Not even a year had passed since my engagement, but I found myself looking back on the months before I became committed to Hadi with the longing of an aging woman, pining over her lost youth. If only I hadn't been so hung up on getting married young and proving to the world how desirable I was, if only I'd ignored the istikhara's results, maybe this could've been my plan. I could've followed Ibrahim to a far-off place and met someone who liked to study as much as I did. But it was too late.

This must be why all premarital touching was forbidden. It trapped you. Even if the ceremony Jidu performed for us was a dissolvable, temporary mutah, nothing could undo the kisses and embraces. Now I'd never be able to claim that I was a good girl to another man. Maybe worse, I'd never be able to remember the sweetness of those firsts without a sting of regret.

I looked up, but my eyes only caught the top of Ibrahim's dark, curly hair. It was enough for him to broach the subject—too much for him to look at me while he was doing it. "I can't," I said, this time as an apology. "I didn't work this hard to get a good reputation to throw it all away."

Ibrahim met my gaze, but his resolve to persuade me had been replaced by worry. He had no argument for this. Soon the future would offer us examples of Iraqi American friends who'd broken their engagements and married other people, who'd gotten married and divorced, who'd had a string of boyfriends and girlfriends and later chosen one to marry, but for now we had nothing but the rules we'd intuited from our parents and their immigrant friends. There was no greater Iraqi population to compare ourselves to, no sense of popular culture. Our Iraq was the one that lived on in our parents' memories, frozen at the moment of their 1970s departure, immune to time.

Now I wanted to comfort Ibrahim, to convince him I knew what I was doing. "I'll be fine. If for some reason, I can't go to graduate school, it might turn out to be for the best. It's not like I can wait forever to have kids. And with Baba's health the way it is—at least this way, he'll have time with his grandkids."

This reasoning resonated with me in a way I hadn't expected. The mere mention of Baba's health brought with it the pressure of tears and the dreadful images my mind kept at the ready. A fatherless bride. Grandfatherless grandchildren. I closed my eyes to block out any more. Hadi loved me. Nothing about our relationship was so bad that I'd leave it at the risk of never marrying, never having children. I decided that not only would I stay engaged but that I would also marry Hadi next summer. I needed access to Hadi if I wanted to fix him, but I didn't want to rush my wedding planning either. Since our engagement had left me with few memories that satisfied my dreams of a sweeping romance, at the very least, I wanted to look back on a beautiful wedding.

That afternoon, I pulled Hadi into his room, knowing that the gravity of our problems had bought us the privacy to work out our concerns. We sat on the chairs pushed against the wall of his bedroom. Hadi looked down, his shoulders slumped. His body was prepared for me to tell him that I was leaving, and this posture of surrender sent a ripple of ire under my skin. My mind railed, *Fight for me, man! Where's your strength? Am I really going to tell you I want to marry you? You, who I want to throttle and shake?*

But with my mouth I said something else entirely. "I think the best thing we can do now is work together to figure out what you should do next, whether it's medical school or something else. But that means, this school year, you're going to have to study around the clock to bring up your grades. And then, I think, we should probably get married earlier rather than later so that I can help you stay on top of everything."

Hadi looked up, and his face brightened. "I think that would really help," he said.

A wave of relief washed over me. I had spared myself so much discomfort with nothing more than my simple acquiescence. Now I wouldn't have to tell Hadi I wanted to leave. I would not break his heart or disappoint his parents. My family would not have to deal with an awkward goodbye, the question of whether to pack up our bags and leave that day or whether to stay until the next morning and pretend that this was not the end to a decade of friendship with the Ridhas.

I took Hadi's hand in mine, and his skin felt like a rescue from all the things I could not bear to confront. Then I leaned over and kissed him, both resenting and appreciating this kiss that adhered us together, that would not let us fall apart.

CHAPTER 18

WOMEN IN ISLAM

Back at school that fall, I reunited with my MSA friends in the library and announced that I was getting married next summer, a few months after my twentieth birthday. Both Amina and our mutual friend Sura had shared that they'd gotten engaged over the summer, and I was grateful not to be mourning my past while my friends were looking forward to their futures, especially this quarter. My MSA sisters and I weren't merely studying together, but we were enrolled in the course on women in Islam, as well.

We had agreed that we needed to be in that classroom as a group to deal with the stereotypes about women being forced to wear the hijab, genital mutilation, and nonconsensual arranged marriages. Six of us, including Amina and Sura, signed up to be there to raise our hands and object, "Not all Muslim women live like that. Look at us. We are Muslim women, too. How come nobody writes about Muslim women like us?"

My MSA sisters were all high-achieving students. The majority were studying to be doctors and engineers just like their hard-working, professional mothers who'd overcome language barriers and carried on working as physicians and engineers in the United States. Only three other women, besides myself, had chosen majors in the humanities, but our unconventional choice only motivated us more. We had to prove to our immigrant communities that success was possible outside of the sciences.

The day we watched a documentary about the feminists who threw off their veils in an Egyptian train station in the 1920s, Amina addressed our class first: "Those women were clearly responding to the hijab as some sort of symbol of patriarchy, but most of us wearing the hijab today do so for our faith. No one forced us to wear it. This was our choice, an expression of our freedom. You think women who walk around in a bathing suit, obsessing over their weight and cellulite, are free? We're the ones who are free from judgment and unreasonable beauty expectations."

Then for emphasis, I added, "Just because I don't cover my hair, it doesn't mean I don't believe in it. I have always tried to live by my own standards of modesty even if I am not ready to wear the hijab yet. I don't wear sleeveless shirts, and I stay away from skirts that go above the knee."

A week later when the topic of female circumcision arose, we exchanged exasperated looks. Sura took the lead with, "Look, you have to stop and consider the way religions work. You have a faith, and you have its practitioners. Islam can't stop its adherents from clinging to unfortunate cultural relics. Female circumcision predates Islam, and it is practiced almost exclusively in Africa. This is a horrible deviation from Islamic teaching."

By way of proof, Amina explained, "In Islam, both men and women have an equal right to sexual pleasure." To the doubtful glances that followed, she said, "Yes. Islam is always being written off as a misogynistic religion when it is such a progressive faith in regards to female sexuality."

Islamic teaching held that regular sex was essential to a healthy marriage, that you earned God's favor or *thawab* for sleeping with your spouse, and that women had a right to experience an orgasm. When our wedding nights arrived, we would wear sexy lingerie of every color and style, wax every hair-covered surface, and know that the physical moments we shared with our spouses were halal, permissible and blessed in the eyes of God.

When the discussion moved onto the topic of arranged marriages, Sura strategically rested a diamond-studded hand under her chin and said, "It is just so much more complicated than that. Like I just got engaged last month to my brother's roommate. I didn't know this, but he'd liked me for years. He was waiting until he finished college to tell me, and no, we didn't date before he proposed, but I don't feel like I needed to date him to know. And when he asked, it was really sweet. He cried. I cried."

Our classmates nodded with interest, as if Sura was an exhibit at a museum. Without skipping a beat, Amina added, "I think most people in this room would think I'm having an arranged marriage because my parents introduced me to a guy a few months ago. We talked over the summer and got engaged a few weeks ago, but I would never consider myself as having an arranged marriage. I want to marry my fiancé. He is smart and good-looking. He's a total catch, and I hate that just because I'm Muslim, my parents can't just introduce me to someone without people thinking it was a setup."

I chimed in, "Amina's totally right. I met my fiancé when I was six. We grew up together. We both liked each other, and he asked me to marry him before his parents asked for my hand."

For the purposes of this course, my current ambivalence toward Hadi was irrelevant. We'd just finished reading *A Wife for My Son* by Ali Ghalem, and the novel depicted the stereotypical arranged marriage, complete with a distasteful bloody sheet scene. Outside of class, my MSA friends and I criticized its author. What type of a Muslim would write stuff like this? So what if disgusting things like this happened? We needed literature that made us look like the normal people we were, with educated parents who asked their daughters' opinions on who they wanted to marry, and sent them to expensive private colleges, and would never dream of insulting them by checking their wedding-night sheets. With Ghalem confirming my classmates' worst assumptions about Muslims and Arabs, I had no choice but to keep my angst to myself. The last thing I wanted was to confirm the views my fellow Muslims and I were working so hard to discredit.

It was the same reason why I never mentioned my Shia identity in class—image control. I didn't want to add sectarian differences to a conversation that was already so rife with misunderstanding, that years later still circled back to the movie *Not without My Daughter*. The irony of erasing my own individuality to challenge stereotypes was entirely lost on me. I may have only been nineteen years old, but I took seriously the responsibilities that came with representing my religion. This was not only a class but also an opportunity to change the way eighteen people thought about Muslims. Beneath every raised hand, every argument my MSA sisters and I made, I could hear us whispering this unspoken plea: "Remember us after this course ends and when you're listening to the news. Please remember us."

CHAPTER 19

A DAY FOR ME AND THE GIRLS

A Lebanese sales associate named Samira ushered Mama, Mrs. Ridha, Lina, and me into a fitting room as big as my dorm room. While they got situated on the armchairs pushed up against the wall-to-wall mirrors, Samira asked me what kind of dresses I wanted to see. Amor was not the kind of store where customers were allowed to rifle through the dresses on their own. I told her not to bring anything sleeveless or strapless and that I liked full skirts, preferably tulle.

It was winter break, and Mama, Lina, and I were staying with the Ridhas for the weekend while we went wedding-dress shopping. Because Wedding Dress Shopping Day was a special occasion, Lina and I had spent the better part of last week deciding what I would wear. I now slid out of my carefully chosen outfit, an angora top paired with a houndstooth pencil skirt. On the carpeted platform in the center of the room, I stood in suede heels, nude hosiery, and a matching set of lacy underwear because I didn't want Mrs. Ridha discovering that I was a cotton-granny-panty kind of gal. Now was her opportunity to get a peek at the body that her son was marrying, and I didn't want her to be disappointed—even if Hadi didn't want her seeing me undressed.

Hadi hated that Islamic custom allowed any woman to see my body, while he, the soon-to-be husband, was literally stuck waiting in the car. If Hadi had it his way, Mama, Lina, and Mrs. Ridha would be sitting in the waiting area outside. I'd stick an arm out of the fitting room and grab the oversized dresses, and the clothespins to secure them, right from Samira's hands. "Now that I am getting married, you may no longer see me in my undergarments," I'd call out. "Not even you, woman whose uterus was once my home!"

In anticipation of this weekend, Hadi and I had reenacted the following telephone conversation nightly.

He'd say, "How would you feel if you knew I was changing in front of other people?"

"Be my guest," I'd reply. "Be free. Be naked if you want." *Just leave me alone.*

Apparently my lack of interest in keeping Hadi's nakedness all to myself was hurtful. In a wounded tone, he'd say, "I don't see why you don't want our bodies to be something special, just between us."

"I don't see why you are asking me to do something that our religion doesn't even ask of me. Even girls who wear the hijab do whatever they want in the company of other women."

Sharing a fitting room with a girlfriend, sister, or mother was female bonding at its finest. This was the equivalent of me asking him not to watch sports with his male friends. Ever.

"This has nothing to do with religion," he'd finally say. "I've always thought of our bodies as a symbol of the private life we share together. I know you're the only person I want to see me, and I thought you'd feel the same way."

At the time, I could have gagged on Hadi's love and all the things that we were only going to share with each other. I had heard so much about boys and their different needs and indestructible reputations that I never stopped to consider what it might have felt like to be the kind of Muslim boy who had grown up eschewing such cultural double standards, holding onto our religion's ideals of the virgin couple through high school and then college. Surely, Hadi was carrying his own special brand of expectations into his first relationship with a woman, but I did not have the maturity to recognize that. His extraordinary sentimentality only baffled and frustrated me.

While normally I wouldn't have given a second thought to being in my underwear in the company of other women, that morning I relished my small act of defiance. It was a day for me and the girls. We'd do what ladies did in fitting rooms—admire and gripe about our bodies.

Samira came into the room and hooked a bundle of dresses on the door. She took one look at me and said to Mrs. Ridha in Arabic, "Congratulations. Your daughter-in-law has a beautiful body. Your son is very lucky."

Mrs. Ridha laughed. "We are the lucky ones. What he wouldn't give to be seeing what we are seeing."

This elicited laughs from everyone except Lina, who crinkled up her nose with disgust.

"I hope he doesn't like big boobs, because what she has will barely fill a hand," Mama said. Her tone was light, and it set off another round of laughter, but this was not meant as a jab. Iraqis do not value directness. We say things we don't mean so that people will correct us, we refuse things we are offered to be polite, and we never ask for what we want without apologizing for it profusely. My big nose and small chest were marriage liabilities, and this was Mama's way of acknowledging this, of saying, "Now you've seen everything we have to offer."

My MSA friends and I could argue all we wanted about how Islam shielded women from unforgiving standards of beauty, but Mama's comment reminded me how far the Western ideal of the slim but buxom femme had traveled, how universal it had become. On the few occasions when Mama had commented that my future husband might be disappointed by my small chest, I'd taken offense and said, "You're my mother. You're supposed to tell me that whoever marries me should accept me the way I am." She'd looked at me as if

I was being naïve. "Men like boobs," she said. It was silly to pretend otherwise.

Mrs. Ridha now made a shooing gesture with her hand to dismiss the topic. "You think anybody could ask him such a question? Hadi thinks everything about Huda is perfect. One time, I asked him, 'If Huda wanted to change her nose, would you accept it?' He got so angry. I told him, 'Don't worry. Nobody is trying to change her.'"

This was another arena in which Hadi's love suffocated me. Among friends, I was used to moaning about my big nose and the way it leaned to one side, my dimply thighs, and my fleshy stomach. For the most part, these were invitations to contradiction, but Hadi objected to the practice entirely. He said things like, "Hey, I love your _____. You can't talk about it like that," and I'd follow with something I never expected to defend, my right to criticize myself.

Samira slid a series of dresses over my head and clipped them closed. There were several nos, a couple of maybes, and then gasps. "Now this, this is something special," Mrs. Ridha said. The dress had a satin bodice with long sleeves and a skirt made of fine tulle whose underlayers were dotted with clear sequins that danced in the light while its top layer was intricately embroidered along the bottom edge and train.

"Beautiful," Mama agreed.

I smiled. I twirled. I did a little dance because that was what you did when you tried on a dress that you liked. You checked out how you looked while dancing in it. It had a lovely swish.

No. Wait. It was too soon for this kind of excitement. My ring had taught me a valuable lesson about patience in shopping.

"This is off the shoulder," I said to Samira.

"We'll specify in your order that you want the sleeves on the shoulder."

"Can that be done without pouffiness? I don't want any pouffiness."

"Of course."

"Do you guys really like it?" I asked Mama, Mrs. Ridha, and Lina.

"You're beautiful," Mrs. Ridha answered, "so whatever you wear is nice. What matters is that you like it."

"I like it, but how much is it?" I said, turning to Samira.

Samira's lips moved with computational noises, and then she said aloud, "Three thousand for the dress, and then there will be additional fees for alteration and the custom sleeves."

Now it was my turn to gasp. My ring had cost less.

"Don't think about the price," Mrs. Ridha said. "The important thing is that you are happy."

And I was happy in a way that surpassed the glee of finding the perfect dress. I'd been taught that it wasn't enough to marry a man because you loved him. You had to love his entire family. This moment felt like proof that I was making the right decision. I may have questioned how I felt about Hadi, but I loved Mrs. Ridha. Not because she was buying me the most expensive article of clothing I'd ever owned, but because she understood that I was not just a wife for her son but a girl with dreams, some reasonable, most not, but all aching to be made true.

Samira gathered up my hair and fed it through the opening of a rhinestone tiara. Staring at my reflection, I felt content, not just with my dress but also with my choice. Life was so much easier when I thought only like an Arab girl, who was happy to be marrying into a good family, who was free to love her spouse before her wedding but under no obligation to do so, who knew her love didn't have to be ready yet. It hadn't had a chance to grow.

Back at school, I felt as if I'd been cut in half with zigzag scissors. My sophomore year, I roomed with Aysar, one of two Iraqi American girls I'd met on campus (the other Iraqi girl happened to be Aysar's cousin and the person who introduced us). Aysar didn't hang out with the MSA crowd, and she wasn't looking to get married while still in college. In her company, I felt nostalgia for things I had not yet lost. My wedding date had been set for the summer, and seven more months of life as a single girl didn't feel like enough.

I loved living with Aysar. We called the lone sink at the front of the room our kitchen. We brewed tea every night in a dormitory-violation Mr. Coffee and coordinated our bathroom trips so we could talk and visit with our neighbors as we walked down the hall. We danced to loud music, and rather than stop when we grew tired, we held onto the back of our desk chairs and moved only our behinds while saying breathlessly, "Must keep dancing."

Aysar was exactly the kind of friend an obsessed-with-grades student needed. She made me write my term papers on her computer so that I wouldn't have to stand over my Brother word processor, loading its typewriter with paper and printing out one page at a time. She brought me soup when I was sick and insisted that I take the occasional study break to have dinner off campus or catch a movie. And whenever I got back from the library, Aysar was waiting for me with music on and tea brewing.

I joked that Aysar was the best wife and that it was a shame I hadn't been born a man, because I would've made such a good husband. I wanted to be the one in the couple who worked, whose goals and ambitions determined where my future family lived. But instead, night after night, I sat on the sidelines and coached Hadi to find research projects that would lead to the kind of undergraduate publications I hoped would get him an acceptance into medical school. And while all this struck me as unfair, it didn't seem unbearably so until one evening when Aysar and I were stretched out on our beds, taking a moment to relax after dinner.

"We should go to Europe for spring break," Aysar had said. "A girl trip before you get married."

Aysar and I would've had an amazing time in Europe. She'd say, "Let's go to a club." And I'd say no, but then she'd insist and I'd have to go along with her because it wasn't safe to separate. By day, we'd sit in cafés and people-watch and laugh until we cried. "You may be beautiful and stylish," we'd say to the well-dressed passerby, "but you don't have any shops with the word 'mart' in it. You can't buy underwear, auto parts, and milk all in the same store." And we'd live on salads and bread and cheese, the kind of food that didn't fill Hadi but the kind that would make me feel so healthy, so light, so free.

"I can't think of how I'd ever be able to do that," I said without looking at Aysar. This admission felt heavy, deadening.

All this time, I'd believed getting engaged was my ticket to freedom, but I'd never felt so constrained. I'd merely gained another person to answer to, a third parent who had an opinion on who I studied with and changed in front of, whose career path would dictate where I would live and go to school. It was one thing to defend my culture and religion to my peers, to explain its principles and ideas in class after class, but it was quite another thing to own this fractured mind, to hear the American voice within me whisper, *You are too young, much too young to be tied down, to limit yourself for any man*, and my Muslim voice console, *This is just fine. You are marrying the right guy. God Himself told you this.* If only I knew then that this dichotomy was confining me, too, cleaving my thoughts into two sides where my every misgiving was an American idea and therefore risky and dangerous, and my every reassurance was a Muslim idea and safe and good.

✿

CHAPTER 20

THE PROOF OF OUR YOUTH

Hadi blamed the physical distance between us for the tension during our phone conversations. He insisted that all we needed was one day out, one day to prove that our lives together could be fun. His mother was planning a reception to welcome his sister Jamila's new baby in January. Since my family would be coming for the occasion, he had asked his parents that we be allowed to go out alone the day before the party.

I told him he had to plan everything, hoping that this day would capture my heart and, once and for all, quiet my mind's incessant chorus of regrets. It never occurred to me that this was too much to expect from one day, one moment, one man. Our wedding date had been set for the end of July, and I needed something to reassure me that my decision to stay with Hadi hadn't been a mistake, that even though Hadi still hadn't gotten any interviews to medical schools and I had no idea what he was going to do after he graduated in June, there was something so romantic and wonderful about us that we were meant to be together.

My family and I arrived at Hadi's house on a Friday night. We would be taking over Hadi's room, my parents on the bed, Lina and I on a stack of blankets on the floor. That night, Hadi walked me to the door of his room and told me that he was looking forward to tomorrow and that I should dress casually. My body let go of tension I hadn't realized I'd been holding. Hadi had put thought into this. He'd planned.

The next morning, I slid into the kind of outfit I rarely wore but Hadi said I looked cutest in—jeans, tennis shoes, and a sweatshirt—and then I repacked my bag because our families would stay at the Ridhas' beach house in San Diego that night. I expected to find Hadi waiting for me in the kitchen, but only our parents were seated at the marble slab table, sipping their tea, dipping pita bread in *lebne*, or wrapping it around slices of Syrian cheese and bundles of mint.

"Sit down and eat," Dr. Ridha said.

And because Hadi was nowhere to suggest otherwise, I sat and felt some of the day's excitement fizzle. There were girls whose boyfriends picked them up from their homes and whisked them off to fancy brunches and dinners, and then there were girls like me, who had breakfast with their future in-laws on the day she had come to think of as her first and last date before getting married.

When Hadi showed up in the kitchen a half hour later, he was dressed but not ready to leave. He whispered something in his mother's ear. A moment later, he was in the garage. Then he was out of the garage and saying, "It's not there."

After more directions from his mom, Hadi went back into the garage and returned with a cooler in hand. He set it down on the counter and bent toward his mother's ear again. I stuffed a piece of cheese into a triangle of pita bread and watched Mrs. Ridha leave her chair and pull bread, mayonnaise, and cold cuts out of the refrigerator.

When Hadi and his mother set to work, making sandwiches for our day out, I excused myself and headed to the hall bathroom. There I took a series of deep breaths so that I would not cry. This was the first date Hadi had planned for us, and he was packing us a picnic with his mommy. *Dear God*, I prayed, *why can't we do anything that makes me feel like an adult who is old enough to be getting married?*

I wanted to call Mama into the bathroom, but I already knew what she'd say. That I expected too much from the boy. That I wanted to marry someone who'd never had a girlfriend but wanted him to act like a man who had been out with a thousand women. That I wanted an American-style date, but that we weren't Americans and Islamically we shouldn't have been going out alone anyway. That because I was born in America, I equated being an adult with doing things without parental involvement, but in Iraq, some people lived with their parents their whole lives and there was no shame in that.

Listening to her imaginary talk was enough to send me back into the kitchen with a vow to be patient, to give Hadi a chance. He'd never taken a girl out before. He didn't know how pathetic this seemed.

When I came back to the kitchen, Hadi was lining up our sandwiches next to two canned soft drinks in the cooler. He smiled at me. He was excited, proud of himself for the day he had planned. Hadi slid the cooler closed and announced that he was ready to leave.

"Why are you leaving now?" his father asked, getting up from the breakfast table. "It will be time to pray in a half hour. Pray and then go."

Hadi looked at the clock and then looked at me. This was the practicing Muslim's midmorning outing dilemma. When you only had less than an hour to the afternoon *dhuhr* prayer to spare, you had to decide whether you wanted to wait and pray at home or leave and spend the day wondering if you should (a) find a quiet place where you could pray without drawing an audience; (b) miss your prayer, feel guilty about it, and make it up when you got home; or (c) rush home to squeeze in the prayer before sunset when the evening prayers would become due.

But now that Hadi's father brought it up, the choice was no longer mine to make. Opting for anything but staying would have declared an indifference to my daily prayers and an eagerness to be alone with his son. "It's up to you," I said and then looked away, setting about clearing the breakfast table and helping with the dishes. No more discussion of our leaving followed, and so I finished in the kitchen and returned to the bedroom, where I took off my socks to make wudhu and covered my hair to pray, before finding Hadi in the hallway.

"We're leaving," Hadi announced. This brought our families out of their rooms to bid us farewell.

"Why are you in such a hurry?" Dr. Ridha called out from his bedroom doorway. "Wait until Jamila and Bashar leave."

Hadi's sister and his brother-in-law were leaving their baby with Mrs. Ridha and spending the day at an amusement park. I couldn't understand what their departure had to do with ours and apparently neither did Hadi.

"Why would we wait for them?" Hadi asked while approaching his father. "We're not going out together."

"And what's wrong with you all leaving at the same time?" Dr. Ridha's voice was calm and level. I knew this tone; it made any inflection on the other end of the conversation sound unreasonable and defensive.

"But we have our own car," Hadi said, involuntarily completing the effect.

With the same evenness, Dr. Ridha answered, "There is no rush now. I said wait for them and go out together."

The negotiations had ended. Any reply now would imply that we had some kind of inappropriate rush to be alone together, and so we waited and waited because the catch in all this was that Hadi's sister wasn't ready. She had a baby to nurse, milk that had to be expressed, a diaper to change, and a bag to pack because she and her husband would be spending the night together at a hotel before meeting us for the elaborate reception Mrs. Ridha had planned the next day.

When our moment of departure finally arrived well over two hours later, our families gathered at the door and kissed us on the cheek as if we were leaving on a transatlantic journey. Hadi's mother reminded him that we'd all be going to the beach house that night, and then she gave Hadi something to return to the electronics store we'd be passing on the way.

We settled into Hadi's brother's car, since Hadi's car was still grounded in the garage. The clock on the dash read close to three o'clock, and this alone made me feel as if our day was done before it even started.

"Sorry about that," Hadi said.

I didn't answer.

"I'm happy to finally be with you," he said.

An uneasiness had constricted my throat, and all I could offer in return was a tight thank-you. Hadi and I were children around his father, and children weren't supposed to get married. Adults got married.

After a tense, quiet drive, we joined a winding two-lane road that I hoped signaled our arrival to our destination. When we still hadn't stopped thirty minutes later, I feared we were lost.

"Where are we going?" I asked.

"I'm sorry. I thought we would've been there by now."

"Where is there?"

"It's an old gold-mining town. I was going to take you there because I know how much you like history, but I think the friend who gave me directions might've made a mistake in telling me how far away it is."

Of course, he made a mistake, I thought, because this day was doomed from its outset.

"It'll be getting dark soon," I said.

"What do you want me to do?"

"I don't know, but it's almost four. Even if you found this place now, everything will be closing soon. And I'm hungry, and soon it's going to be too dark to have a picnic."

"Should we stop and look at a map?"

"I guess," I said.

Hadi pulled into a wide turnout and parked to the side of a scraggly oak tree. He fanned out the map across the steering wheel.

"I'm sorry," he said after a moment. "I don't know exactly where we are right now, but it looks like we still have a ways to go. Even if we keep going, I don't know that we'll be able to make it down there before dark."

I watched Hadi fold up the map, feeling terribly burdened by this truth: Hadi had no tricks up his sleeve, no rescue in the works. Our date was officially a bust, and this on the day when I'd seen such proof of our youth. Already reduced to a child, I didn't know if I could talk myself out of crying.

Hadi stepped out of the car, got the cooler out of the trunk, opened the door on my side, and said, "Come on. You're hungry. There's more room in the back."

After we'd settled into the bucket seats, the cooler between us, Hadi added, "This wasn't how things were supposed to turn out."

"I know," I said. "Things are always supposed to turn out differently, but somehow they never do."

"The day isn't over yet. We still have to get back to San Diego. We can return my mom's stuff, and then maybe we can have dinner on the way."

"I don't know." I preferred to think we'd never gone on a date than to think our one date had gone so badly.

"Let's go. I'll call my mom when we get to the store and tell her we're stopping for dinner."

"Okay," I said and reached over and squeezed his hand. Maybe this would be one of those funny, romantic dates—the kind of day where everything goes wrong in the beginning but turns out right in the end.

The gods of California traffic, however, had not smiled upon us. It took us over an hour to get to the electronics store. By the time we finished the return and arrived at the pay phones outside to call Mrs. Ridha, it was nearing seven o'clock. Seven on the day of my only date, and we still had not gone anywhere. I had pinned so much hope on this day, but to Hadi's parents this was just another day to sit down, have a family breakfast, run errands, and, for reasons beyond me, orchestrate a simultaneous departure with his sister.

Hadi picked up the receiver and unraveled the tangled metal cord. "Wait," I said. "I'm having second thoughts about dinner."

In spite of my protest, Hadi's fingers went to work, punching in his calling card number.

"Hadi, we've been out too long, and our parents won't understand that we've spent the entire day in the car. All they'll think is that we had the whole afternoon together and still want more."

"It's fine," he said, pulling the cord taut in his hand. "I'll talk to my mom."

No one picked up at the beach house. Next he called home, and his mother answered. I listened to Hadi's side of the conversation, and when he hung up, he filled in the blanks. His mother decided she had too much to do before the party to go to the beach house. All the women were staying home that night, but our fathers were driving to San Diego with our things so that we wouldn't have to drive all the way back to his parents' house.

"Let's go straight to the beach house then," I said. The last thing I wanted was to upset our fathers.

"No, don't worry. My mom said it was okay, and besides our dads just left. They won't be at the house for another hour and a half."

I was too nervous to have dinner at a restaurant with table service, and so I pointed to an Italian place in the strip mall across the street. After ordering at the counter, we sat in a booth where I picked at my airport-quality rigatoni, a ball of disappointment lodged in my throat. I'd been a fool to think I could have the Muslim American love story of my dreams. At the end of the day, we were just two Muslim kids from families who believed outings like this were just unnecessary opportunities for sin.

"We are getting married in six months," I said, on the verge of tears, "but it was too much to ask for this one day. I just wanted us to have one special day to remember."

With an almost panicked fervor, Hadi pleaded for one more stop. "The day isn't over yet. Let me take you to Coronado Island. The bridge is beautiful at night. We can walk along the beach, stop for ice cream."

"There's no time."

"Who cares about the time? They made us waste time at the beginning of the day, and if we get in trouble, I'll deal with it."

"I don't think it's a good idea," I said without explicitly refusing. The allure of the day being made right was too irresistible. If we went to the beach house now, I didn't know what I'd tell myself about our engagement to make it tolerable.

But back in the car, I could not take my eyes off the clock.

"This is farther than I thought," I said. "It's getting late." Fear had conquered me. There was nothing Hadi could do in the next hour that would cancel out what had happened during the day, nothing that would be worth handling the questions about where we'd been.

"Don't worry," Hadi insisted. "We'll be quick."

We sat on a rock near the entrance to the beach on the Hotel Del Coronado's grounds for all of four minutes before I said we should go. Not only did the beach at night scare me, but also my stomach was cramping with anxiety. I could hear a clock ticking away in my mind; I could hear Dr. Ridha saying, "Where were you?" as soon as we walked through the door.

I stood up. Hadi said, "Can I at least give you a hug before we leave?"

I walked into Hadi's outstretched arms with my arms flat at my sides. He wrapped his arms around me, but I did not return his embrace.

"I give up. Let's go." He stood, wiped the sand off the back of his pants, and said, "My ring."

"What about your ring?"

"It flew off my finger and into the sand," Hadi said, dropping to his knees, patting the ground around him.

"You've got to be kidding me. We were supposed to be back a half hour ago."

"You think I don't know that?" he said, digging around the periphery of the rock.

"Oh my God." I brought my hands up to my mouth. "There's no way you'll find it. Nobody ever finds anything in the sand, and it's dark and it's late . . ." My voice trailed off, and instead of dropping to the ground and helping Hadi look, I leaned back against the rock and panicked. "We are so doomed. I knew we should've gone back. This is a sign. There's something wrong with us being together."

Now we'd have to tell our parents we'd been to the beach at night. The beach of all places. They barely allowed us to go out alone, and we were at a place notorious for making out and sex. Oh the disgrace!

"There is nothing wrong with us being together. It's cold. My fingers must've shrunk, and the ring was already loose to begin with. Let's go inside the hotel. I'll call home, and we'll see if they have a metal detector or flashlight or something."

Hadi's suggestion filled me with dread. I hated how we appeared as a couple to people outside the Muslim community. What would the employees in the hotel think when Hadi said he lost his ring and we looked like teenagers? To the average American, we were two stupid kids, with the words *breakup* and *future divorce* written all over our foreheads.

Leaning on the darkly stained wood-paneled front desk, Hadi told our story to the hotel night clerk. She sucked air through her teeth, the way people do when they are about to tell you the thing you've asked for is impossible, ridiculous even. She suggested we rent a metal detector and come back tomorrow.

Between searching for the ring and walking back to the hotel, we'd lost another hour. It was now past ten. There was nothing left to do but call home and confess. At the pay phones by the lobby bathroom, Hadi called his mother. He explained what had happened and asked her to get the message to Dr. Ridha that we were going to be late. Hadi wasn't about to call his dad and get a sneak preview of the lecture that awaited us.

We drove home over a lit bridge, an ocean of blackness below us, but the beauty of the view was lost on me. The entire drive home, I cried at the injustice of it all. This was an engagement I didn't want anymore, and now I was going to be given a lecture intended for a boy and girl who were in love, who'd stayed out too long, having fun. Now I was returning to a house full of men, with no moms to intervene.

When we pulled into the driveway, I felt a blaze of shame go up within me followed by a desperate urge to run. I wasn't used to getting in trouble. I didn't know how to steel myself to face an angry adult.

At the sound of the engine, Dr. Ridha opened the front door. As soon as we stepped out of the car, the lecture began. "This is absolutely unacceptable. You two should not even be out together alone, and then you were out so late. You made us both very, very worried."

We walked into the house, our heads down. Dr. Ridha pointed to the stairs that led up from the entryway into the living room. We followed, and he continued. "I don't like this at all. I am very disappointed in you, Hadi. This is somebody's daughter, and you are responsible for her. This is a sign. You should not be going out together alone. That's it. No more of this."

I had frozen in front of the couch, my eyes meeting Baba's as he stood by the dining room table. I knew instantly that he was not upset but confused. He looked shocked, as if he had not expected Dr. Ridha to be so angry.

"I want everybody to go to bed now. We'll discuss this more tomorrow."

I gave Baba a half smile and then rushed to the room where I'd be staying before anyone noticed that I'd started to cry. Before I had a chance to close the door, Baba appeared.

"I'm sorry. I just asked Dr. Ridha why you were so late. I didn't know he would get so much angry."

And then I got a flash of what this evening might have been like for Dr. Ridha. Without Mama around to keep Baba in check, his anxieties had gotten the best of him. Baba was the type of person who needed to know where every member of his family was every second of the day. He'd probably asked Dr. Ridha where we were and when we'd be back at least a dozen times. Dr. Ridha must have grown increasingly uncomfortable that he didn't have an answer, that it was his son who was causing my dad so much worry.

"It's okay, Baba," I said through tears because there was no point in explaining otherwise. I knew that bewildered look he'd worn standing by the table a few minutes ago. It was the same did-I-do-something-wrong expression that transformed his anxious face whenever Mama snapped at him for calling her too much at work or for using the overhead paging system to find her in public places.

I sat on the edge of the bed and blew my nose into the tissues I'd grabbed off the dresser. Baba could not stand to see me cry, but he never knew what to say to comfort me either. That night, he stood beside me awkwardly, his hands folded behind his back, and said, "I was so much worried, but I did not want to make you sad. I wish your mummy was here."

He put his hand on my shoulder, and an urge to shelter Baba from my sadness overcame me. "I'm fine," I said. "I just feel bad, that's all. We weren't trying to be late, and I was having such a terrible time."

Baba said, "You want to call your mummy?"

I shook my head and said I'd go to bed instead. But I stared at the ceiling, feeling the weight of my own future pressing down on me, and could not fall asleep. This was not the life I wanted. Not the engagement I wanted. Not the boy or the kind of father-in-law I wanted. But I was too far into things to get out now. The hall had been booked, the date announced. How I wished the mattress would swallow me whole.

The next morning, I got ready for Jamila's reception as slowly as possible. I camouflaged my puffy face with makeup, pinned my hair into a French twist, and painted the nails on my still-trembling hands. When I had nothing else left to do, I filled the hollow that yesterday's crying had left behind with a deep, steadying breath and went downstairs.

Our fathers were seated at the dining table, eating pita bread with cheese. Hadi sat at the table too but without any food in front of him.

"I'm glad you're here," Dr. Ridha said as soon as he saw me. "I have something very important I want to tell the both of you today, here in front of your father."

He cleared his throat and continued. "After the dawn prayer, I woke up Hadi, and we went down to the beach where he lost the ring. I raised my hands and prayed to Allah, *subhanallah wa ta'ala*, to help us find it. Then I started to pick up handfuls of sand, like this . . ."

Dr. Ridha brought up both of his hands until they met to form a bowl shape. "I shook my hands so that only the sand could pour out. I did this again and again until I found this at the bottom of my hand." He reached into his pocket and produced Hadi's platinum band.

I looked over at Hadi for confirmation, but his expression was hard to read, a mixture of frustration and helplessness. And who could blame him? Who on earth could find anything in the sand? Maybe Dr. Ridha did have some kind of direct line to God.

"Now I'm going to keep this ring for a time because I think Allah, subhanallah wa ta'ala, has done this to remind us that a man and woman should not be alone before they are married."

"But, Baba," Hadi said. "I bought tickets to a show tonight a long time ago. We were going to go with Jamila and Bashar so we wouldn't be alone. I asked Mom, and she said it was okay."

"You'll have to give them away then. I told you, I do not think it is right that you two go out together anymore."

Tickets. This was the first thing I'd heard about tickets. Hadi did have more planned for us. He was trying.

I reached for a piece of bread. I needed something to stare at so no one would see my thoughts crushing me. Yesterday had been a punishment from God. Hadi did have another trick up his sleeve. Later he would tell me that he'd gotten us tickets to see *Cats*, but the only thing I'd have to show for it would be the memory of its denial. What was this household, where one man could make a decision for everyone despite the person's wishes and wants? This imbalance of power felt foreign, alien. I didn't understand how two families, so similar in religion and culture, could be so different. After all these years of friendship, it never occurred to me that there would still be sides to the Ridhas I had not seen, family dynamics I'd never witnessed. I wondered how much of the Hadi I knew was colored by the role he played in his family; I wondered how he might have appeared to me had I known him as a man first and the Ridhas' son second.

❦

CHAPTER 21

CRISES A, B, AND C

Now that Dr. Ridha had made his stand, Hadi and I only saw each other when our families visited for a weekend. Since we couldn't go out alone together anymore, we stole kisses and gropes, but once alone, I'd turn over each embrace in my mind, burning with the shame of sneaking around and the irony of it all. Our families were like the state of Iran, expending an extraordinary amount of effort to keep us from being an unmarried man and woman out in public only to leave us with nothing to do inside but make out.

Back at school, I struggled to come to terms with this boy I never failed to kiss but wasn't sure I liked and the elaborate wedding we were planning. Almost nightly, Hadi and I bickered over the phone regarding three areas of disagreement.

CRISIS A: IS IT MY BODY OR YOURS?

This argument touched on several matters (whether or not I'd get a massage prior to our wedding, how I'd style my hair that day, who we'd spend time with before we left for our honeymoon), but the one that received the most argumentative attention was the question of who would see me first on the day of our wedding. I believed Hadi should wait for me at the end of an aisle, like a proper Hollywood groom, maybe shed a tear the first time he saw me. Hadi thought that we should exchange a private moment prior to our wedding. He likened waiting at the end of an aisle to being the last person to see a present intended for him. I accused him of treating me like an object and of being jealous and controlling. Hadi accused me of being unsentimental and being more interested in our wedding than our future.

CRISIS B: YOU ARE TOO BORING.
YOU ARE GOING TO RUIN MY WEDDING.

In April, Hadi's aunt threw us a bridal shower in a Lebanese restaurant. For the entertainment, Mrs. Ridha hired a well-known Persian dance troupe led by an agile, somewhat elfin man in harem pants. During the final song, the spritely dancer pulled us both to the center of the dance floor. He motioned for us to follow him as he wove through the tables, shaking a tambourine, and although Hadi cooperated, his body was tense and tight. Since my vision of my wedding featured an excited, happy groom, Hadi's bridal-shower presence concerned me. During our nightly phone calls, I reminded him that he had to become an eager dancer before our wedding, whether it was natural to him or not. Hadi argued that not all people expressed joy by dancing or laughing or other more public displays of glee. Some people, he said, are happy quietly. This, I informed him, meant that he was dull. And for added measure, I told him he didn't make me laugh enough. He was not funny, and in his company, I was doomed to a humorless life.

CRISIS C: WHAT THE HELL IS GOING TO BECOME OF US?

By the end of spring, it was apparent that Hadi would not be going to medical school in the fall. He would be graduating in a few weeks, and he had no admission, no job, and, for the moment, none of my respect. The invitations had been sent out, and the thought of calling off the wedding at this point was anathema to me. The Ridhas were equally loath to accept Hadi's pursuing a different path, and so after discussing several options, our families decided that come September I'd overload on units so that I could graduate at the end of my third year. Meanwhile, Hadi and I would live together close to campus. Under my supervision, he would work, take more classes, and reapply. The following fall, we'd go off to graduate school together.

Even though I'd been the one to suggest the plan, I made sure to let Hadi know how much I hated it. Where would he even find a job? How would I know which graduate school to apply to if I didn't know where he was going to get into medical school?

I never told Hadi that I was so overly critical of his academic history, because I was terribly insecure about my own achievements. Although I could make As by studying around the clock, I could not bring in anything more than average scores on standardized tests. To me, this proved that I was an academic imposter who had duped her teachers through hard work. I wanted to marry someone who'd help me keep up the charade, a genius on whose intellectual coattails I could ride. Together we'd talk about smart things, keep smart company, and no one would ever know that I'd been raised on sitcoms. But now Hadi's situation had pegged us as an average couple, the kind of people who went to no-name schools.

Since I blamed Hadi for crisis C, I decided that this made him ineligible to participate in the negotiations of crisis A or B. Whenever we argued, I paraphrased this finger-pointing tirade: "You didn't do your part so you have no right to make any demands on our wedding plans. Because of you, I have to go into my wedding with a black cloud of doubt hanging over my head. The least you can do is give me the party I've always wanted."

As long as I had my dream wedding, I believed there was still hope for Hadi and me. Then I could cast off our engagement memories, plot down our ceremony and reception as the opening to our love story, and wait for our newlywed years to redeem us. First Valentine's Day, first birthdays, first anniversary—these moments would be the chapters of an even better story.

In the weeks leading up to our wedding, the shopping alone was enough to make me think my strategy was working. Of course, I wanted to get married. Hadn't I picked the floral arrangements on gold stands; the tiered fondant cake; the flower girls' ribbon-and-pearl dresses; the bridesmaids' entire ensemble, from their blush dresses to their rhinestone tiaras and white gloves?

The only thing left to covet now was the family reunion I had hoped my wedding would inspire. The last time Mama and her six siblings had been in the same place was her 1971 wedding, but I also knew just how unlikely this possibility was. With the exception of one sister who lived in the United States, Mama's siblings were spread between the United Kingdom and Lebanon. One of the sisters in Lebanon still had her Iraqi passport, and coordinating summer bookings and visas to the United States was always a tricky and fickle business.

But then it started to happen. My aunts and uncles each called to say that they were coming. This, in itself, shone like an omen that Hadi and I were meant to be together. Our union was so blessed that a veritable miracle was taking shape in its honor. The concerns I had about marrying Hadi were irrelevant when I compared them to the sweet anticipation of Jidu's face that first moment when all his children were in the same room again. First, we'd cry. Then we'd stay up late, laughing, chatting, and reminiscing. At my wedding, my aunts, uncles, and cousins would dance and clap and make me feel as if I was the most important person in the world to have ever gotten married. Picturing all of this made me giddily happy. I could fix my relationship with Hadi later, but there was no way to go back in time to change a wedding. And right now, these visitors, flowers, favors, and dresses all made me feel as if a sorcerer's hand had gone to work, rendering my girlhood dreams into reality.

Then one morning, when Mama and I were lingering at the table after breakfast, discussing how to coordinate trips to the airport, how many vans to rent to haul us down to Los Angeles for the wedding, she said, "I'm going to tell you something Jidu told me before I got married. You leave your house in your wedding dress and you come back in your *kiffin*."

I felt a faded memory come into focus. I'd heard this from Mama before, during her marriage talk. Out the door in a big, puffy dress, only allowed back in a papery funeral shroud. I shook my head. Did she really think she needed to tell me this now?

She sensed my annoyance. "It's only a way of saying that this family doesn't believe in divorce."

"I grew up in this family. You think I don't know that?"

I had crossed a line with my tone, but Mama didn't call me on it.

"There's no need to get angry. If you know it, you know it," she said and moved on to asking me where I thought we should take everybody, Disneyland or Universal Studios.

I gave an opinion while trying to name the rock of tension sitting in my gut. This was more than annoyance. This was umbrage that my mother felt the need to warn me of the finality of marriage. For the past year and a half, she had watched me accept and swallow a list of troubles. She, of all people, should have known just how much I understood the irreversibility of my commitment to Hadi. Leaving Hadi hadn't been an option when we were engaged, and it was no more of an option now.

CHAPTER 22

A BRIDE IS WITH US

Aweek before my wedding, my family pulled up in two rented vans to Hadi's family's three-bedroom San Diego beach house and unloaded our cargo: twenty-six people, their luggage, and extra bedding. The beach house would serve as Bride's Family Headquarters until we relocated to the hotel where our reception was being held.

As we went about the house, carrying in bags and boxes, we continued the happy noisemaking we'd begun in the car, the clapping, the tambourine banging, and the ululating whistle, because this too was a part of the wedding celebrations. The groom was being brought his bride.

Mama assigned all women and children to the master bedroom. The men would sleep in the living room (Hadi among them until he left for his parents' full-time residence). And two couples would get the remaining two bedrooms: my grandfather and his wife, out of respect for their age, and my uncle and his English wife. It wouldn't be fair to expect an English woman to rough it Arab-style.

Jidu was the last to get down from the van; he was at his heaviest and needed time to clear the gap between the step and the ground. Standing in the doorway, I held out a hand for him, smiling at an image of him during the drive. He'd encouraged us to play the cassette tapes my cousins had brought along even though he was too observant to listen to music on any other occasion. "A bride is with us," he'd said as if that was reason enough for merriment and music. From our seats, we'd shimmied our shoulders and sang along, and Jidu had clapped, his hands meeting together and separating in jaunty little bursts.

I led Jidu through the door. Hadi stood in the foyer and greeted Jidu with a salaam that Jidu returned along with a warm, "Hello, Baba," and a kiss on the forehead.

"I'll tell you something," he said to Hadi in a conspiratorial whisper. "We're giving you the best girl. This is *Hadeytallah*."

Gift from God. That was Jidu's nickname for me. He took both our hands and said he wished us all the happiness in this life and the next; he wished for us to see our grandchildren and our grand-children's children. And then letting go of Hadi's hand, he said to me, "I carried your mother and every one of my daughters on their wedding day, and inshallah, inshallah, if God gives me the strength, I will carry you."

I kissed Jidu's hand and led him up the stairs, my heart warm with anticipation. Jidu would carry me, and I would join the ranks of his daughters, my mother and my aunts, women I admired.

That night, after dinner, we played the same cassette tapes, this time from the living room tape deck. We danced. We jumped. We made conga lines around the couch and squeezed in for group pic-tures that had to be snapped at least a dozen times with different cameras because of closed eyes, missing photographers, and wiggly children.

We did this night after night. Hadi never danced. He had to be coaxed into the pictures. Most evenings, he sat on the stairs and watched us, neither smiling nor unsmiling. Everything about my family being together was exactly how I'd pictured it except for him. I wanted Hadi to charm my aunts and uncles, to smile and laugh so heartily that my family would congratulate me on finding such a great guy. I hoped my family's approval could cure me of whatever conflict still lingered in my heart. Their arrival had already brought me such peace with getting married. It was precisely because of my wedding that these people, who had not been under the same roof at the same time for over twenty years, had come together, and I adored being a part of this huge, noisy clan. I just wished Hadi blended in with us better, too.

On the third night of our stay, I approached Hadi on the last step, a castigatory hand on my hip. "Why are you just sitting here?"

"This isn't my kind of thing."

"What do you mean by 'this'? This is a celebration for your wedding, and you're the groom, and you're not even acting like you're happy."

"I'm not a happy groom just because I'm not dancing and clapping?"

I scoffed as if Hadi was being ridiculous. "Pretty much. That's how most people show they're happy."

"Well, that's not how I show that I'm happy, and if I am not happy enough for you, I can go back to my parents' house early. I don't have to stay."

Hadi's suggestion intrigued me. If Hadi wasn't going to impress my family, at least he could leave them with fewer reasons not to like him. And I would enjoy everyone's company more if he wasn't here looking so disinterested, trying to pull me away every chance he got to talk or kiss or sneak a hug, and it would be so much easier to show up to my wedding, convinced I was making the right decision, if I didn't have all this proof day after day of how much our personalities differed.

"I don't want you to leave," I said with feigned reluctance, "but maybe you'd enjoy spending more time with your family before the wedding, too."

Hadi knew exactly what I was implying without my saying it. Although he had planned on going home over the weekend, he left the next day. I knew he was hurt. After months of bickering, months of me worrying about school and telling Hadi he should have tried harder, now there was this proof that what I wanted most from our wedding was not him but the party, these people. But instead of sympathizing with my soon-to-be-husband, I blamed Hadi for being too available. He'd created no scarcity with his love, no sense that it was a precious commodity. I was doing Hadi a favor by hinting for him to leave. I was strengthening our love's economy by giving it room to grow.

The day before my wedding, my entire clan and I filed out of our rental vans in front of the Regal Biltmore Hotel in downtown Los Angeles. At the hair salon, I got a blowout from a stylist who gave me a piece of advice for my rehearsal dinner: "Drink as much as you want tonight. Just take two Tylenols before you go to bed. You won't even feel hungover the next day."

I looked at the girl in the mirror—brunette, fair-skinned, hazel eyes. I could have been any girl, Italian, maybe Greek. I knew the hairdresser didn't see me—the twenty-year-old Muslim girl who'd never had a drink in her life. I smiled and nodded at his drinking tip. I would play the part of the Western bride as long as I sat in his chair. Today, the day before my wedding, I did not have the energy to convince anyone that Hadi and I were childhood sweethearts, nor did I want to answer any questions about our marriage being arranged or if I loved my future husband.

When my hair was done, I took my smooth, curl-free locks upstairs to the suite all my aunts and girl cousins were sharing. There, I played a different part, the Arab girl bride who let her aunts tell her she needed bigger, flashier earrings and brighter lipstick to go with her long, black sequined gown, who used one of their fancy headscarves as a shawl to cover her exposed shoulders. Then I headed downstairs, eager to see the preparations in the ballroom.

As I opened the hall's towering double doors, I squealed with true delight. The tables had been set with white and gold linens, and tall gold bases awaited their floral centerpieces. Diana, Nadia, and Aysar were already there, rushing toward me with arms open wide. I hadn't even finished hugging them when Hadi showed up in a pin-stripe suit, his hair freshly trimmed, carrying a dozen long-stemmed red roses in a gold box. Listening to my friends' collective "Aww," I felt a surge of certainty. I wanted this boy in a suit giving me beautiful things. My friends seeing it. This hall filling up with our out-of-town guests, a mix of family and friends. I crumpled up our old story and threw it away. This wedding would set our love story free.

CHAPTER 23

❀

LOVE HER, BOY, LOVE HER

With a comb in one hand and cigarette in the other, Dariush, proprietor and Beverly Hills stylist extraordinaire, transformed the giant ball of back-combed fuzz on my head into a sleek updo.

"You're a very pretty girl," he said in a thick Persian accent. He stubbed out his cigarette and added, "You should have a nose job. Such a shame a nose like that on such a pretty face."

I should've resented having my flaws pointed out to me on my wedding day, but I didn't. Dariush was a genius, and there was no sense in distracting him over something as small as my pride. Dariush secured my rhinestone headpiece and then got to work on my face, gluing on individual false eyelashes, painting a thick line of black eyeliner over the evidence, trimming my eyebrows, and filling in my lips with a shimmery neutral. When I looked into the mirror, I felt triumphant, transformed. This was not the subtle, natural beauty extolled in American bridal magazines. This was a look straight from satellite television, the dramatic-eyed Arab bride.

Back at the hotel, in a staging room that had been set aside for us, Mama helped me slip into my dress. Then she stood, taking me in, tears in her eyes. "Such a princess," she said before leaving to get Hadi. I'd given up on my see-me-at-the-altar dream after I realized he was going to see me for the pictures anyway.

When Hadi first laid eyes on me, it was nothing like the moment

I imagined. He made no gasp, no jump for joy, or other cinematic gesture. He merely took my hands, his lips spreading in a wide smile, and said how he couldn't wait to spend the rest of his life with me.

"Me, too," I said, and I meant it. I loved Hadi in a tuxedo, the way the coat jacket filled out his shoulders and the way his bronze skin stood out against the bright white of his dress shirt. Standing there, taking in my groom while embraced by sheets upon sheets of tulle, I felt as if I were wearing the brand-new pages of our story together.

Still holding my hand, Hadi led me to the ballroom so we could pose for photographs. All the tables had been set; small gold boxes filled with chocolates sat at the top of every plate; and floral arrangements full of fragrant gardenias, white roses, and sweet peas were perched on every stand. Our multitiered cake stood in a corner balcony. And the family and friends who made up my eight bridesmaids, among them Jamila, Lina, Diana, Nadia, and Aysar, had lined up in front of the photographer, a vision of pink, sparkly tiaras and little white gloves. Everything was exactly as I'd imagined if not better.

After their group picture, my bridesmaids stepped away from the photographer and circled me. They told me I looked beautiful, and I told them the same. I marveled at Lina's curly locks secured in a French twist, a rhinestone bracelet pinned into the curve. It was such a careful detail, something so small but so lovely that I felt myself expanding into the beauty that surrounded me, into this moment and place where everything was right. There was no room for nervousness. No space for regret. No time for doubt. Today was perfect, and the memory of all this wonderfulness would be the balm for my and Hadi's uncertain future.

We took pictures for an hour, and then we lined up outside the closed doors of the adjoining hall where we'd be holding our ceremony. When the sound of the DJ playing an airy, jazzy tune drifted toward us, the flower girls entered, followed by my eight bridesmaids, then our grandparents, my mother and brother, and Hadi and his mother. For my grand moment, the doors closed and then reopened to the sound of the wedding march—not because any of this was customary in any way. It was just iconic, something I coveted for no other reason than that I wanted to feel as if I was living out a scene from the movie *Father of the Bride*.

With Baba at my side, I walked down the aisle slowly, pausing for photographs, pressing down on Baba's arm when his pace quickened. I felt rooted by the attention of our family and friends, alive and centered. I wished the aisle was longer. I wished I could walk with the weight of a bouquet in my hands, my legs pushing along a petticoat and a dozen layers of tulle, for hours.

Hadi met me at the end of the aisle and gave my father a kiss on each cheek before taking my arm. Before us was a raised platform holding our wedding *sufra*, a decorative spread of various symbols: a mirror for our bright future, colorful spices to guard against the evil eye, painted eggs for fertility, a piece of flatbread for prosperity, and a bowl of honey and two large cones of hardened sugar for our life to be sweet.

Now Hadi and I walked around the sufra and sat on the velvet loveseat his mother had shipped from Egypt. The Seyyid who was marrying us stood by the microphone to our side, wearing a black turban and a freshly pressed black robe that opened to reveal a long, white gown underneath.

I could not concentrate on the marital advice the Seyyid offered our guests; the anticipation roaring through me was too loud, too distracting. But as soon as I heard him calling me by name, asking me to accept the terms upon which our families had agreed, my mind became focused. I kept quiet as I'd been trained, waiting until he'd asked me five times in honor of the Prophet Muhammad, his two grandsons, and their parents. The fifth time, Mama gave me a nod, and with words I'd been rehearsing since I was twelve, I told the Seyyid that he was my representative, "*Na'am, inta wakili.*" The women brought their tongues up to the roofs of their mouths. Their ululating ring made it official.

But a critical piece of Americana was missing. I had wanted a you-may-now-kiss-the-bride moment. It was just as iconic as the wedding march, just as necessary. Dr. Ridha approached the microphone to make an announcement to our guests about where they would be gathering to say the evening prayers, and Hadi took the opportunity to get his father's attention with a loud "psst." Dr. Ridha leaned over us. Then, back at the microphone, he said with a chuckle, "Hadi would like to kiss his bride." There was laughter, and I was peeved. This wasn't supposed to be a funny moment, something we had to nudge our families to remember. We pecked on the lips, and there was more ululating before our relatives lined up to present us with their gifts of twenty-two-karat gold necklaces, earrings, bracelets, and rings.

Our evening went on like this, something American, something Arab. Shortly after the gift exchange, our entire bridal party stood behind closed doors again, this time waiting to walk into the reception hall. For this entry, we were pure Arab. The Lebanese band struck up a typically Middle Eastern tune, and in typical *zeffa*-style, Hadi and I walked in first, a chain of our relatives behind us clapping, dancing, and shaking tambourines. We circled the dance floor several times before the band took a break, and we went back to being American for my first dance with Hadi, a father-daughter dance, a brief interlude of American pop music chosen by our American DJ. A little "Chicken Dance." Some Spice Girls. A curious choice of the Beastie Boys' "Brass Monkey."

It was as if my daily waffling between two cultures, my uncertainty over why I picked one tradition to observe over another, had put on a dress and some makeup and decided to throw a party. It picked out music and food, trying to fix the regular hotel-fare chicken breast with appetizers of hummus, dolma, and baba ghanoush. Sometimes my two worlds blended for such beautiful effect.

Sometimes they clashed.

In between songs, the DJ took the microphone and called out, "Huda, how did you feel the first time Hadi asked you out?"

I froze, my heart beating wildly. Would I have to take the microphone and explain to the DJ now in front of everyone that we did not date and Hadi had never asked me out? A second later, I heard the first few notes of *I Will Survive*, then the lyrics describing the singer as afraid and petrified. I breathed a sigh of relief. All that had been a culturally insensitive lead-in to the next song.

Our guests resumed dancing. Most of Hadi's family remained on the sidelines, some because they were not much for dancing, others out of a fear of sin and gossip. My family relied on the immunity that being at the wedding of a close relative afforded them (dancing at the wedding of a relative was a sign of affection and therefore understandable), but this was only a temporary reprieve. Regret would consume them later. My uncle would lecture my cousins for dancing while wearing the hijab and lament how we'd represented our family. My aunts would compare themselves to Hadi's aunts, who had steered clear of the dance floor, and beg me to edit them out of the video.

After dinner, the band returned with their tablas and ouds and their Lebanese lead singer. I relaxed, knowing I'd squeezed in all the American things I'd wanted. Now I could enjoy my religiously excused opportunity to dance. It was exactly like I'd pictured—Lina, Diana, Nadia, and Aysar joining me on the dance floor, our heads thrown back, giggles erupting. But now Hadi was retreating toward the tables. I knew I should go after him, ask him what was wrong, but my legs would not follow.

A half hour later, we cut our cake, I tossed my bouquet, and then I grabbed the photographer and went over to Jidu who was sitting at his table. He smiled when he saw me, and without a word, he stood and bent at the knees. He wrapped his arms around the width of my dress, and invoking the name of our first Imam with a strained "*Ya Ali*," he hoisted me up into the air. I planted a kiss on his cheeks. The photographer's bulb flashed, and he put me down.

When it was time to hit the dance floor again, Hadi stayed back, talking to his cousins, but I marched straight into the shadow of the glimmering disco ball. As the night wore on, tired bodies drifted back to their seats, but my loyal friends and I kept going. I didn't listen to my aching feet and back. I wanted to take advantage of every minute, every second.

Hadi tapped me on my shoulder. "My back really hurts. I'm ready to go."

"It's too early," I said. "I'm not ready for the night to end."

He looked at me agape. "How can you say no? I'm telling you I'm in pain."

But I refused again because I didn't care about Hadi's sore back or the deed that awaited us. This was what I wanted. This poufy dress. This crown. I didn't want to take it off yet. I would never wear it again. I would never be a bride again.

"If you go back out there, then we're not doing anything tonight," Hadi said.

"Fine," I answered because I didn't believe him. Once we got upstairs, Hadi would change his mind. He was a guy after all. Wasn't sex all they wanted?

I went back to the dance floor and joined the flower girls whose exhaustion had made them hyper. We were the only ones dancing, but this did not deter me. As the bride, I, alone, set the mood for this party. I owed it to my guests to dance, and this was not a responsibility I took lightly.

When people started to leave, Mama pulled me away from the dance floor to take photographs with our guests and to say goodbye.

By one in the morning, the only people left in the hall were our relatives, but the spirit of the party had not left them. They lined up behind
Hadi and me, the tambourines and drums reappearing. They clapped
and sang us all the way to the elevator. In Arabic, they sang, "Love
her, boy, love her. Don't be afraid of her mother." And then much to
my chagrin, one of my uncles got everyone chanting in English, "We
know where you're going. We know where you're going."

When the doors to the elevator closed, my ears buzzed after
hours of dancing into the blare of the band. My head pulsed with
the weight of my rhinestone crown. My feet throbbed from the
tightness of my shoes. And my new husband of about seven hours
was angry. He stayed in his corner of the elevator, his arms folded,
without saying a word.

Given the chance, I did not choose him. I did not prove to him
that he was more important than the party.

CHAPTER 24

BIOLOGY

It was over. Still in bed, I turned and looked at my wedding dress draped across a chair, the skirt so full of fabric it practically sat up. All that planning, hoping, and dreaming had evaporated in a few short hours. I would never wear that dress again, never be the guest of honor at such a grand party. Sadness pressed down on me like a giant boulder—a boulder that grew heavier when I thought about how things had gone last night.

Hadi was already in the shower. I leaned over his side of the bed and dialed Mama's room. She practically squealed she was so happy to hear from me. "I wanted to call you before we left," Mama said, "but I was afraid to wake you. How did everything go?"

I knew what she was alluding to, but I didn't have time to get into details. "Fine," I lied, "but our suitcases got mixed up. I don't have anything to wear."

"I wondered what happened to my bag. I didn't even realize you didn't have yours."

Moments later, the doorbell to our suite rang. All I had to wear was my underpants from the night before—my dress had sported its own built-in bra. I dug into Mama's suitcase and pulled on her ratty, old brown housedress, the one I'd seen her mop the floors in hundreds of times.

I opened the door, and she threw her arms around me. When she pulled away, she looked confused. "Why are you wearing that?"

"Because I don't have anything else to wear."

"You mean you didn't even wear your beautiful nightclothes?"

"If I did, would I be wearing this?"

My new bridal set was still sitting in the suitcase on the floor beside her.

Searching my eyes, she asked, "Are you okay?"

I shrugged.

"Did you do it?"

I shook my head.

"That's okay. Not everybody does it the first night. But how come? What happened?"

I picked up the suitcase in one hand, and with the other, I pulled her over to the loveseat in the living room portion of the suite. Then I closed the door to the bedroom in case Hadi came out of the bathroom. He wouldn't have liked me discussing this with my mom.

I sat down next to Mama, but I couldn't bring myself to look at her before I said, "We tried, but we couldn't."

"What do you mean 'couldn't'?"

"You know . . . *couldn't*. I'm pretty sure that I don't have a hole. There's just no way *that* can get in *there*."

It seemed there'd been a misunderstanding on my part. It didn't shrink so as to slip in nicely without hurting anyone. It grew.

Mama laughed. "I assure you. You have a hole, and that does get in there."

"If that's how this is done, then I'd really prefer to have nothing to do with it." I stared at my hands, still too uncomfortable to meet Mama's gaze.

Mama was having a wonderful time at my expense. She laughed until she saw the look I flashed her. Then she worked to suppress her grin. "I'm not laughing at you. You're so cute, that's all. Sex is wonderful. You just have to relax. Maybe you're so nervous that it's making you dry. You know, you could try a little lubricant, and then when you get really aroused, close to the point of orgasm, then he can try."

"Mama!" I said as if the entire word was an expression of shock.

"Come on. We talked about these things." Ever the clinician, Mama never shied away from frank discussions about the body.

"Yes, but it was a long time ago and I wasn't listening." I reached for my suitcase, unsure what to make of all this information. After all the kisses and touches we'd exchanged, I was so confident that my wedding night would be just like the dimly lit, passionate tangle of bodies I'd seen in the movies and that somewhere in all the kissing and moving, the intercourse part happened. I assumed that was how teenagers got pregnant on accident because it was so easy for a penis to slide inside a woman. I had no idea that I would have to play such a conscious role in all of this, that I'd have to oil myself up like some sort of a machine. The entire process struck me as unromantic and far too deliberate. Sex had seemed so easy on film, so inevitable.

I told Mama I'd get dressed and meet everyone downstairs. I set my suitcase on the bed and pulled out the outfit I'd planned for this very day. An off-white dress with pearls around the cuffs. A set of lace undergarments in the same color. We were supposed to check out of this hotel and into another in Newport Beach for the few days until we left on our honeymoon. I thought about tonight and the next night, and the weight of the deed in front of us bore down on me.

I didn't get it. Did the whole world really go around doing this? Why did women talk about the size of *that* as if it was good for it to be big? Wouldn't they want it to be small so it wouldn't have to pierce them to make its way in? And on top of everything, I was so tired. I thought making love rested you, that it was in its own way a kind of sleep. On television, people always looked so refreshed after staying up all night to have sex. But now it seemed that time was time. Sex was sex. And sleep was sleep. Nothing canceled the other out, and now I was tired and my head throbbed. Why did everything have to be so different from how I had imagined it?

I'd heard people say the first time hurt, and then it got better. When we arrived at our suite in Newport Beach, I told myself that all we had to do was get this first time behind us. This, unfortunately, was easier thought than achieved. After a series of failed attempts, I was fed up. We were failing at something so basic, so fundamentally human that teenagers figured it out on their own and in cars. We'd been naked for almost two days in a huge king-size bed, and nothing. It was embarrassing.

That night I resolved to take care of business. "You're gonna have to hurt me," I said. "Just don't look at my face, and get it in there."

"I'd rather not do it at all than hurt you," Hadi answered.

I found this declaration unnecessarily chivalrous. "You don't mean that. Eventually we'll want to have kids."

We talked about the best position from which to proceed as if we were two naked coworkers assigned to the same project.

"Remember," I said. "Do whatever it takes to get it in there."

After a considerable amount of rearranging—me propped up on pillows, no pillows, on my side, on my stomach, on my back—there was a breakthrough, the sensation of being punctured, followed by pressure, fullness, stretching. I wanted him out, and I was going to say so until I saw his face. Such surprise. Wonder. Joy.

I said nothing.

He asked, "Are you okay? Does that feel all right?"

I said, "Yes." A carefully chosen one-syllable word. All I could utter without a grimace, an inflection of pain.

"Do you want me to get out?"

"Up to you," I replied because I wanted him out, but I also wanted to have done this right, for Hadi to feel whatever he was supposed to.

He pulled out, and my entire body relaxed. "Are you done?" I asked.

"That's okay. I can tell it's bothering you."

"No, just do it. We have to do it right this once."

I had to reassure Hadi several times that this was what I wanted before he leaned over me and filled my lower body once again with pressure. Such pressure, such tightness that the entire exchange struck me as completely wrong. It didn't fit in there. It didn't belong.

But then Hadi's back arched, his eyes closed, and witnessing his reaction, his movement quickening, I felt a distracting sense of awe. My body could do this to him.

Hadi drew in a breath and then released a deep sigh. He rested his head on my chest.

I tapped him on the shoulder with an "Are you done?" And to his very grateful reply, I added, "Can you get out then?"

I marveled at the return to emptiness, the relaxation it brought to muscles I didn't know I had.

"Is there blood?"

"No," Hadi said, reaching for the box of tissues.

"Really?" I asked, unsure of how to react, how he would react. "Are you sure?"

"Yeah, you're fine. Not everyone bleeds."

"How do you know?"

"Biology," he said so plainly I wanted to cry. It was as if my entire body had been dunked in relief. We'd finally done it. And Hadi was Hadi, and I was me, and we lived in America, and nobody was waiting to see a bloody sheet, and I was married to a man who knew this was not a cause to question my honor.

"Hadi, women have been divorced for this, and shamed for this, and I know it's weird to mention this now, but I can't help but think that could've been me."

I threw my arms around Hadi. With all the things that had disappointed me over the last year and a half, in this monumental way he had not. If this was a kind of test, Hadi had passed. We had passed.

"Are you okay?" Hadi asked.

"Yes," I said. "But I think I'll take a bath."

I wanted to soak away the soreness within me and think about all of this—the kind of man Hadi had shown himself to be, the couple we were, the sex we'd had. It hadn't looked or felt anything like I thought it would. There were no frantic movements, no passionate grunts, and none of the pleasure I'd experienced with Hadi before. This was a bodily function only shared with another person.

At our wedding, Hadi's parents had surprised us with two tickets to Madrid and then to Málaga. It was a long-held dream come true. I had told Hadi about my fascination with Islamic Spain, the notion that East and West had intersected there long before it had become the defining dichotomy in our Muslim American lives, how the beauty of its architecture proved that the two worlds we straddled had always meant to be melded. What I didn't tell him was that I also had high hopes of looking fabulous there. I'd pictured myself with my hair tied in a bun, wearing big hoop earrings and a red flower behind my ear. We'd watch flamenco and, in doing so, pick up the dance naturally and easily.

It was my first international flight that I was old enough to remember, and I was very impressed with the frequent snacks even in coach: little pieces of toast with cream cheese and olives, some with shaved cucumbers. Hadi and I kept busy playing card games and napping on each other, but as soon as we landed, I panicked.

Standing in front of the luggage carousel, waiting to go through customs, I looked over at Hadi and decided we were too young to be traveling alone. The act of being married didn't suddenly turn us into capable adults. We were in a foreign country, and we needed our mommies and daddies.

Fortunately airports are tailored to inexperienced travelers. We followed the signs and made our way through customs and into our shuttle effortlessly. When the Mercedes van finally neared the center of the city, my heart raced at the sight of the ornate colonial buildings, the narrow streets lined with compact cars on the ground and charming balconies above, and the main streets crowded with taxis waiting to be hailed and with pedestrians heading in and out of small shops. It was so different from suburban California, its parking lots and strip malls. Madrid had more character and personality than any of the heavily franchised cities I'd known. With my airport anxieties now behind me, I looked over at Hadi and itched with an unexpected restlessness, a longing to know the freedom of being on my own in a new place. In front of us sat a group of single women, all in their late twenties. Next to them, we were too young to be married. Dating maybe. But married? The image we presented to the world, outside of our small community, didn't make sense, and it was this image of us I couldn't shake. I felt as if I'd finally arrived to my life's most exciting destination, but I was no longer an exciting person. I was not single. I was not free.

Hadi, on the other hand, went straight to the camcorder we'd borrowed from his parents. He set it up in our hotel room, and later he lugged it to Retiro Park and then on every city tour after. Every time he opened the viewfinder, he addressed our future children and asked me to say something to our unborn offspring. I hated that Hadi was already turning us into fuddy-duddy parent-tourists with a video camera, but admitting as much seemed to establish Hadi as the better parent prematurely. And so on camera, I protested wordlessly. I was grumpy, uncooperative, and sullen.

It was a mood that soon came to color off-camera moments too. I'd expected the same religious immunity that applied to weddings to apply to our honeymoon. I'd packed an evening gown, hoping we'd go out dancing in Madrid. Even though neither one of us had ever set foot in a club before, the image of us dancing together had always defined my mind's picture of what it meant to be grown up and independent.

During the four nights we spent in Madrid, we never went dancing, and I kicked myself for harboring the ridiculous fantasy that merely being in Spain would suddenly transform us into a pair of ballroom dancers. The gown stayed in the suitcase. We came back to our room almost every night around eleven, and even though we had sex on every one of those nights, I pitied myself because of it. I was tired of setting aside so much time every day, sometimes twice, to pleasure-seeking. I had a lifetime of sex ahead of me. What I really wanted to do was to see this country that would only be available for my eyes to see now.

When we later arrived in Málaga, my aspirations for the evening gown transferred to the bathing suit at the bottom of our suitcase. The modest swimwear industry was still years into the future, and so I justified this purchase with thoughts of Jamila and the swimsuits Mrs. Ridha had bought her daughter for her honeymoon in Hawaii. How wrong could it be to bare a little skin, I rationalized, if Jamila's own mother, my mother-in-law, had purchased a bathing suit for her daughter?

From our balcony, the views of the bougainvillea-laden trellis, the shapely pool below it, and the shimmering Mediterranean only a few footsteps beyond seduced me. It couldn't be possible that I'd been brought all this way only to be denied an opportunity to enjoy either body of water. I waited for Hadi to offer that we go for a swim, and when he didn't I hinted.

"I bet you really want me to wear the bathing suit I packed so we can go swimming."

"I do want you to wear it," he said, "but not to go swimming."

"But why else would I wear it?"

"For me. In here."

My blood boiled. I had believed in the Islamic ideal of a woman's beauty belonging only to her husband. I had so ardently defended it to my classmates, arguing that it brought intimacy to a relationship. But now that I was the object of such singular attention, I chafed. I knew I didn't necessarily want to wear a swimsuit in public. I just wanted to break the rules on this one occasion, the way others before me had broken the rules. I wanted Hadi to condone my behavior, absolving me of my guilt, and then together we'd resume our religiously observant lives. But because Hadi was now denying me this one chance to bend, it was him I resented. Not wearing a bathing suit in public was no longer my choice, the way it had been when I was in high school. It was Hadi's decision, Hadi's fault.

Bringing my hands up to my hips, I said, "We came all this way. You don't want to go to the beach?"

"I'm fine."

"But I'm not fine."

"So we'll go."

"We'll go, and what will we wear?"

"Our clothes."

"I didn't come all this way to stare at the Mediterranean Sea in my clothes."

"You want to wear a bathing suit?"

I shrugged because I couldn't bring myself to say yes.

"Why would you want to now? You've never wanted to before."

"Hadi, I haven't been in a hotel pool since I was nine. *Nine*. And it was fun, and I liked it, and I just want to feel that again. Your mother bought a bathing suit for your sister. She took her honeymoon break, and I want my break too."

"That doesn't make sense to me. If something is wrong, then it's always wrong. You can't take breaks from rules. They're there for a reason."

I never imagined I could have this kind of disagreement with Hadi. I'd assumed we shared such a similar background that our religion and culture were going to be the conflict-free areas of our lives, but here we were, one of us willing to break the rules, one of us not.

"I don't even know what that reason is anymore, Hadi. Before we got married, I didn't wear a bathing suit, because I didn't want to show my body to other men, but now that we're married, what's the point? Nobody's going to look at me or ask me out."

"I'm really not comfortable with you wearing a bathing suit."

"I really resent that now that we're married, you get to decide this for me."

"That's not how I see it. I don't want anyone but you to see me. I don't want to go to a pool and have other women look at me."

Other women, please. And because it wasn't cruel enough to think it, I said, "I don't care if anyone sees your body, Hadi."

He looked wounded, and this annoyed me so much I began to cry from frustration. Getting our parents out of the picture, dictating what we could and could not do, was supposed to save us. Our wedding was going to be the new opening to our love story, but here we were falling into our old patterns, losing a precious day in Spain arguing over such muddy issues—religion and privacy, control and love. Each issue felt like a falling tree, crashing into our lives, impossible to get around.

Hours of discussion later, Hadi and I went down to the beach. Instead of a bathing suit, I wore Hadi's shorts that swung below my knees and his oversized T-shirt. I looked ridiculous, I felt ridiculous, and as we walked along the water, I pointed out every topless woman and every G-string and said, "You really think people would've been looking at me when there are people here like her?"

But we got on with the afternoon. We walked in the sand and

gathered the seashells that caught our eyes. Working together on a common task felt like a reconciliation, and we went back to our room with shells in our pockets and our hands linked. That night, however, I struggled to fall asleep. I wondered if this fight meant we were destined to spend our lives together arguing. I wondered why my mother promised me I'd have more independence after I got married when marriage had only added on a husband telling me what to do.

The next day and for the rest of our trip, I did not give voice to any of the thoughts that troubled me. We still hadn't explored any parts of Andalusia, the inspiration behind this entire journey, and I didn't want to waste any more of our precious time bickering. When we finally took the all-day bus trips to Grenada and Cordoba, the architecture filled me with so much awe and wonder I felt too grateful to utter a single, negative comment about our relationship. It had brought me here.

On those day trips, I'd rest my head on Hadi's shoulder on the way going and coming, and we'd take in the fields of sunflowers outside our windows, chuckling at our multilingual tour guide's adorable English and the antics of the tanned-to-rubber, chain-smoking senior citizens at the back of the bus. At the end of the day, we'd have late-night dinners at the Italian restaurant across the street from our hotel, the same overworked waiter serving us every night. And perhaps, sweetest of all, we'd buy sizzling-hot mini-donuts doused with a squirt of chocolate from the elderly couple with the cart on the main avenue.

At the time, it never occurred to me that married life could be a continuation of this pattern. A little bliss. A little strife. Mismatched ideals and conflicting viewpoints. Big clashes and small resolutions. On our honeymoon, these arguments shook me. If we could not navigate our happy, carefree moments without tension, then I feared for our everyday lives, the struggles waiting for us when we returned.

BOOK II

✿

CHAPTER 25

A BIG, FAT ARAB STEREOTYPE

It was my first wedding anniversary, and instead of jetting off to Europe like Amina or loading up my car for a road trip to a rustic cabin like Sura, I was on an airplane, moving to Mexico. After overloading units to graduate a year early, I'd been nominated as the valedictorian of my graduating class, won the History Department's award for best senior thesis, and been accepted to a handful of graduate programs, some with tuition waivers and stipends. Hadi had been accepted into the medical school he applied to as a backup plan, the one in Guadalajara, Mexico.

A flight attendant slid an omelet, the texture and color of a kitchen sponge, onto my open tray table. I picked at my food with a plastic fork. I couldn't cry and chew at the same time.

"Why don't you try to eat something?" Hadi said, slicing into his bread as if he hadn't just uprooted my entire existence. "Maybe you'll feel better."

At first, the suggestion that mere food could offer me some comfort insulted me, but after I sniffled through the first two bites, it appeared that Hadi was right. The omelet was warm, and it filled some of the hollowness inside me. Without intending to, I finished everything on my tray. Refreshed, I turned to the window and cried again.

I had wished for so much of this. I had wanted the adult status that came with being a married woman. I had wanted to travel without heeding Mama's warning that we had to stay together so if we died, we died together. But I hadn't wanted to move to another country and put my education on hold.

Hadi had offered to come with me to graduate school. He said he'd wait out another year, apply again, or maybe pursue a different career path. But I knew we couldn't survive another round of applications together. Hadi was a procrastinator, and I was a generous giver of helpful advice and reminders. We contemplated going our separate ways and meeting up during vacations to resume our married life, but this too would not do.

I was carrying around a heavy bag of resentment with Hadi's name on it. Living with Hadi for almost a year had taught me two things about him: he was brilliant, but he also sabotaged himself. Hadi was a true problem-solver, someone who enjoyed trouble-shooting all sorts of issues—be it a glitchy computer, a clogged pipe, or a flickering light—but when it came to school and applications, he never studied long enough or started anything early enough to have a real chance of success.

I told myself that a few months of separation would turn my resentment into a rift too wide to bridge, but deep down, I also knew that I was afraid to go off to school alone. After years of Mama telling me I had to wait to get married to travel and live on my own, I believed it. I didn't know any Muslim girls who'd gone to school out of state, and now that I was married, it didn't feel very wifely either. The kind of wife I heard the aunties in our community extol was always dutiful and self-sacrificing. The type of woman who went to graduate school alone was independent, strong-willed, and indifferent to disapproving gossip. I had no idea how to pretend I was a woman like that. If I had I wouldn't have gotten married in the first place.

The tissue in my hands had turned to shreds, so I reached for the coarse napkin on my breakfast tray. Less than two hours ago, I had waved goodbye to Mama and Lina wiping away their tears, and Baba standing awkwardly beside them, hands behind his back. At my feet was a bag with all of my acceptance letters to graduate school. Soon I'd have to write to these universities to tell them I wasn't coming, and those letters would be all I had left, each one a tiny diploma, a small salute to years of hard work.

But just when it seemed that I'd reached a new depth of self-pity, a voice from within urged me to get a grip, reminding me that Mama had gone through far more, flying all the way from Iraq to the United States with a husband she barely knew. I was twenty-one years old. I had a college degree, and I was friends with my husband before I married him. Yes, I was moving to a different country, but I was only a three-hour flight away from home, and my family had already bought their plane tickets to see me in a month. *This will be over in a few years*, the voice warned, *and you'll be sorry you didn't have a nice anniversary. Make a good memory for today, and then you can be sad again tomorrow.*

In the days before we left California, I'd entertained two competing and shamefully stereotypical images of what Mexico was going to be like. Either I'd find people in ponchos and sombreros, living in adobe houses with donkeys tethered outside, or they'd be dressed in flowing linen with flowers in the ladies' hair and residing in palatial villas with large balconies overlooking a flowered courtyard.

As we drove from the airport to our hotel, it appeared that only one aspect of my vision had been correct. Guadalajara was a landscape of contrasts. We drove past brick houses with glassless windows and flat tin roofs; past modern buildings and an even greater number of charming, colonial ones; and, finally once into the suburbs, past tall concrete walls, some of them a block long, safeguarded with jagged, broken glass bottles. Every time a gate opened, I craned my neck to get a peek at the mysterious mansion inside, the surrounding walls seeming to imply the home within was too precious to be viewed.

In the taxi, I no longer felt the urge to cry. My eyes were now busy searching out my surroundings for clues as to what my life would be like. Everything had to be taken in: The vendors ladling colorful juices out of large tubs into clear plastic bags they tied closed with a rubber band around the neck of a straw. The intersections where children begged, men wiped down windshields, and clowns juggled. The arch strangely reminiscent of France's Arc de Triomphe. The multilane roundabouts that spoke a language of toots and honks.

Before I was ready for our drive to end, we arrived at our hotel. From our room, I called home to inform my parents of our arrival and then opened up my suitcase to change for dinner. On top was the evening gown and strappy, silver high-heeled shoes I'd lugged on my honeymoon and what was beginning to seem like a symbol of my relentless, impossible hope. Last night while packing my bag with Mama, I had imagined finding a fancy restaurant to celebrate our anniversary, that there in the glory of a romantic moment this unexpected move would be transformed into the grandest of adventures.

How foolish this dream now seemed as I stood in front of all the clothes my mother helped me select and fold. Just thinking of Mama twisted my stomach with a tightness that proved the word homesick terribly apt. For the sake of posterity, I coaxed myself into a cotton summer dress and the same pair of flat, black sandals I'd worn on my honeymoon. I would want a better story of our first anniversary than an evening spent in our hotel room, crying.

Outside, the weather was still warm and inviting even though the sun had begun to set. We walked until we came to an indoor shopping mall, the center of which was filled with children bouncing silver missile-shaped balloons. Instantly I felt my mood lift. The lack of rules inhibiting children's play struck me as very Arab. It reminded me of services at the masjid where all the children wandered about oblivious to the speaker behind the microphone, snacking on chips, climbing over the bodies seated on the floor. Maybe we would fit in here. Maybe we'd fit in here better than we did in the United States.

The only restaurant options were an outdated Mexican diner and the Kentucky Fried Chicken we had passed on the way. Hadi asked me if I wanted to leave and keep walking, but it was getting late, and I was afraid we'd get lost or, worse, find nothing and wind up coming back to the same spot. But when he asked me which of the two places I preferred, I panicked. I could not have my first wedding anniversary dinner at either of those places.

I tried to pass the choice back to Hadi. "I don't know. Where do you want to go?"

"It doesn't matter to me."

"You always say it doesn't matter. Today I need it to matter."

"That's not what I meant. It's just that you care about where we spend special occasions more than I do."

I started to say, "Let's just go to the di—" but then traveler's anxiety overcame me, and I suggested KFC. It took a lot more language to sit in a restaurant than it took to order fast food.

We stood back before entering the line, staring at the lit-up menu. The options were limited enough to make the choices decipherable, but that still didn't solve the problem of what we would order. Up until that moment, Hadi and I had only eaten halal meat, but there wasn't going to be any halal food in Mexico. We hadn't discussed the issue. Were we going to be vegetarians, or were we going to start buying store-bought meat?

I said, "If we aren't getting chicken, then that pretty much leaves biscuits and mashed potatoes. And the coleslaw, but you don't like that."

"The gravy is probably meat-based, so you'll have to tell them to skip it."

"Mmm. Mmm. What a dinner," I said.

"I'm fine with that. Go ahead and order."

"Me? Why me?"

"You're the one who speaks Spanish."

"I do not. I took Spanish in high school. Everybody knows that you don't actually speak the language you studied in high school."

"But you still know more than I do."

"Is that how it's going to be here, too? Me taking care of everything? Fine. I'll order."

I stepped into the mazelike line, fuming. As the line thinned, I rehearsed, "*Puré de papas, bisquets*," but how do you say "gravy," and how do you say "I'd like"? Do I just say, "*Quiero*, I want . . ." or should I say, "*Puedo tener*, can I have . . ."?

Standing in front of the cashier, my mouth went dry. A language barrier was all it took to make a teenager in a paper hat intimidating. I'd never actually produced Spanish words for another person's ears. In my mediocre Spanish classes, we read and took tests, but even our teacher spoke to us in English. Now this boy was going to think I was so stupid.

"*Buenas tardes. ¿En qué le puedo servir?*"

I already didn't understand, but that was okay. All I had to do was tell him what I wanted.

"*Quiero*," I said, "*purè de papas sin* gravy." I prayed that he knew the word *gravy*, but his expression was blank.

At once, I grew uncomfortably warm. I took a deep breath and then tried another approach. "*¿Habla inglés?*"

He shook his head, and I searched for a thought basic enough to translate into Spanish while sweating through my dress. Gesturing to the bowl I created with my hand, I said, "I don't want the thing on the potatoes."

"Ahh," he said as if he now understood. The flames of discomfort that had lit up around my ears cooled down.

I carried our order back to the table where Hadi was sitting. Still standing, I peeled back the lid on the mashed potatoes. There was gravy all over it. I sank into our bench.

"You didn't tell them we don't want gravy," Hadi said, surprised. "I thought I did."

"Take it back," he suggested as if it was the simplest, most obvious solution.

"I can't."

"What do you mean, you can't?"

"I just can't," I said, feeling tears sting my eyes for the hundredth time that day. How was I going to manage my life here? We couldn't even order dinner, and we still had to find a place to live, get around in taxis, buy housewares and maybe furniture. I felt as if someone had switched on the lights in a dark room, and suddenly I could see what it meant for my parents, Hadi's parents, and all our family friends to have moved to the United States. Had they really gone through moments like this and survived?

I pushed a plastic spork through its wrapper. "Just scoop it off and eat around it. Please. If you really love me, you'll just eat it."

On the way back to the hotel, I held Hadi's hand because the sky had grown dark and cloudy and the sidewalks were uneven. Hadi said, "Watch out for that crack."

I looked down, and in that moment a fat rat scurried in front of us, its long tail sweeping the dusty sidewalk. I let go of Hadi's hand, then screamed and jumped up and down in place as if trying to shake off the rodent's memory. Then it started to rain. This was not a gentle rain that arrived with a soft, warning drizzle. This felt as if the sky broke open and poured its entire contents upon us. Hadi took my hand again, and we started to run, but my feet kept slipping out of my sandals.

Hadi looked back and said, "You had to wear those shoes. You still haven't learned about the elements."

There was a levity to his tone and a smile on his lips, and I knew exactly to what he was referring. On our honeymoon, every time a pebble rolled into my sandals or my toes got covered in dust, he'd say, "That's why I always wear closed-toed shoes. To protect my feet from the elements."

He thought he was being cute bringing this up now, that this moment would remind me of happier times and lighten my mood. I didn't appreciate it. My mood was so heavy it would have taken wheels to make it budge.

By the time we got back to our hotel, we were soaked, but still we stopped to look out the window. Jagged bolts of lightning cut through the night. Thunder roared. And through the window opposite us, rain pummeled its way through the space between the panels of the courtyard's clear glass roof, the fronds on the potted plants flattening from the pressure and the tile floor disappearing under water.

"Oh my God. It's a hurricane," I said. This was it. The roof of the hotel was going to blow off, and we were going to die tonight.

Hadi said, "It's just a summer thunderstorm. I'm sure everything will settle down in a bit."

But the only thing that settled down that night was the storm. As soon as all our first anniversary deeds were done, gifts, kisses, and bodies exchanged, I started crying again, straight onto Hadi's bare arm. He tried to comfort me, promising me that things would get better as soon as we found a home, but I wasn't thinking that far ahead. I was feeling the full weight of what I'd lost.

After all those years of encouragement from my professors, their assurances that I had great academic promise, I had followed my husband like a big, fat Arab stereotype. My mind pounded with a thought so seditious it frightened me. If only I'd waited, it said, I could've married someone else from our community, someone who wouldn't have pulled me out of school. I could have had my dream Muslim American love story and my career, too.

CHAPTER 26

❀

TRYING TO MAKE A LIFE

The next two weeks passed as an odd amalgam of pleasure and pain, of feeling as if we were on vacation but not. Parts of our days were spent trying new restaurants, walking to the mall, and watching that summer's blockbusters from the plush leather recliners at the nearest cinema. There was a thrill to each of these activities, within them delightful moments of discovery. In Mexico, you could buy a drink and a big tub of popcorn at the movies without it costing more than your ticket, and you could eat avocados every day without it being expensive. *Nuez* or nut ice cream and yogurt were now my favorite flavors, and the *bolillos* at the grocery store, pulled straight from the oven, gave the notion of fresh bread new meaning. However, in the midst of all this loveliness, we still had to make daily trips to the university; wait in long lines to apply for Hadi's student visa; return with stacks of passport-sized photographs of Hadi from every angle and photocopies of every piece of paper that ever had his name on it; pay a slew of bills for his tuition, books, and supplies; and apartment hunt.

Many days felt as if they were one long chain of Kentucky Fried Chicken moments. Every time we got into a taxi, ordered at a restaurant, or went to see an apartment, there was always one critical word I did not know and could not find in my dictionary. High school Spanish had not prepared me to say things such as the following: "Where is the water tank?" "Is it a gas or electric water heater?" "Are we responsible for filling up the gas tank?" "Does the apartment have a working telephone line?"

That is until we met our new landlord Fernando. Fernando spoke perfect English, and for that we loved him. "So the utilities are included?" Hadi asked, finally taking the lead of our apartment hunt.

"Yes, electricity, gas, and water are all included, and I think you will find our accommodations very comfortable. All the furniture is here for your convenience. My brother has a furniture factory, so that is why all our furnishings are very *de lujo*. I think you say 'of luxury.' And the bed coverings are new. All you have to do is bring your things."

A segment of one of Guadalajara's obscenely large homes, Fernando's apartment had the original mansion's front door—an imposing stained-glass masterpiece—and the original kitchen, which was a large room with a six-burner gas stove, a tiny refrigerator, and a nearly bedroom-size pantry. A wall of smoky mirrors divided what must have once been an enormous living space, and to the side of that wall stood a bathroom and our only bedroom. But it was a move-in-ready place with an English-speaking landlord. Suddenly it didn't seem to matter that the rent was as much as our apartment in overpriced California. After a stressful two weeks of bickering with each other and changing hotels, this odd but beautiful apartment answered our prayers.

A week later, Hadi left for his first day of school. I waved to him from the marble steps outside our front door and then returned to our apartment with a gnawing sense of loss. This was the first time since kindergarten that I was not attending school.

My first week at home, I slept much more than I intended. In the mornings, I'd look at my clock and think I could've gone to two classes in the time it had taken me to wake up. Then I'd stare at the contents of my closet and wonder if it was worth getting dressed when I had nowhere to go. I'd conclude no and sit back down on my bed with the books I had assigned to myself. But reading alone, without tables full of other students at my side, was lonely, so quiet and pitiable that I'd turn on the television for company and then find myself sucked into episodes of *Santa Barbara* dubbed in Spanish.

On the days we needed groceries, I took a bus into town and bought whatever my hands could carry, including a newspaper to look for jobs. Soon my family's upcoming visit gave my shopping a different purpose. I needed mats for them to sleep on, bedding, and more towels.

We'd been in Mexico for one month when Mama, Lina, and Ibrahim, who had another month of break before he started back up at school, arrived at my door in an airport taxi (Baba had decided to come in a few months to give me something to look forward to after they left). For the five days they camped out on the mats I'd laid out around our living room, that feeling of being on vacation returned. Hadi would leave in the morning for class, and we'd wake up at a leisurely pace; have a breakfast of bolillos, Oaxacan cheese, and some fruit; and then call a cab to take us to the tourist attractions in my *Lonely Planet Mexico* travel guide. In their company, I didn't dread using what little Spanish I knew. As a part of his graduate studies, Ibrahim had been traveling all over Europe and the Middle East, perfecting his Arabic, picking up Italian and Turkish, and now I felt equally adventurous sharing how I, too, was making my own way in another country, picking up another language. Seeing Guadalajara through my family's eyes was validating: it was an exciting tourist destination, its unique *artesanías* worthy of bringing back home as souvenirs, its architecture the perfect photo opportunity. I enjoyed my family's company so much I wished I still shared my daily life with them. Not this husband who didn't get my intellectual pursuits the way Ibrahim did, who didn't need my big sisterly advice the way Lina did, who didn't cook our meals and help wash our dishes and ask me how I was feeling the way Mama did.

Now more than ever before, I wanted to talk to Mama. I knew the circumstances that had brought Mama to America, but I wanted to hear exactly how her heart felt, how she got used to missing her family, how she found the courage to continue her education in her second language. But we rarely had a moment to talk. The days blurred past, filled with shopping and sightseeing. On the last weekend of their trip, Hadi and I rented a small Nissan Tsuru to take Mama, Lina, and Ibrahim through the heavily forested, winding roads to Puerto Vallarata. Because Hadi was the only one among us who knew how to drive a stick shift, he drove the entire weekend, a roundtrip of over four hundred miles, but I did not repay his kindness with gratitude. I picked on him the whole time, for wearing socks and laced shoes to the beach, for keeping his shirt tucked into his pants, for being too stuffy.

Mama tired of my attitude and scolded me to "back off the boy," but I couldn't escape the thought that soon she would be leaving with my brother and sister and that I had to stay in Mexico with Hadi—the man I was married to but who was not related to me, not my family. I belonged with them, too.

After Mama, Lina, and Ibrahim left the following Monday, I cried alone in my apartment, choked by its emptiness, the memory of them at my breakfast table. This was what I had rushed into; this was my ticket to freedom and my grand, sweeping love story—eating breakfast alone in Guadalajara, not being enrolled in school.

Our first year of marriage I had been so busy, overloading units so I could graduate early and go off to school with Hadi, that I hadn't felt the full weight of domestic life. Hadi had been the one with a more flexible schedule. He'd worked, shopped for groceries, cooked our meals, and done our laundry, but here the unrelenting cycle of shopping, meals, and dishes was all mine.

Hadi had been the better housekeeper. To keep food fresher, he'd store it in a Ziploc bag that he'd close right up until the corner, where he'd insert a straw to suck out all the air. He folded all our socks in half so as not to tax the elastic, and he folded all our towels the same way so that they'd fit better in the closet. To me, these tasks were too inconsequential to be given any attention. I placed the toilet paper onto the roll whichever way it came into my hand. I closed the shampoo bottle without waiting for its shape to be restored. I sealed sandwich bags shut without squeezing out the excess air first and balled up our socks without any regard for their longevity.

Hadi could not understand my haphazardness. He'd pause in front of a stack of folded clothes and ask curiously, "Is there a reason why you folded some of these shirts with the sleeves to the side and some with the sleeves behind?"

"There's no reason, Hadi," I'd say. "Some people do things without thinking about them."

"Okay," he'd say with his arms raised up in surrender. "Just trying to see if you'd found a better way of doing something."

And this was the real kicker for me. I did have a better way of doing things when it came to school, but all last year, Hadi never asked me if there was a reason why I outlined every chapter I read or why I started my term papers weeks before. No. He just went to work and put towels and food storage first, and this was where it got us. Hadi was the student I had wanted to be, but he wasn't studying the way I would have studied.

"Shouldn't you be doing something for school?" I'd ask every time I caught him without a book in front of him. But my constant reminders made us argue far more than they inspired Hadi to work. I knew I needed something to fill my time, something to get my mind off Hadi's study habits and my longing to be back in school.

The following week, I took the bus to the local university and signed up for Level II Spanish classes, but being in a classroom made everything better and worse all at the same time. Tucked behind a wooden, one-armed desk, I missed the furious scribble of notes I'd had in college, the sense that I was fulfilling a calling. Now I was learning how to say "elbow" and "eyebrow" and describing my class-mates as having very skinny elbows and very dark eyebrows. And while I valued the opportunity to learn a language, I wanted to leave the classroom with an idea worth contemplating and defending, something I could discuss over coffee with friends. Now my only classmates were sophomores and juniors in college, studying abroad. They attended classes by day and partied by night. They were living with Mexican families who gave them meals and a room. I had a husband. I paid rent in Mexico and shopped for groceries. I was not visiting; I was trying to make a life.

We'd start the school day with a two-hour grammar course, followed by a two-hour conversation class in which Señora Gonzalez, a matronly woman with cropped hair and full cheeks, stood in front of the blackboard and posed a strange mix of both banal and thoughtful questions for each one of us to answer in Spanish.

"What is your favorite sport and why?"

"I like the basketball because the balls are very beautiful. Very orange."

"Who is someone you admire?"

"I admire my mother. She is a very good person. She is short and nice."

"What will you tell your friends about Mexico?"

"It is a country with very nice people and very good food."

Then she turned to me and said, "Tell us about something important to you."

"The history is very important. If we understand the history, we are going to be more sensitive people."

"Why you don't say your husband? Your family?" the girl next to me interrupted in broken Spanish. Revealing a mouth full of shiny braces, she added, "You always giving big answers."

"Yes, that too," I said and nervously seesawed my pencil against my thumb. Suddenly, I saw how my classmates viewed me. I was the annoying girl with the lofty ideas, trying to turn a Spanish class into a seminar.

CHAPTER 27

THE ASPIRING DOCTOR'S WIFE

Hadi loved it when I visited him on campus, but I hated watching other students going on with their careers when I didn't know where I was going with mine. I hated being asked what I was doing to fill my time because taking Spanish classes sounded so small, so accessible, so unrevealing of my 4.0 GPA. And, most of all, I hated meeting the female medical students. They were aspiring doctors while I was the aspiring doctor's wife, and a handful of them, I soon discovered, were Muslims, one of them who wore the hijab. I had thought I had to get married so I could go to graduate school in another state, and these girls' parents had been willing to send them out of the country for the sake of their education.

The day Hadi introduced me to Marjanne, an Iranian American woman in his class who also happened to be from California, I hit a new low. She was friendly and warm, but none of that made an impression on me. What stayed with me was her reply when I told her I'd been taking Spanish classes.

"You know what you should do?" she asked, her eyes widening with excitement. "You should make sandwiches and bring them around during lunch. God knows, I'd buy them. The only thing close by is that taco stand, and I'm scared to eat there."

"That's something to think about," I said in a tone Marjanne mistook for sincerity.

Pulling her long, crinkly hair over one shoulder, Marjanne added,

"I think that would go over really well. Don't you, Hadi? Bring some turkey or pastrami sandwiches in a little basket. People would buy that right up."

Hadi was wise enough not to respond. I forced a smile, and we excused ourselves from Marjanne's company. Later that afternoon, Hadi and I walked home in a dangerous quiet, but as soon as Hadi closed our front door behind us, I exploded. "Do you see what I've been reduced to here? People think I'm some little wifey, sitting around at home, waiting to cook for everybody."

I wouldn't have minded making sandwiches had I still been enrolled in a degree program. Then any of the cooking I did could have been something extra, an added talent, but here, the suggestion made me feel so provincial, so married off. I thought all of us Muslim sisters were on the marriage track together, and now Islam wasn't the excuse; it wasn't the reason. It was one thing to have sacrificed my education to uphold God's law and quite another to have clung to rules unique to my family.

But then a few weeks after meeting Marjanne, an Indian American guy in Hadi's class introduced me to his wife, Zoya. They'd gotten married on one of his visits back to India. Zoya had been eighteen years old and right out of high school. They'd already had their first child, a chubby, blue-eyed toddler, so cute I had to keep myself from squeezing the rolls in her thigh when I first met them. This was more like it, I thought, during the first dinner we shared together. This was what I'd been taught to expect—marriage and kids first, school worked in later.

But over an exquisitely prepared biryani and fresh roti, Zoya told me she was the youngest of three sisters and there'd been no pressure on her to marry. "I loved him," she said. "Otherwise, I would have never left my family back in India."

I couldn't imagine declaring that I loved Hadi with such confidence. After so many years of being told it was ayb to be interested in a boy, it still felt shameful and wrong. And here was Zoya, raised among Muslims but so confident in her love for her husband. She wasn't running away from any stories about what Muslim love was or trying to prove she had an American love story. She'd married the man she wanted to marry and was going about her life, an amazing cook, a talented seamstress, and, later I would discover, a capable math tutor.

I hadn't expected this move to Mexico to raise so many questions about my own culture and community. All of my MSA sisters from college had grown up with rules so similar to mine if not more, but the Muslim women I was meeting in Mexico had been raised with such different boundaries. I soon became good friends with the hijab-wearing medical student who told me her parents had few reservations about letting her study in another country. Now she was in her last year, planning on becoming a pediatrician. She'd mastered Spanish, and she showed me all around town with total confidence, bargaining down our taxi fares and answering jovially any questions about what order she belonged to when our drivers assumed she was a nun. Then, there was the student in Hadi's year who declared at the Friday afternoon prayers that she was heading to the airport to pick up her boyfriend, her white, American boyfriend, named Steve. She made the announcement plainly, without even a hint of secrecy or shame.

Back at our home, I called Mama, confused. "I see all these Muslim girls in school here, and I don't understand why you didn't want more for me. Why didn't you want me to go off to school and become something?"

"That's funny," she said, "I always compared myself to my cousins who were becoming doctors and wondered why Jidu didn't want us to finish school before we got married. But I really thought I was giving you more. I wanted you to marry someone younger. I wanted you to finish college. I just wanted to keep you safe, too."

"Yes, I know, if we fly, we fly together, so if we die, we die together."

"Of all the things I've told you, this is what you remember?"

"That's the kind of thing that leaves a pretty big impression on a kid."

"When you've seen as much death as I have at such a young age, you don't take life for granted. I guess it gave me some comfort to think if you were married, you'd always have another set of eyes watching over you."

After we hung up that night, Mama's words stayed with me. I attributed so much to our religion and culture that I rarely allowed her the everyday motivations of instinct and fear. And she was right; no matter how confused I was about my feelings toward Hadi, I'd married someone I'd grown up with and considered a friend. I had an elaborate wedding and graduated from college. I'd already had more. I only wished there'd been less concern for my reputation and our friendship with the Ridhas, and less istikharas, so that this could have felt like enough.

CHAPTER 28

❖

AN EDIBLE
IDENTIFICATION CARD

Baba arrived in Guadalajara with a small Middle Eastern grocery store inside his suitcase. Wrapped among his pajamas and undershirts were a sack of basmati rice; a vial of saffron strands; a couple of jars of grape leaves and tahini sauce; and a few bags of pita bread, bulgur, and pine nuts—everything I'd requested before he left.

Although Hadi and I had found a rather large Lebanese restaurant in town, owned by a Lebanese immigrant family and appropriately named El Libanes, eating Middle Eastern food didn't feel as important as making it. I needed our apartment to be filled with the nutty smell of rice, the food on our table to act as an edible identification card, declaring who we were to our friends and visitors.

I'd never felt so American and even more specifically Californian as I did living in Mexico. In this third space, it didn't matter where my parents or Hadi's parents were born. Since we spoke English, most Mexicans accepted us as American students, our names registering as foreign rather than particularly Arab. And, among the other American medical students, our shared spoken language and the common experience of having lived in the United States were enough to bond us to a community of expatriates we might not have had anything in common with stateside.

Sharing our food, and even Baba himself, felt like a way to introduce our new friends to the people we'd been before we moved here.

Even though Baba would only be in town for a few days, I'd invited all the Muslim medical students over for dinner—a mix of American-born Indians, Pakistanis, and Egyptians, and a few of our other American friends. In preparation, Baba and I took a taxi to an open-air market where Baba delighted in the reminders of his tropical island life. He drank coconut water straight from a fresh coconut and loaded up on papayas, guavas, mangos, and avocados. "You know in Zanzibar," Baba said, "we used to eat avocado like a dessert. We put the sugar and scoop it with a spoon."

As we meandered through the dusty aisles, Baba spotted a familiar dry bean. With the scoop, he poured a few into his hand and said, "This is similar to the bean they used to make *mbaazi* in Zanzibar. Let us make it for your guests." Baba paid for the beans and a few serrano peppers to season the coconut-milk-based stew, and I felt an unexpected stirring of pride. Being in Mexico had opened up a window into my father's memory; it had conjured up stories I may not have heard otherwise.

After we got back home, Baba, Hadi, and I worked together to prepare the next day's dinner. Baba soaked the beans. I roasted eggplant for baba ghanoush. Hadi chopped the onions for a tomato-based marga and the rice I'd use to stuff the dolma. I marveled at how comfortably we worked together.

In Mama's company, my heart stewed with a warring mix of blame and resignation. It was so easy to look at the istikharas Mama made and her affection for Hadi and make her responsible for my decision to get married. It was even easier to picture myself as Mama, a woman making the most of a relationship that was picked for her while striving to reach her educational goals. But here in Baba's company, I was forced to remember things I often forgot, that Baba had not wanted me to get married, that he'd repeatedly offered me an out and I was the one who had reassured him that this was what I wanted, that I'd been so caught up with the business of becoming a bride.

It was a remarkably short-lived burst of awareness. Hadi's presence as a host began to annoy me as soon as our guests arrived for dinner the following evening. The assalamu alaikum he offered our Muslim friends was far too quiet to make them feel truly welcome, and instead of facilitating introductions between our guests, he left Baba alone to fill up all the conversational space in the room with his favorite stories from his medical school days in India and in Iraq. First, Hadi disappeared to set up the drinks and the ice chest. Now he was back in the kitchen again, leaning over me as I scooped rice onto a platter, asking me if I needed help even though several women were already standing around, waiting to do the same.

"You need to go sit with everybody," I whispered.

"I'm just trying to help," Hadi said in the same hushed volume.

"The biggest way you can help me is by taking care of our guests," I said.

As I watched Hadi walk out of the kitchen, his shoulders sagging from my rebuke, I tried to shake off a sense of extreme exasperation. I had been the one to strike up friendships with the wives of the medical students, to seek out the Muslim community at the Friday prayers held in one of the student's living rooms, and to make the calls inviting over these guests. All Hadi had to do was talk to our company, and now this dinner that was supposed to be about Baba's visit and this food was turning into another one of my assessments of Hadi, another occasion to simmer with regret. I had seen this shyness at my prom. It would have been so easy to let Hadi go then, to explain to Mama that we were not a match. I had wanted an outgoing spouse, someone at ease in a crowd, someone who could fill up a room with chatter like Baba.

Throughout dinner, I glanced over at Hadi, trying to guess what impression he was making on our new friends. It appeared as if he'd made his way into a conversation with a few of our guests, but this didn't please me either. I thought about how slowly Hadi told stories, his habit of including every detail, and I feared that he was boring our company. I imagined our couple-friends going home and talking about us, wondering why I'd picked such a dull husband.

It startled me that I could entertain such a horrible thought, so cruel and judgmental while flattering myself that I was somehow the better catch, but still I could not banish the idea from my mind until much later that night when all our guests had left and the dinner dishes were washed and then put away. Baba and I had settled onto the de lujo couch in our living room, and he said, "You are right, Hudie. This Hadi is a wonderful boy."

I couldn't imagine how this evening that had irritated me so much had left Baba with such a positive impression. I prodded Baba to show me what my insecurity hadn't allowed me to see. "He's a bit shy though."

"It's not bad to be shy," Baba said. "Imam Ali used to say, 'Speak only when your words are more beautiful than silence.'"

"I've never heard that."

"Oh, yes. Sometimes to have the good manners, one must say less."

Hadi's introversion had always struck me as a burden, something that I had to compensate for with cheery conversation. I had never once considered the virtues of reticence or that people might appreciate Hadi's thoughtfulness and sincerity, the way he carefully weighed everything he said before he spoke. I didn't consider it, because I forgot that Hadi was his own person whenever we were around other people. He became an accessory, completing the look I wanted to project, subject to the same merciless scrutiny with which I studied myself in the mirror.

I scooted in closer to Baba and rested my head on his shoulder. Our conversation drifted into the kind of long silences that I expected when I was with Baba but resented when I was sitting next to Hadi. I puzzled over this stark contrast—the judgment I reserved for my spouse and the clear, uncomplicated affection I held for my family, and I hoped that one day I'd learn to love Hadi with the same acceptance, the same forgiveness.

CHAPTER 29

———————————— ❀ ————————————

I LOVE HUDA.DOC

I decided to take a break between Spanish II and Spanish III to enroll in a two-week certificate course, being held downtown, in teaching English as a foreign language. I hoped that I'd make friends in the class, maybe find a job after, but there was no real potential for companionship among my classmates. They'd all flown in for the course, their sights set on teaching posts in other countries. And I soon discovered that teaching a language had the same boring quality as learning one. It only put me on a different side of the desk.

I knew I didn't want a job where I had to teach English, but I also didn't know what I'd do after I'd taken all the levels of Spanish if I didn't teach. Go back to watching *Santa Barbara* dubbed in Spanish, to pretend reading the academic book I'd left marked at page fifteen for a month?

Daily I left class feeling more alone than before I'd started. Coming downtown every day had only made me more aware of Guadalajara's largeness and my lack of a purpose within it. Here in the bustling *centro* nothing was familiar, not the streets, the bus routes, the restaurants, or the shops. Because of the intimidating newness of the downtown, I'd arranged for a taxi driver from my neighborhood to give me rides. Some mornings, I had to call him to wake him up. Some afternoons, he didn't show up, and I had to call him from a phone booth along one of the downtown's quieter cobblestone side streets.

On the Friday after my first week of class, I called my driver for the better part of an hour, but nobody picked up. A neatly dressed, teenaged delivery boy had seen me on the phone, on his way to drop off a package and again on his way out. He asked me if I needed help, and when I explained about my neighborhood taxi driver not showing up, he said that he had a delivery in my area and offered to take me home.

I wrestled with the idea. I could take a ride from a clean-cut young man, with a friendly smile, who was a stranger, or I could take to the corner and try to flag down another man of undetermined age, size, and disposition who was also a stranger and who would probably rip me off. What was the difference, I rationalized, between riding home with this guy and a taxi driver? At least with this guy, I wouldn't have to haggle down the price or, more truthfully, accept whatever price he named. Even though I had been in Mexico for almost two months, I was still too timid to bargain. The most I could muster was a frown at the driver's fee, and after a reluctant "*bueno*," I'd invariably get in the car and spend the entire ride berating myself for my complete willingness to be had. It would be so nice to skip that inevitable sequence this one time.

And this guy was cute. It seemed unlikely that such a handsome kid with dark brown wavy hair, neatly trimmed around the ears and neck, and a disarming smile could be capable of anything dangerous. Wasn't there some sort of psychological study that showed good-looking people didn't do bad things? Wait. No. It showed that women, like me, were more likely to think that good-looking men would not do bad things.

I tapped one foot nervously and smoothed the front of my skirt. A few noisy, worn-out cars rumbled past along the rocky road. Maybe I should just ask him if he had any criminal intentions toward me. If I called him on it, he'd be way too embarrassed to try to rob or kill me later.

So I said the only thing I knew how to say in my Level II Spanish. I asked, "Is it safe?" or at least that was what I thought I asked. I might have asked him, "Are you sure?" The word for "sure" and "safe" was the same, *seguro*, and I couldn't remember if I had used the right form of the verb "to be" to convey the correct meaning.

"Of course," he said, waving his hands in the air as if offended by the question.

I knew then I had gotten the question right, but I also felt a sudden twinge of guilt for asking. He was a nice kid, fresh from his mother's hugs and kisses, washing and ironing, and I had just been an obnoxious traveler.

That was when I got into his car and scooted along the fabric seat toward the door. I put my bag in my lap so I could beat him with it if necessary, clicked my seat belt into place, and then slid my hands around the door's slender handlebar.

My hands were still there when he looked over at me and asked, "Are you always this nervous?"

I eased my grip and said, "A little. But it is good to be careful, no?"

"*Claro*," he replied. "I have sisters."

"*Mira*. You understand," I said, my eyes fixed on the road. The part of me that feared for my safety relaxed, but another part of me stayed prickly with discomfort. As much as I'd rationalized taking this risk, it did not change the fact that I had little experience being in the company of men who were not related to me.

At least I picked a good driver. I watched him maneuver his way through the downtown's cacophony of horns and checkerboard gridlock with ease. Not bad for somebody who could've only had his license a year or two at the most. I was terrified to drive in Mexico, but this kid kept one hand on the wheel, the other on the gear, while looking so calm he might as well have been driving a minicar around a track in an amusement park.

He introduced himself as Antonio and asked me how I liked Mexico.

"I like the people," I said. "They are very good. I like the architecture. It is very beautiful. I like the food. It is very delicious."

I smoothed my skirt again, pulling it taut over my knees. I hated the flatness of my speech in Spanish, its toddler-like simplicity.

We continued to have a typical local-meets-foreigner conversation, and I arrived home a half hour later unharmed but heavy with guilt. I couldn't tell Hadi I'd taken a ride home with a delivery boy I'd met on the street.

Hadi came to the door, gave me a hug, and asked me about my class. My resolve not to mention the delivery guy did not waver, but I itched to pick a fight. I never would've done something like that had I not been put in this position of having to take taxis all over the place, of having to dig for ways to fill up my time.

"Bad, like usual."

"What's wrong? Did the taxi forget you again?"

"Yes, but that's not what's wrong. What's wrong is that I'm taking these stupid classes to teach English instead of being in school, studying history."

"Here we go again," Hadi said. "It's all my fault. I messed up in school, and I brought you here. Is that what you want to hear?"

"No," I said with exaggerated offense. "I just want you to appreciate how hard it is to be here."

"You always say that, but there's no way to make up for bringing you here. I could say thank you all day long, but it wouldn't change anything."

For an hour, we went back and forth, with me insisting that this interruption in my schooling was the end of my career, and with Hadi insisting that things would work out. Our argument moved from the doorway to the bedroom to the bathroom. We argued as I washed my face and changed. And then, I gave up. I started the fight, and I was the one to walk away. I said I had to make dinner and left the room.

We didn't talk the rest of the night. We'd had this argument so many times I should've tape-recorded one, labeled it "the Mexico Fight," and played it whenever the mood arrived.

After Hadi went to bed, I sat down in front of our laptop, prepared to send an email full of complaints to a friend about my impossible life. Because our dial-up internet connection was so erratic, we wrote all of our emails in a word-processing program, before logging on and then sending off everything at once. There, I saw that the last saved file was titled "I love Huda.doc." Without contemplating whether or not I was invading Hadi's privacy, I opened it. Filling up an entire page was that one line over and over again. I love Huda. I love Huda. I had heard Hadi furiously typing while I was in the kitchen making dinner. I had assumed that he was sending an email, complaining about me. And this was what he was writing.

If only Hadi had been merely my boyfriend—not a husband whose future was so tangled up in mine—this gesture might have melted me. I might have sought him out and covered him with kisses. All these years, I'd regarded the temporary nature of a boyfriend with such disdain, but now I understood the value of that kind of a relationship, its appeal. What a gift it was to be able to experience what you did not want in a relationship and then walk away.

That night, as I drifted off to sleep, I imagined myself married to a man whose ambitions equaled my own, our life together in a prestigious university, never having left the United States. At first it seemed a dream come true, the mutual achievements, the shared time reading, the interest in each other's research, but then I considered what it might be like to be married to someone who had expectations of my success, someone who resented me for holding him back, someone like me.

I sat up in bed and looked over at Hadi. I watched his hand, resting flat on his chest, rising and falling with every breath, and I wondered if being married to me was not the grand gift he allowed me to believe it was.

The following Monday, I sat on a bench in the Plaza de Armas, glancing up at the circular gazebo at its center, its intricate iron railings and Hershey's Kiss–shaped roof. Hungry pigeons pecked the surrounding grounds in a furious rush, trying to eat their fill before the children, running about, chased them away. In every tree-shaded corner, vendors grasped giant balloon bouquets or stood behind stalls, selling potato chips doused in a squirt of chili sauce and a spray of lime.

A warm breeze pressed against my skin, the sun illuminating the tiny hairs along my arms. If it was possible to fall in love with a location's weather, then it was happening. In the two months we'd been here, the weather was rarely warm enough for me to break a sweat but still not cool enough to make an always chilly person like me uncomfortable. Even when the sky clouded over and burst with rain, it still didn't get cold enough for me to need a jacket.

It hit me then that if it wasn't for the English course and if it wasn't for Hadi bringing us down here, I wouldn't be downtown right now, enjoying the sunshine's embrace, about to reach into the waxy paper bag in my lap and pull out a hot croissant stuffed with Mexico's creamy goat's milk caramel, *cajeta*.

That was the problem with Mexico. Every time I tried to write it off as the cause of all my problems, it slapped me with a beauty that made me feel as if I should shut up and be grateful to be here, seeing its sights, tasting its food, feeling its weather.

After I'd dusted the last few crumbs of croissant off my hands, I grabbed my bag, crossed a busy street lined with horse-drawn carriages awaiting tourists, and passed through the imposing doors of the cool and musky cathedral. The cathedral's yellow dome and pointed towers dominated the entire downtown. It was a symbol of Guadalajara, its silhouette painted on every taxi, and it was coming to dominate my entire experience of the downtown, too. There was something about the elements of my life that it fused together, giving me hope that there might be some reconciliation for me, an Iraqi American Shia Muslim, in Catholic Mexico.

Inside, I felt at home in the warm glow of the candle light, surrounded by the smell of melting wax, comforted by the passionate whispering of prayers. When I'd first started going to Catholic schools, I'd struggled during Mass. Coming from a religious tradition that forbids iconography and the consumption of alcohol, it was startling to attend services with the image of a bloody, tortured Jesus pinned to a crucifix hanging above me, to watch my classmates taking sips from a large chalice of wine. But year by year, I grew accustomed to the Mass, and even though I never actively participated, there were certain songs that touched me, prayers that I had inadvertently memorized, homilies that spoke to values I knew Islam and Christianity shared. Now rather than Guadalajara's cathedral feeling strange to me, it felt familiar, and its statues, crucifixes, and artwork were things that I recognized.

That afternoon, I stood in front of the glass case holding the statue of Santa Inocencia. She was dressed in a long, frilly communion dress and lying down along a bed of white satin covered in amulets, photographs, and written petitions. The older woman next to me bowed her head and whispered a prayer over her arthritic, interlocked hands. When she was finished, she turned to me and said, "She is a martyr. When she took her first communion, her father killed her because he didn't want her to accept Christ."

I nodded solemnly, as if she were the first person to tell me this.

"You can pray to her. Ask her for anything," she added, her hands still intertwined.

I didn't want to disappoint her, so I lingered in front of the glass case a little bit longer, thinking about this woman and how those very same words could have been spoken by a member of my own family. I could hear my mother, my grandfather, my aunts and uncles referring to one of our Shia tradition's martyrs in the same way, saying, "Ask them for anything. God may be able to deny you and me something, but He cannot deny them."

Now Santa Inocencia brought to mind the story of Ali al-Asghar, the Prophet Muhammad's six-month-old great-grandson. When his father, one of the Shia tradition's most revered saints, Imam Husayn and his army were surrounded in Karbala, they were cut off from their only source of water. Imam Husayn pleaded for a drop of water for his crying son, and the sight of this baby, the Prophet's own flesh and blood, withering away from dehydration made the opposing troops restless. To quell the impending mutiny, an arrow was sent flying into the baby's throat. Every year on the anniversary of his martyrdom, an empty crib is carried during the lamentation rituals in his honor. He, like Santa Inocencia, is a focal point for prayers, for mourning undeserved losses.

A crowd formed around the glass, and I stepped away only to stop in front of a statue of a weeping Mary, robed in black. Imprinted on the placard beneath her was the title "La Dolorosa, the Sorrowful." She was the first mournful Mary I'd ever seen, and she reminded me of the stories of Fatima az-Zahra, Imam Husayn's mother. She is said to appear at every service where her son's name is mentioned. Fatima is our symbol of a bereaved mother, and in Mexico, Mary represented the same.

I felt an affinity here that I hadn't even felt among my MSA sisters. During the winter semester of last year, the religious studies professor who specialized in Islam taught a class specifically on Shiism. Several of my Sunni Muslim friends had signed up, but I could no longer sustain the face of unity that had meant so much to me in our women in Islam class. When my friends raised their hands and argued that the Shia practice of taking to the street and beating your chest in the name of a martyred Imam wasn't true Islam, I had to raise my hand and explain that this was merely an attempt to experience the suffering of a beloved icon and hero. When they objected to the Shia use of human imagery in their art, I had to clarify that doing so was not a form of idolatry but of storytelling and commemorating. When they argued that the Shia regard for their saintlike Imams was incompatible with Allah's oneness, I had to suggest Imams were merely vessels through which one communicated with the divine. But I sensed that here, in this cathedral, no such explanations were necessary.

I continued to wander around the edges of the cathedral, but my mind itched. Mexicans added a mournful streak to their faith that felt so familiar, so Shia. All my life, I had toggled between my school life and home life, feeling too Muslim and Arab in one and too American in the other. But here the dominant culture's rules were not the same ones I'd defined myself against for so long. Here a grandmother had told me to pray, and her devotion had felt like home.

CHAPTER 30

❋

A MATTER OF LIFE AND DEATH AND GOD HIMSELF

Over the next few months, Hadi and I fell into something of a Guadalajara groove. I finished Level III Spanish, and from it, I gained both confidence in going around the city and an unexpected sense of pride. While Hadi had not quite picked up Spanish yet, he was taking Spanish classes on the weekends and consistently scoring above average on his medical school exams. When he came home, he practiced his clinical skills on me, checking my ears and throat, palpating my abdomen, and listening to my chest. Although we both had diarrhea all the time, this became an ongoing joke between us, an experience we came to refer to as simply "explosion." And, finally, the time I spent with the American wives of medical students, grocery shopping together on the weekends and attending their monthly book club, opened my eyes to two important things:

1. Marriage was a great equalizer. For all their romantic dates and surprise proposals, these American women still wound up in Mexico, cooking, cleaning, food shopping, and doing laundry just like me.
2. Babies were the answer. The majority of the wives were mothers or soon-to-be mothers, and I didn't see them fretting over their stalled careers. I was certain these women

spent their days cuddling their glorious babies, never lonely or bored. My own mother had said my brother had cured her loneliness after she came to America. It was so obvious that I should have a baby, too.

But when I shared my plan with Hadi, he squashed it with unwelcome reason. "Our lives are so unsettled here," he said. "Do you really want to bring a baby into this? How would you feel if the baby had diarrhea and had to be taken to the hospital for dehydration?"

I put my hands on my hips to further convey my indignation. "Just because our stomachs are weirdly sensitive, that doesn't mean our baby will be like that, too. There are plenty of people having babies here, and I only know of one woman who had to take her baby to the hospital with dehydration."

Hadi looked at me as if he had concerns for my sanity. "You do know you're not supposed to have kids because other people are doing it?"

In a childish, mocking tone, I said, "Yes, I know we are not supposed to have kids because other people are doing it," and because that wasn't immature enough, I accused Hadi of not letting me do anything. "It's like you're telling me, 'Don't go to school *and* don't get a head start on having kids.' What is this purgatory?"

In the weeks approaching winter break, Hadi and I revisited this argument several times, each time circling around my plans to go back to school, with Hadi saying he didn't want us to have a kid if we were going to put our child in day care in a few years, me arguing that my mom had gotten through school by bringing me to class with a little coloring book, and Hadi concluding with what was another issue entirely. "Is it really wise to bring a child into a relationship that we still haven't settled into yet?" he'd ask. "Most of the time, I'm not even sure you like me."

This question was directly tied to another, more pressing, topic we'd been debating—how we'd divide our first trip back to California. I wanted to go straight to my parents' house and stay the entire break, maybe return to Guadalajara at the same time as Hadi so we could share a cab on our way home. Hadi, on the other hand, believed we should travel together and split the time between both our parents' houses. We were husband and wife, he argued, and that was what married people did. To drive the point home, he added, "And you want us to have kids? If we had a baby, would you take the baby away from me for a month, too?"

Both discussions filled me with the urge to shake him, hard. The precise reason I wanted to go to my parents' house was because I needed a break from being married. If we actually had a baby, then we could talk about the fair way to split our vacation time, but for now, all I wanted was to shop with Lina, dance with Aysar, and giggle all night with Diana and Nadia at a sleepover.

In the end, I agreed to fly back to Hadi's parents' house a week before we were scheduled to return to Mexico. Hadi tempted me with the possibility of packing up his brother's old car and driving it down to Guadalajara (Hadi didn't want to ruin his car on Mexico's potholed roads). We'd have to share the car, and I'd still take the bus to the Spanish classes I'd resumed taking at the local university, but at least there'd be no more hauling duffel bags of clothes to the Laundromat, no more plastic bags of groceries cutting off the circulation on my wrist while I gripped the pole on a crowded bus.

My first few days home were a blissful show-and-tell. I showed off the haircut I'd gotten the day before I left, the clothes I'd purchased just for my arrival, my new Ricky Martin CD, and Spanish skills. But the days that followed brought no long-awaited respite from my irritable bowels. No joy in seeing how my friends had moved on with school, work, jobs, homes. No satisfaction when I visited my former professors without any research interests to share. I'd salivated over the idea of being home for weeks, and now that I was here, I felt buried under a heavy, stuporous funk, one that had turned particularly sour right after Mama's weekend phone call with Aunty Najma. Mama had passed along the news that two of my cousins who lived in Lebanon would be studying abroad, one at a university in Scotland, another in England.

Although I went through the motions, visiting with friends at sleepovers and girls-only dance parties, I felt cooped up in my head for the remainder of the break, trying to unravel this mystery: if I was the one who was born in America, how had I wound up living the more culturally traditional life?

At night, I'd lie in my bed, feeling as if my room did not belong to me. I was no longer the girl who'd chosen cherub throw pillows, a print of Victorian ladies in a café, and a wrought-iron bed. All through high school, I had been drawn to all things Victorian; it had been so easy to insert myself into Victorian love stories with all their restrained, unspoken love. But how foolish had I been to not realize that I would have never been the protagonist of one of these stories. I would have been the Mohammedan, the exotic Oriental, or the native savage.

Now more than ever, I wished I was in school so a professor and a class discussion could help me analyze how familial, cultural, sociological, and religious forces had intersected to drive me to this choice I did not own. I wondered if I had an arranged marriage, a forced marriage, a working-things-out marriage, or a marriage reaching its end.

The last possibility twisted me with heartache. If I attempted to undo my marriage now, the only future I saw for myself as a divorcée was manless, sexless, and childless. I questioned the wisdom of throwing away a life with a kind man and an equally promising father when all I really wanted was a do-over—to go back to being the girl who had lain in this same bed, filled with hope for her future—and to choose school over marriage, to choose to live my own life before agreeing to live my life for another.

As my time at home approached its end, I dreaded seeing Hadi's family, but refusing to go would have required an explanation I was not capable of giving. On the appointed day, I took an hour-long flight to Southern California. Mrs. Ridha picked me up from the airport alone because we'd be going straight to a baby shower for a mutual friend. On our way, she told me that Reem Salaam had gotten divorced. Soraya Ahmed had broken off her engagement and was already engaged to someone else.

I stared off into the crowded highway, my gaze blurring on the glint of sun that bounced off the car in front of us. Reem had gotten married the year before me. I had admired her beautiful dress, the way she'd danced and smiled the entire night. Soraya had announced her engagement six months ago. She must have been as unhappy as I had been, but instead of suffering through it, she'd had the courage to walk away. Now she had the chance to be happy again. Why did she have the strength to leave when I didn't? Did she value herself more?

With my eyes still focused on the road, words left my mouth, words that surprised me. "I thought a girl with a broken engagement could never get remarried."

"Why not? These things happen."

"But the way we were taught, it seemed like a girl had only one chance."

"No," Mrs. Ridha said, glancing in her side-view mirror as she changed lanes. "It's not like that. Because you young people were born here, we wanted you to understand the way our people think. We did not expect you to listen to everything we said."

Mrs. Ridha's words pierced me. My engagement, my marriage, my life in Mexico suddenly felt like a tragic Shakespearean mis-understanding. I'd thought our community's code of conduct was a matter of life and death and God Himself, and the entire time, our parents knew that this wasn't necessarily the case, that they were saying things to keep us away from the dangers to which they assumed America made us vulnerable, but still understood that we might do something else, maybe even expected it.

I wanted answers to a thousand other questions, but even more than that, I didn't want Mrs. Ridha to see me ruffled. So I waited, thinking of something I could say that would make her explain more without giving away the impact her words had on me.

After a long pause, I said, "I don't know if you know this, but Hadi never said anything to me at my prom. He didn't even tell me I looked nice, but I felt like I had to marry him because we'd gone out together." Fearing that I'd gone too far, I added, "Not that it's a problem, but you know, then. That's how I felt."

"Who thinks like that? Of course, we wished you'd marry Hadi. From the moment I met your family, I loved your mother, and I always thought that, mashallah, you're just like her—good in everything. But because I knew your family takes istikharas about these things, I understood that it didn't matter how much we loved you or Hadi loved you. It may not happen."

I was quiet. Although Hadi's parents were so similar to mine on paper, they were different in practice. During this year that I'd spent as a part of their family, I was surprised by how seldom they turned to istikharas to make decisions. The Ridhas might have undertaken one a year if at all, but my family made several a day—if not by turning to the Quran, then by counting off on the *sibha* or prayer beads my father kept in his pocket. They looked to the istikhara as if it were a divinely inspired coin toss. Should I stay home sick today? Should I accept this invitation? Should I take this medication, eat this food, buy this product?

Marrying into the Ridha family had made me see my family's reliance on the istikhara as curious and idiosyncratic rather than devotional, and now it was forcing me to question something so much more painful to doubt—the istikharas that had determined my own marriage. They made me agree to Hadi before he'd even asked for me, before I'd even attempted to make a decision about him in my own heart. In that sense, those istikharas had violated the practice's most basic conditions—that those requesting it be torn by indecision, that they hold a question as an intention in their minds. From the outset, Mama had been clear that these istikharas were hers—that she'd framed the intention from her perspective—and yet I'd accepted their outcomes as if God Himself was speaking to me.

I felt like a fool to be discovering now that the Ridhas never felt they had spoken for me; they had been aware the entire time that this relationship may not happen.

To my silence, Mrs. Ridha added, "And yes, Hadi did tell me he never said anything to you at your prom, and I was really surprised. I thought you kids grew up here, you knew what to do."

And right then, on a greater Los Angeles highway, a view of the world as Mrs. Ridha saw it crystallized in my mind—a world where a mother thought it would be great if her son married her best friend's daughter. It shamed me to think of how willing I'd been to stereotype not just my culture but Mrs. Ridha herself. I'd so willingly accepted this story of being claimed since childhood that I'd failed to see that the trope of the matchmaking mother didn't fit Mrs. Ridha at all. The truth was what it had always been—she truly and sincerely loved me.

My talk with Mrs. Ridha quelled my restlessness for the rest of my stay. The first few days, Hadi and I gathered the things we didn't have in Guadalajara but wanted—a television for the living room, a stereo, a VCR, and a desktop computer—but when it came to actually packing his brother's four-seater hatchback, Hadi took over. He enjoyed the challenge of making things fit into tight spaces; it was a real-life brain teaser complete with rules he refused to break. No space allowed between objects. No items could go up front by the driver or the passenger. Nothing could block the rearview mirror. Nothing could be left behind.

Before we set off the next morning, Hadi showed me around the car, proud of every nook and cranny he'd managed to utilize, and then we set off, Hadi's eyes fixed on the road ahead and my eyes fixed on a guidebook that warned of checkpoints, bandits, police officers looking to be paid off, and the general hazards of driving at night—wayward cows, unlit roads, and the lack of roadside assistance.

For three days, we drove by day and stayed in hotels by night. Every threat we'd been warned of went unrealized, but the possibility of danger draped over us like a blanket that narrowed our world to each other, the cozy security of our car. Hadi and I got along in this world. Here our roles were simple and defined, our living space limited and undemanding. It was peaceful in the car. The views shushed me. Once again, I couldn't complain about living in Mexico when it had brought me to this terrain that wound us through wet, grassy flatlands; tree-studded mountains; lush rain forests; colorful roadside shrines; and small villages with cobblestone streets and brightly painted churches.

But those days we spent in the car were only a passing reprieve. That winter semester, Hadi and I fell into a turbulent routine. We'd moved into a new apartment after Fernando surprised us with a sizable hike in the rent. We bought furniture, curtains, and a refrigerator—each one a challenge for my developing language skills. I took Level IV Spanish by day, tutored children in English after school, and taught adults at an English language institute at night. But having more to do didn't make me happy the way I thought it would. On the contrary, tutoring and teaching filled me with dread. I didn't want to coax six-year-olds out from under the table or lure them to learn with promises of a cookie. I didn't want to plan lessons for adults who rarely showed up to class and were too tired out by their day jobs to study. And I blamed Hadi for it all.

I was a twenty-one-year-old, facing the monotony of married life without having known the wooing that was supposed to precede it. I was certain that if only the circumstances of my engagement had been different—had I been whisked off on exciting outings and been surprised with a storybook proposal—then maybe I would have been too in love to feel such regret.

On Valentine's Day and a few months later on my birthday, my hopes rose that the perfect gift or outing would break the spell of constant rumination. But when each occasion opened with Hadi asking me what I wanted to do that day, I felt crushed, as if he was announcing that we were officially a boring married couple, news that was all the more disappointing because we'd never had the chance to be an exciting unmarried couple.

I'd always imagined married life as the beginning of a newer, better me. I would become a woman straight out of the glossy images of a bridal magazine. I'd eat dinner at a table set with matching china and flowers, and this would be my new normal, not dressing up, not playing pretend. I'd load our dishes and clothes into their respective appliances, wearing cute, working-at-home clothes because I'd no longer be the type of person who put on her pajamas as soon as she got in the door. I'd go on vacations at Beaches Resorts, holding hands with my spouse as we emerged from the waves as if we were two gods of joy, casting light on the world with our shiny, toothy smiles.

Even on ordinary weekends, I'd find these bullishly persistent hopes rising. Before we went to bed, I'd think that this was the weekend that we'd wake up early, dress in stylish clothes, and go out exploring.

But no such shift ever arrived. Our weekends invariably disappeared into all the tasks of self-maintenance. We slept in, we did laundry, we grocery shopped, and we had sex. It puzzled me that this act of intimacy that had once seemed like the ultimate goal of marriage, its reward and its prize, had become part of the routine of living, a constant, like feeding and bathing ourselves. Before marriage, I'd pictured sex as a special event, the ending to a fancy night out, something that required its own attire of satin and lace. In reality, sex was more of a naked activity, ripe with fluids and smells, but unlike every bodily function I'd attended to in the past, this one was a team effort, requiring so much unexpected conversation: "I can't breathe," "Your elbow is on my hair," "You're squishing me."

When I had been in school and too busy to pay much attention to our sex life, my eyes were always on the clock, my mind constantly calculating: *If this isn't going to go anywhere, then I've got to find an excuse to get out of this cuddle. If it is, then I've got to get things moving so I can be back to my books in under an hour.* Hadi had complained that I was pushing him away, but I ignored his concerns. I was the first crush, the first girlfriend, the first female body in his life. There was no way I'd ever be able to satisfy that much need, that much want.

But now that time was no longer a constraint, I found myself marveling at the trickster that was desire. It pulled Hadi toward me even as I pushed him away. It had driven me to do too much with a boy too soon and then stranded me in a relationship and a life for which I was not ready. Maybe if I hadn't kissed Hadi before we got married, I would have broken off my engagement and stayed in college another year, rooming with Aysar, my future still a bright, blank page.

What made even less sense to me was that I could be so riddled with regret and confusion and still wrap myself up in Hadi, day after day, week after week. How could I enjoy sex, linger in Hadi's arms after, and then moments later fold up in shame and accuse that same intimacy of trapping us together? Was I some kind of animal, using Hadi, and then released from desire, returning to my senses? Or was this alone some kind of proof that we were in love and always had been? Did my body know something I didn't?

One Sunday morning that was quickly turning into the afternoon, I rested my head on Hadi's chest, wishing he would say something that would make me forget all the doubts I'd been having, something that would make me believe once and for all that our story together had been a tale of childhood sweethearts, that we'd been drawn together like magnets.

"Tell me how you always loved me," I said.

Hadi stroked my hair. "I've always loved you."

"Even from that first time you saw me when I was only six years old?"

"I don't know about that. That was before I'd even started to like girls, but I thought you were nice."

I lifted up my head and looked up at Hadi with a disapproving glance. Our lives together could be crumbling, and he still wouldn't just tell me what I wanted to hear. Regardless of the circumstance, he stuck to the facts.

"Okay, but as soon as you liked girls, you loved me, right?"

"I did."

"So when would that have been? Do you remember the exact moment?"

"I know that summer when you guys stayed at our house while I was away at camp, I was jealous that everybody else got to be with you and I didn't."

"So," I said, pausing to do the math. "That would've been when you were going into the eighth grade and I was going into fifth. You loved me then?"

"All the boys loved you then."

"And you wished that you could grow up and marry me?"

"I wished it every day."

"Did you have dreams about me?"

"I did. I used to look forward to going to sleep so I could dream about you."

For a brief moment, the present went quiet, and I could see Hadi the boy pretend-marrying Lina in the park, the small things he'd given me, the captivated way he used to look at me without ever saying a word.

I leaned in and kissed Hadi as if to try on the idea that it had always been him. I plucked away the memories of our families and the pressure of their friendship. I pictured myself falling in love with Hadi of my own accord and willed this revised memory to stick, to become my reality.

CHAPTER 31

※

SHIA HERETIC

For our first Muharram as a married couple, living at a distance from our families, I wanted to do something that proved we were as committed to carrying on our religious traditions as our parents had been. The only Shia community I knew of was in Torreon, Mexico, over an hour away by plane. Ibrahim had stumbled upon a reference to the community in an academic paper, but I didn't have an address or a telephone number, and there was no trace of the Shia community's masjid on the relatively new internet. All I had found online was the number to an Islamic center in Mexico City and the name of the man who'd founded it.

I was still so immersed in my conservative MSA's culture that I truly believed it would be more appropriate for Hadi to call. Hadi loathed making phone calls in English, let alone in his developing Spanish, but I insisted. "You're the man," I said. "I make all the other calls here, and I'm just asking you to make this one, little phone call when you are the one who is supposed to be doing the talking."

Hadi didn't sigh as much as he exhaled forcefully before picking up the phone on his desk. I left the room so I wouldn't feel the urge to tell him what to say. Later, when he came to find me, he had not just the number but also a funny story. "The guy said, 'Brother, I must warn you that the community in Torreon is Shia.'"

We laughed at this glimpse of how the wider Muslim community perceived our tiny sect, and we made all sorts of jokes about what

245

Hadi could have, should have said. "I know, Brother! I'm a Shia heretic myself!" Or perhaps, "All the more reason to go, Brother! These people must be converted!"

A few weeks later, Hadi and I boarded a small commuter jet to Torreon. After a short flight, we made our way to our hotel where the masjid's architect and founder met us in the lobby. I had to resist the urge to rush him with a hug. Standing before me was a Spanish-speaking Baba, the same height, the same build, the same thinning white hair, and a beard just like the one Baba grew after he came back from his Haj pilgrimage.

He was surprised by us, too. He took in Hadi without any facial hair and me without a hijab and said, "I thought anyone who would fly all the way from Guadalajara to come to the masjid would be like the people you see in Iran."

I remembered something he'd said on the telephone, how we were welcome to visit the masjid and remember Imam Husayn but that they were a community of Mexicans and that there would be no *golpeando*, no hitting. Mama's yearly Ashura pilgrimages to Southern California had made traveling for this occasion feel like something ordinary and expected, the very least one could do, but only now did I see how our journey must have appeared to a man in this quiet Mexican town with a Shia community of less than a hundred people who, our host would later tell us, rarely attended the masjid. He must have assumed Hadi and I were spirited with extraordinary religious zeal, the kind of Shia he'd seen in images from Iran, beating our chests and demonstrating in the streets.

He took us out to lunch where he introduced us to his wife and his unmarried daughter. Speaking in a mix of Spanish and English, he told us the story of his parents' immigration to Mexico in the early 1900s from Lebanon. Like Hadi and I, both he and his wife were born to Arabic-speaking, immigrant parents. They, too, had grown up with a handful of other families that shared their beliefs and found each other in this incredibly small pool of "people like us." He lamented that there were no similar prospects for his daughter in their shrinking community. He, himself, had not been particularly interested in religion until a serious car accident renewed his faith in God. During his recovery, he taught himself to read the Quran by following along while listening to recitations on cassette tapes.

That night, we met again in the masjid, a simple but beautiful mosque, complete with arches, a dome, and a minaret. The building amazed me; it was so unlike any of the community centers, converted churches, and industrial buildings we had in California. It had taken a move all the way to Mexico for me to finally pray in a proper mosque.

After reciting our evening prayers as a group, we sat in the large, open prayer space where I counted eight people besides Hadi and myself. We sat without any partition to separate the men from the women, and taking in the scarves loosely draped over the heads of the few women in attendance, their short-sleeve shirts and ankle-revealing skirts, I was glad I'd left my abaya back at the hotel. I was the only woman in the room to observe the Ashura custom of wearing head-to-toe black as a sign of mourning, and I already felt overdressed in my black scarf, blouse, and skirt.

Our host gave a brief speech in Spanish on the significance of the day of Ashura. He told the story of the battle of Karbala and of Imam Husayn's martyrdom, and although the content of the retelling was the same, the story felt stripped down to its bones without the Seyyid's passionate and sorrowful reading, and his frequent pauses to sob into the microphone. Here there was no crush of crying bodies, sitting shoulder to shoulder; no rhythmic poetry following the sermon, set to the percussion of hands upon chests; no Styrofoam boxes piled high with rice and a saucy, lentil *qeema* to be distributed after the services.

Mama would have wanted me to pay attention to my prayers,

my heart heavy with emotion for Imam Husayn, but absent of the rituals that had defined my experience of Muharram, I felt more longing than faith. Without Mama and these familiar traditions, I didn't know what to bring to this day, what feelings, what prayers. I feared that I had gotten married and left home before learning enough from Mama to pass on my language and religion.

Even with our yearly pilgrimages to a community that received a steady stream of arrivals from abroad and that kept Arabic alive on our tongues, I knew less about the Quran than our host who'd grown up in such cultural isolation. What was to stop my kids from becoming just like his daughter, with even less Arabic words lingering around in the corners of their minds, perhaps even less committed to marrying someone who shared the labels that had once defined their grandparents?

My gaze fell on Hadi seated on the floor, concentrating on our speaker, and I took comfort in our shared identity, in knowing that we'd work together to carry on these traditions. In all my doubts as a newlywed, I had questioned my insistence of marrying an Iraqi, Shia—surely marrying another Muslim would have been enough—but now I saw the wisdom of my youthful prejudice. Hadi and I were bound together by so much more than our shared childhood; we shared the same history.

The next day, after the short flight that carried us back to Guadalajara, I spilled every memory of our short visit into a disorganized word-processing document. I wanted these scribbles to become my purpose in Mexico. I had an image of this community becoming my future dissertation, my time in Mexico taking on an instant and tangible source of value. But as soon as I reread my observations, the logistics of doing any further research daunted me. I didn't know anything about doing fieldwork, nor did I have the Spanish skills to conduct interviews, and it wasn't as if I could keep flying back to Torreon.

Ibrahim could turn anything into research. He would have written a paper on just this weekend's visit, but truthfully, I hadn't wanted to reach for my notebook while I was there as much as I'd wanted to mull over what this visit had shown me about my own identity and all its layers. I wondered if this was a sign that I didn't have the same passion for history, but doubting yet another plan for my future felt as circular and painful as my marriage angst. I had to stay committed to this career path. I had to be certain about something.

CHAPTER 32

THE LOVE I MISSED

I'd found an even better purpose for my time in Mexico than research. Charity work. A wife of one of Hadi's classmates had told me about a woman who'd volunteered the entire time her husband had been in school and about how she'd done so much good before she left. I loved the sound of those words, "so much good." It was the perfect antidote to the sense of aimlessness that had beleaguered me since our trip to Torreon, a way for my time here to have meaning.

It was the fall, after our first summer visiting California. I'd hung my head in shame when friends asked me what I'd been up to. I heard a voice in my head saying, "I flew to a mosque in Mexico and took some notes that I don't know what to do with," but just imagine if I could have said I had been caring for sick babies in a hospital, building low-income houses, or working with children in an orphanage. These commitments spoke of renunciation and thoughtful choice. They said, "Yes, you may be in graduate school, but that path is not for me. I've chosen to make a difference in the lives of the less fortunate."

After weeks of phone calls, I found my way to the tall metal gates of an *internado* outside Guadalajara where I'd offered to give English lessons to the girls who boarded there. Some of the girls were orphans, but most of them were children of poverty, taking their meals and going to school from the internado during the week and going home on the weekends.

At the small, metal door to the side of the gate, the director, a brusque, unsmiling woman named Viviana, motioned for me to enter and led me straight to the homework room where twenty-three girls from ages five to thirteen sat hunched over notebooks. As soon as we entered, the girls stood up in front of their chairs and said, "Buenos días," in unison. They wore mismatched combinations of hand-me-down clothing. Their eyes covered the entire spectrum of brown, from nearly black all the way down to one pair of striking hazel, and their hair was uniformly cropped just under the ear. My heart swelled. I had never seen anything as beautiful as the faces before me.

Gabriela was the first to walk away from her table and take my hand in hers. She looked up at me with deep brown eyes, a nose sprinkled with freckles at the bridge, and asked, "*¿Còmo te llamas?*"

I told her my name was Huda and nodded when she answered, "Joya?" I couldn't take the risk of children mishearing my name. I'd recently been informed by a mortified woman that my first name sounded distressingly similar to *joda*, the command form of the verb *joder*, "to fuck."

Following Gabriela's move, the rest of the girls abandoned their notebooks on the tables in front of them and surrounded me. Their little hands reached out for my hands and up to feel my hair, and as I answered their questions about my curls, my laundry detergent, and my funny accent, I vowed to stay with these girls until the day I left Mexico.

What I didn't know was what I was doing in the classroom with the girls. Not only was I an inexperienced teacher, but I also had no knowledge of how an internado ran, what the children were like, or how they learned. During my first week, every time I tried to organize the girls into games to teach vocabulary, they begged me to write things on the board so they could copy the words into their notebooks. When I relented and threw things up on the board, they pleaded with me to grade their notes and draw them pictures that they could color.

But in spite of our slow starts, by the end of the week, English fever had swept the internado. There were exchanges in every corner of "What is my name?"; "How are you?"; and "Good morning." The alphabet song rang through the courtyard. And I was falling deeper and deeper in love with these girls who fought over my lap before class, cupped my chin in their hands, stroked my hair, and caressed my cheek; who performed choreographed dances for me before lunch; and who cried on my shoulder when they missed their families.

At the end of each day, thoughts of the girls stayed with me. Some days these thoughts soothed my own disgruntled spirit, and I floated home thinking, *To hell with grad school. The work I am doing here is far more important*, and other days, I came home feeling heavy and lost. I'd spend my evening hours picturing Mariana's broken soles, Lucia's wild cries after a weekend when her mother failed to come for her, chubby-cheeked Carla asking me if she could pretend I was her mother, and Ariana trying to tape her long, stringy locks of hair back onto her head after getting her hair sheared because of lice. Come nightfall, these images wrapped themselves around me tight, squeezing away all hope of sleep.

But as much as my time at the internado unsettled me emotionally, it quieted me maritally. Being around so much deprivation made me question my right to complain about *anything*. Growing up, I'd shared a home with my parents, siblings, grandparents, and visiting relatives. I'd eaten meals at a dining room table, with family at my side. I'd been educated in private schools, I'd graduated from college, and I had a husband who loved me.

I started to pay closer attention to the things Hadi did. I wondered if they were a kind of love that I had missed. Wasn't it love to irrigate my ears when they grew so clogged up with wax that I could barely hear? Wasn't it love to squeeze out the in-grown hairs on my leg as if we were a couple of grooming chimpanzees? Wasn't it love to wage war against the bands of invading cockroaches that crawled up our drains and into our showers and onto our counter-tops? Wasn't it love to deal with the cat-sized rat that had been living under our stove when it showed up in the kitchen in search of its next meal?

In those weeks, my attitude toward Hadi softened enough for him to recognize the change. "It's like you hate me a little bit less," he said one evening after dinner.

I laughed and feigned innocence. "What are you talking about? I never hated you."

A breath of levity had been blown into our relationship, and with that, Hadi took on a new confidence, a willingness to make me laugh. That fall, we'd gotten new upstairs neighbors, an American medical student, his wife, and their three children. Right away, it was clear that we were not going to be instant friends. This couple embodied almost every stereotype about Americans that embar-rassed me in Mexico. Rather than attempt to learn Spanish, they spoke English only at a higher volume. Their first order of business was to install a huge satellite on our roof so as not to interrupt their access to American football and reruns of *M*A*S*H*. And, in well-dressed Guadalajara, their children often ran around barefoot and without shirts. Our landlord once inquired, "Are your neighbors— what do you say? Okies?"

Sound traveled so clearly between our two apartments it was as if both units were connected by giant megaphones. Because we did not want our new neighbors to hear us griping about them, Hadi and I took up something we'd never done as a couple before—speaking in Arabic. Until then Arabic had been a language solely reserved for parents, grandparents, and our parents' friends. Since we'd picked up the language entirely from our elders, our speech lacked youthfulness; we had no slang, no way to sound under fifty. The phrases that came out of our mouths felt as if they'd been lifted directly off our parents' tongues: "Black on my face" and "Long live the hands that prepared this meal." To avoid this sudden verbal aging, Hadi had started speaking Arabic with an American accent, and this had me in stitches. Rendering such an inflected, guttural language flat was hysterical.

Every time a giggle escaped my lips, he'd say, "You're so cute when you laugh." Then he'd add, "See, I can be funny sometimes."

Hadi grew so committed to keeping me laughing he agreed to spice up one boring Sunday by trying on all his misfit clothing, the too small, the too colorful, the clothes family members had brought back from abroad with random English words and American cartoon characters, such as Mickey Mouse and Wile E. Coyote. This was something he'd sworn off doing because of the giggling fit it had sent me into the last time we'd cleaned out his closet. Now Hadi tried them all on for me, the thin yellow golf shirt that showed his nipples, the too-tight Lakers sweats, the rip-off Members Only jacket from Iran, and he strutted around our room as if on a catwalk while I laughed so hard on our bed that my sides ached and my eyes watered.

And since Hadi had taken up finding ways to make me laugh, the evening he sat me down in front of the television and told me he had a video for me to watch, I was certain it would be a comedy. He'd borrowed *Life of Brian* from a friend last week, *Robin Hood: Men in Tights* the week before. But now he offered a preamble that confused me. "I thought this might help us, but you don't have to watch it if you don't want to."

A blurry FBI warning later, a sex therapist appeared on the screen, a mousy woman in Sally Jessy Raphael glasses with a billowy poof of blond hair, speaking in hushed, soothing tones about becoming comfortable with one's body.

I gave Hadi a curious look. He put up his hands as if to declare innocence and said, "It's up to you."

I returned my gaze to the screen, perplexed. This man could barely coordinate his special occasion shopping, and he'd planned ahead and actually bought this the last time we were in California. My cheeks grew hot. Hadi had voiced his concerns over my lack of interest in sex, but I assumed the fact that we still managed to do it with some regularity made up for my reluctance. Merely considering otherwise rooted me in my place. I was no longer the sole proprietor of all the gripes and quibbles in this relationship, and to discover this just when I thought things were getting better between us was both novel and terrifying.

I'd hinted to Hadi at the guilt I felt over the intimacy we'd shared before we got married. I'd asked him questions like, "Don't you think it's terrible what we did?" and "Doesn't it make you feel rotten that our parents think we were so good when we were so bad?" To his answers of "No. We loved each other, and we were getting married, if not already married in the eyes of God," I'd argue back, "Of course, you don't feel bad. You're a guy."

Hadi had taken offense to my answer—he said it was as if I was implying men had no judgment when it came to sex and that I continuously discounted the ceremony we did with my grandfather when Hadi truly believed that had sanctioned our time together—but I didn't apologize and admit that the real problem was that I was ashamed. That I believed, as the woman, I should have been the one to push him away. I should have kept the big kiss the DJ requested at our wedding to a restrained peck. And, yet, even without me stating any of this, Hadi heard it all.

That evening, listening to Dr. Susan discuss taboos and shame, I felt called out for clinging to things that I knew intellectually were not right. I did see my naked self as dirty. I did see sexual desire as something far more sinister than a natural biological drive. I did steal peeks at the clock to make sure Hadi hadn't spent too much time with my stinky *that*. And I never admitted to Hadi (or to myself for that matter) what I wanted or what I liked.

Dr. Susan introduced us to three couples who'd be demonstrating the points she'd discussed. Taking a look at the average couples on the screen, I prepared myself to be disgusted by their nakedness but found that I was relieved. These people looked just like we did when we had sex. They changed positions and had bad haircuts, jiggly bellies, and splotchy thighs. This was fascinating, a revelation, the adult equivalent to the book *Everyone Poops*.

I didn't make eye contact. I held onto a throw pillow, and Hadi fiddled with the tangled fringe on the chenille throw blanket draped over the couch's arm.

After the video ended, Hadi said, "I hope you don't think I was trying to say anything with this video. I just thought it might be helpful."

The idea that sex was something that could be "helped" overwhelmed me. I didn't want sex to become a point of discussion or an area for improvement. I wanted it to stay relegated to a small, tidy corner of my life where I ideally never had to confront any of my childhood hang-ups.

"I don't know if you get what it's like to grow up hearing all these things about how a woman is supposed to be around a man," I said. "It's hard to go from being told not to talk to boys and not to be interested in sex to, 'Okay, everything is allowed now. Go have sex all the time.'"

"I've never heard that."

"Why would you?" I said, suddenly defensive. "You're a man."

"No, that's not what I mean. I just think maybe you're confusing messages for unmarried women with those for married women. We're married. It's good for you to want to be with your husband."

"I know that, but when you've been told 'no, no' for so long, it can be hard to switch that off."

"Okay, but this isn't just about sex. I'd be happy if you touched me more. Anything. A hug, a pat on the hand. I know you care a lot about where we go and what we do, but for a guy, that's how we feel loved."

This wasn't the first time Hadi had told me this, but I'd always dismissed the suggestion as irrelevant. What could touching him more really fix? Now I wondered what would happen if I listened to Hadi for a change, if I tried to offer him something other than steady proof of my unhappiness.

I scooted in next to Hadi on the couch and rested my head on his shoulder. He brought up a hand to stroke my hair and said, "See, now this is the best. I just want you to let me love you."

"I know," I said and prayed that I'd find the way to love him back.

CHAPTER 33

A FAMILY OF THREE

At the internado that winter, a few of the older girls approached me, first Natalia with her darkly stained two front teeth, then Miranda with her smooth white skin and baby-like whisper, and finally Rosa with her reddish-brown hair and freckled nose. They nudged each other until Rosa asked me, "We've started preparing for our confirmation. Will you be our sponsor?"

I'd told the staff that I was not Catholic, but they simply chalked this up to another aspect of my foreignness. I was an American; I spoke English; and I was a Muslim, which was something like being Jewish, *verdad*? But I didn't know how these girls would take to discovering I was different from them in yet another way. I gathered up their hands in mine and said, "I would love to be your sponsor, but I can't, because I'm not Catholic."

They nodded slowly, curiously. Then Rosa tilted her head and asked, "Then what are you?"

"*Soy musulmána*," I answered, feeling the sense of oddity that had struck me many times before in the girls' company. In America, I was a minority, but here I was a symbol of the United States and the English language.

"Do you believe in God?" Rosa asked.

"Yes," I said, and this elicited no vocal reaction, just a shrug and a dash back to the homework room.

Mama had asked me on more than one occasion if I had told

anyone at the internado that I was Muslim. I'd told her that I'd mentioned it and that they didn't care. The internado may have been a Catholic institution with the girls going to chapel every day and nuns boarding with the girls, but our days were too busy to discuss the faith I practiced at home.

"You should tell them again," Mama had said, "so they can see that there are good Muslims in this world."

But what Mama didn't realize was that the internado wasn't a part of this world. Behind its tall gates, there was no television blabbing on about the ills of Islam, no internet, no newspapers. (That was until 9/11. Then even those tall gates wouldn't keep one of the girls from asking me during a return visit if all Muslims were terrorists.) At the time, however, I would've had to make the issue of my faith relevant because as far as the internado was concerned, I was just Joya, the *norteamericana* who wore the same jeans, jacket, and tennis shoes every day because it made her feel guilty when the girls asked her how many shirts, shoes, and earrings she had.

The internado had done exactly what I needed—it had filled my days and my thoughts with something other than myself. After realizing how behind the children were in their regular school classes, I scrapped English lessons in favor of working with them in small groups on math and reading. Some days, I stayed behind for bath time and for lunch, but this meant I was there long enough to see the director, Viviana, losing her temper and spanking the children or, on one occasion, threatening the girls who did not follow the rules with punishment by electric chair. I was there to watch their bodies freeze in terror while I looked on speechless.

At night, I dreamed of the internado and confronting Viviana. Some nights, I'd see myself in the office, telling her that things had to change. Other nights, I saw the girls pleading with me to do something. In the mornings, guilt would unfurl inside my chest. I'd tell myself that the only way I could be more useless was by not showing up, but still I struggled to stay awake long enough to get up and get dressed.

I was certain that I was unwell, plagued by some kind of worm or bitten by a traveling tsetse fly. When Hadi was home, I'd pick his brain with questions like, "Do you think I could have African sleeping sickness? How about chronic fatigue syndrome?" It never occurred to me that this sudden onset of overwhelming drowsiness might have had something to do with my failure to speak up, with the knowledge that I'd been presented with the first real moral dilemma of my adult life and chosen silence over action.

Finally, I'd get out the door, the hilly walk to the bus becoming more and more taxing each day. A walk that used to take me fifteen minutes took thirty, and as I walked, I'd think about my decision to get married, to give up school, to remain silent in the face of Viviana's ridiculous threats, and these thoughts consumed me with an emotion I'd never had cause to feel before—pure self-loathing. At the bus stop, I'd struggle to catch my breath while an undercurrent of thought babbled below my awareness. *Get pregnant*, it said. *Then you would have a reason to visit the internado less. The girls would love the baby. You could put the baby in one of those little backpack things and cut your visits to the girls down to twice a week.*

Over the last few months, Hadi and I had gone through the last two tapes in Dr. Susan's video series, and although I'd never admit this to him, he was right. I'd needed someone to normalize sex—to separate it from the shame and guilt that had been such a part of my identity as a virgin. None of our issues disappeared—this wasn't a cure by any means—but now that our sex lives had improved, we argued with less tension, less defeatism. I wished somebody had told me to trust that if I gave in to my body more, my mind would get there later; that there was a direct correlation between the quality of our lives in and outside the bedroom; that the more sex we had, the better we'd get along.

Around the same time, I reached the end of my tolerance for the adult acne that covered my face with hard, red welts. It had been a problem ever since I'd started taking birth control pills. Facial products hadn't helped. Switching brands of pills had not helped. I could pretend people didn't notice the red mounds on my face when I was back home because Americans, for the most part, refrain from commenting on a person's appearance. But, in Mexico, a culture where feminine beauty is paramount, maintaining this illusion was not an easy task. Some days I felt as if everyone, from Viviana to my Spanish teacher to women on the bus, had an opinion or a remedy for my affliction. Try oatmeal. Douse each pimple in alcohol. Why is your face still like this? Did you try the oatmeal? Wash your face with a *jabón neutro*. Go see the cosmetologist Maria Sánchez Villañueva at her clinic.

I didn't try everything they suggested, but I did go see Maria Sánchez Villañueva. She happened to be conveniently located in the strip mall a short bus ride away from my house. She wore a lab coat, called her clients patients and her office a clinic, and offered a wide array of services from waxing to wrapping women in gauze to help them sweat off their weight. On our first meeting, she explained to me that cosmetology was much more advanced in Mexico, and I desperately wanted to believe her. But after a series of painful zit-squeezing facials with one of the clinic's many assistants, I began to question the merits of her treatment. I told Hadi I wanted to see if it would help to stop taking the pill.

Months later I still had acne but less, and it delighted me to know that I had a chemical-free body that could now safely house a baby. I nursed the fat-chance hope that I could convince Hadi to try for a baby on Valentine's Day. That would be romantic, memorable.

And it worked. All of it worked. After I found out I was pregnant, I felt as if my body was a sacred vessel nurturing my salvation. My days at the internado were more tolerable because I knew that soon

I'd have reason to cut my hours. Hadi whispered to the baby every night while I applauded myself for choosing such a good father for my unborn child. I followed my baby's weekly development online, doodled little fetuses on paper, thought of names, and longed for the baby who would end all my loneliness, my struggle to find purpose.

Two months later, I saw the first drops of blood that told me that all this specialness, hope, and relief were threatening to leave me. The results of the ultrasound were bleak—the technician found no signs of life, only an empty sac. The doctor said it was likely a blighted ovum, but still he advised bed rest, saying he'd seen stranger things happen. From my bed, I prayed fervently for a miracle, but every time I got up to use the bathroom, I was met with more blood. Two weeks later, my womb released a small sac that I eyed with horror. It was my twenty-third birthday, and my body had dropped what should have been my beloved in the toilet. Hadi tried to comfort me with science, with the cold, hard truth that we'd never really had a baby to lose, but this only made my grief feel unfounded and illegitimate. I was mourning who we had been when we were pregnant. For ten weeks, we'd been a family of three.

My miscarriage happened before the start of Hadi's spring break, and we decided to keep our plans to visit our families in California. I wanted to get away from the sadness that had moved into our house, but it followed me on our trip. There was the loss of the good news we'd hoped to deliver, the loss of the baby as a topic of conversation between us, and the loss of the excitement over our new roles, Hadi as dad, me as mom.

When we returned to our apartment a week later, the sadness was still there—in every place where I'd slept and sat, and where I lost the baby that never was and never would be—only now it was much worse. Before, my sadness had been tied to hope of a miracle. Now it had taken dread as its companion.

I'd have to go back to the internado, to dealing with Viviana. When I'd started to miscarry, I'd called to say I wouldn't be coming in for a while, but I couldn't bring myself to explain why. Saying the words would've made me weep. Instead, I'd told Viviana I had hurt my back because it was also true. Bed rest had left me with a pinched nerve. Her reply stung like an unexpected slap on the face: "Don't deceive me, Joya."

The night before I was supposed to go back to the internado, I lay in bed and wondered how I'd face Viviana. Would I finally find the words to talk to her about spanking the girls and her empty threats of dramatic punishments? I feared being disrespectful. Not only was she older than me (I had been raised to never talk back to my elders), but also the spanking issue felt like a murky gray area. As time went on, I'd seen everyone on the staff, except for the soft-spoken Madre, give a child a swift swat on the bottom for one reason or another, and although I had conversations with a few of the other staff members about alternatives to spanking, I didn't know if my role as a volunteer entitled me to do anything more than offer ideas. I bristled at the accounts of Western feminists traveling in Middle Eastern countries, trying to liberate their oppressed women, and I didn't want to be the one doing what I'd accused them of—disregarding cultural context, exporting values.

In the dark of my room, contemplating all this, my heart did something it had never done before: it fluttered in a way that left me queasy. I got up to get Hadi and found that the few steps to our office had left me breathless. Hadi sat me down in his office chair, took my blood pressure, and listened to my chest.

Hadi was not at the top of his class when it came to his coursework, but he excelled in anything applied, such as his clinical rotations and his surgery class. With the bulk of his academic coursework finally behind him, Hadi had a newfound sense of confidence. It was as if he'd been waiting for the chance to learn by doing, rather than reading, his entire life. This was something new for us—Hadi, the owner of a body of knowledge that I benefitted from; Hadi, the one who was helping me. All this time, I had been so preoccupied with what I gave up to come here that I rarely stopped to consider what I was gaining. One day soon Hadi would be a doctor, answering questions and comforting so many of our friends and family.

Removing his stethoscope's ear tips from his ears, Hadi told me that my heart was racing and that I should skip going to the internado tomorrow and go see his cardiology professor instead.

Three days later, after an in-office EKG, a twenty-four-hour engagement with a Holter monitor, and an echocardiogram, Doctora Gomez, with the strappy high heels and matching beaded necklaces, called me into her office and told me everything looked normal.

"*¿No tiene angustia?*" she asked.

I thought for a minute and said, "No, no anxiety."

Not one of the storms that had raged in my mind for the last two years occurred to me. Not my giving up graduate school or moving to Mexico. Not my marriage. Not the internado or the miscarriage or the unanswered prayers to save my pregnancy that made me question whether God was the wish-granter I'd believed Him to be. In my mind, anxiety was something a person was aware of, a conscious state of unrest. It had nothing to do with the unsettling, dissatisfied whispers that coursed through my body. That was just my life.

That summer, I flew home for Lina's high school graduation, torn between a sense of pride and betrayal. She'd chosen to attend UC Berkeley, the same college where my mother had locked the car doors and turned around before my campus tour began. Only five years later and Mama's expectations had changed so much. Mama didn't talk to Lina about marriage or getting engaged with any regularity. If somebody asked of Lina's availability, Mama said things like, "What's the rush? She's still studying."

As much as I wanted to be done with remorse, this shift in Mama boggled my mind. Lina had been granted the freedom that Mama had raised me to believe was only available through marriage. It was one thing to meet other Muslim women in Mexico, to see how differently they had been raised, but seeing the rules changing within my own family, and after such a relatively short period, filled me with a longing to go back in time.

When Lina gave her valedictory address, all I could see was myself on the stage. Five years ago, my mind had been focused on the boy in the audience, on marriage, but it was because of marriage that today I had to smile and tell my former teachers what a wonderful experience living in Mexico was, how I loved the people, the language, when a different truth hounded me. I had earned a high school and college diploma to become a wife to a man whose career path had swallowed mine. I had nothing to show for my time, no advanced degree, no baby. Before I left Guadalajara, Hadi had found out that he had failed the first step of his medical boards by one point, and the news crushed me. No matter how much he excelled in his clinical work, the academics still kept him down. Now Hadi would have to retake the exam, and later when it came time to apply for residencies, he'd stand little chance of getting through the competitive selection process to get his first choice. Most likely, my graduate school plans would have to wait once again, but what hurt more was the overwhelming sense that progress was impossible for me. I took one step forward in accepting my marriage only for some news, a failed exam or Lina going off to Berkeley, to come along and set me even further back.

That night as I struggled to fall asleep, a haze of unease cast itself over my room. It was an angst I had not yet learned to identify as anxiety. All I knew was that I felt misled. I'd thought following all the rules guaranteed me the scripted life I'd imagined for myself—the accomplished husband, the His and Her degrees, the bright and beautiful children. I had no idea that growing up was not so much the process of accruing a career, spouse, home, and child, as it was this particular journey to reconcile what you dreamed of with what you got.

When I awoke, I did my best to disguise my restlessness with makeup and a hair-dryer, jeans and a new top. Diana and Nadia were coming to see me, and for one day, I needed to pretend I was still in college, to forget that I was married.

That afternoon, Nadia and Diana filled the living room with the kind of laughter that drew their heads back, their long, black, flat-ironed hair falling behind their shoulders. They looked polished, beautiful, and happy. We hugged constantly; we squeezed each other's hands and reiterated how much we'd missed one another, how good it was to be together again.

And then we had lunch. Nothing unusual. Just the rice, kabobs, and grilled tomatoes I'd prepared that morning, but it didn't sit well with me. For perhaps the tenth time since I'd arrived, I was hit with diarrhea. My stomach rebelled when I was in Mexico, and it retaliated when I left.

I spent the rest of the evening in the bathroom, missing out on conversation, missing out on my one girl's night of the year. In between bathroom runs, I sat at the end of the sofa, my stomach cramping, my behind sore, and my nose unable to clear itself of that vile odor.

"Oh, Hudie, are you okay?" Nadia and Diana took turns asking.

"I'm fine," I insisted and tried to catch where we were in discussing Nadia's applications to medical school, Diana's choices of physical therapy schools, their engagements, and when they might start planning their weddings.

My gaze landed on Nadia's and Diana's rings. Their rocks could've eaten mine and still had room for dessert. While it didn't surprise me that Diana had the kind of proposal we'd always dreamed of—the fancy dinner, the walk along the ocean, the boyfriend down on one knee while presenting her with a velvet box—I couldn't believe that Nadia, my sister in Islamic rules and limitations, had gotten her dream too. Nadia, the girl who'd been so focused on school, so resigned to consent to whomever her parents' chose, had met a Muslim boy through her Muslim community. And although they'd gotten engaged the traditional way, with both families meeting and consenting, Nadia was in love. "Oh, Hudie," she'd once sighed to me, "do you ever catch yourself thinking about the moment of Hadi's creation and just thanking God that he exists?"

Listening to Nadia and Diana, I felt last night's thumping ache return. *This is where you should be,* it nagged. *You should be in school. You should be falling in love and marrying someone now. You should be talking about dresses, and rings, and weddings in the present, not in the past. You should've never had the opportunity to get pregnant, let alone lose a baby.*

When Nadia and Diana left a few hours later, I made another dash for the bathroom and then returned to the same spot on the couch, now next to Lina and Mama.

Mama looked over at me and said, "Tummy still making you miserable?"

That was all it took to beset me with tears that captured my voice. Lina brought tissues, and Mama stood above me, prodding and waiting until I finally sputtered, "All my friends are happy, and all I have is diarrhea."

I heard how funny this sounded, and I released a loud, ugly snort that might've turned into a fit of laugh-crying but didn't. This was my life, my body that I could not trust. Over the last three years, I had been no stranger to self-pity, but tonight was a new low for me.

Mama was usually the first person to laugh at an inopportune moment, but she did not so much as giggle. She rested her hands on her hips and released a low, long tsk. "I thought you were happy seeing your friends. Where is all this coming from?"

I grabbed another tissue from where Lina sat on the floor, clutching the box in her lap, a stricken look on her face.

"Mama, I haven't been happy in so long. I just can't take it anymore."

"Can't take what?"

"Him."

"What about him?"

"He's bringing me down. Look at Nadia and Diana. I'm just as smart, Mama. I should be in school just like they are. It's not fair. You let me get married so young, but this . . . this is the age I should've gotten married at."

"But I thought you liked Hadi."

"No, you liked him, and I listened to you. You made istikharas for me before I even had a chance to figure out if I liked him on my own."

She sighed and brought a thoughtful fist up to her chin. "He was so young. I never imagined you'd have problems."

I thought of Mama and Baba's almost twenty-year age gap. That was what had been important to my mother, youth. As long as she'd found me someone close to my age, she assumed I would be protected against the things she'd suffered from: the specter of early widowhood, a father who could not keep up with his children, a man who fell asleep at every back-to-school night.

"Being young also comes with being immature," I said.

Mama shook her head, and I took this gesture of sympathy as permission to say something bolder. "Since I can't get a divorce, sometimes I wish I'd just die or he'd die so at least one of us could start our life all over again."

At this, Lina burst into tears. Mama looked over at her. "Why are you crying?"

"I don't want Hudie to be this sad."

Mama's lips twisted in a tight knot, and her eyes watered. She'd never seen this fatalistic side of me. "Nobody has to die. You can have a divorce."

"What about, 'Out of this house in your wedding dress and only come back in your kiffin'?"

Mama took the seat next to me on the sofa and let out a sad, slow tsk. "You kids always take everything we say so seriously. Parents say things to keep their children safe, to guide them to make the right choices, but I don't care about anything more than your well-being."

It was the same sentiment Mrs. Ridha had expressed to me last year, and with it returned the same untethered feeling I'd had in Mrs. Ridha's company. I wished I'd understood the perils of basing my whole understanding of my culture on my parents and their immigrant friends before I got married. I had shaped an entire world from the things our older generation said, but their memories still held the experiences of an entire population of people. Even if those memories were frozen in time, at least they were of a diverse Iraq, filled with both the rich and the poor, law-abiding citizens and errant criminals, artists and scientists, the secular and the devout—whereas I only knew them.

"I can talk to his parents," Mama now added, placing a gentle hand on my leg.

"I don't want that. I don't want anyone to know until it's official. Not them. Not Baba. We may get over this somehow, but if they know we're having trouble, they'll never forget."

"You don't have to go back. Just stay here."

This suggestion snapped me back into the life I'd left behind, the stuff I had in my house in Mexico and the girls at the internado; even Hadi seemed entitled to some kind of an explanation.

"No, I have to go back. The one thing I promised my girls was that I would not leave without saying goodbye."

"If you are this unhappy, you really don't have to. You can send them something, call."

"No," I said, the helplessness I'd felt only seconds ago giving way to a sense of purpose. The girls would not be back from their homes for over a month, but I needed that time to gather my things and talk to Hadi. "I'll go back and tie up loose ends, and then I will come home."

"Do you want to make an istikhara?" Mama offered, her tone measured and careful.

I thought another no would emerge from me, resounding and clear, but the prospect of having this decision taken out of my hands was so appealing that I paused. If the istikhara came out good to leave, I'd feel not just validated but vindicated—as if God Himself had given me permission to leave. But what if I got to Mexico and wanted to stay? Would I then blame any future obstacle in my life on my failure to heed the istikhara's warning? And, if it came out bad for me to leave, would I, forever, blame the istikhara for forcing me to stay?

"No," I said with renewed certainty. This time, this decision had to be entirely mine.

Mama, however, could not resist the pursuit of closure. Instead of consulting God, she confided in Jidu that I'd been struggling, and the next day, when we were alone in the car, she told me that Jidu didn't like the idea of me getting divorced.

"That doesn't surprise me," I said coolly, my hands fixed on the steering wheel. "No one thinks divorce is a good idea." And as if to drive the point home, I added, "If Jidu thought divorce was a good idea, he wouldn't still be married to Bibi."

Mama shrugged as if she was surrendering to me on this point and said, "I'm just letting you know. You make your own decision."

I said that I would, but I could feel Jidu's disapproval taking root in my mind. An istikhara may not have been made, but still a judgment had been rendered, a judgment that I dreaded having to defy.

✿

CHAPTER 34

HOW TO FIX HADI AND ME

How did a woman actually go about walking out on the man she'd been living and sleeping with for almost three years? Would I ask Hadi to take me to the airport for a tearful and senti-mental goodbye, a nostalgic last kiss? Or would I gather up all my things in a fit of anger and call a taxi?

During my last week in California, I'd thought almost exclusively about how to initiate our breakup. At first, I assigned myself home-work. I read through a stack of self-help books on how to save a mar-riage that were directed to people who'd had previous relationships and gotten married for love and who still complained of infidelity, boring sex, and falling in and out of love with their spouses and in love with someone else. And then I decided to sort out my feelings on my own. Maybe I was meant to lose the baby because God knew we weren't staying together. Now I could go back to school, and even if I never remarried, I could always come back to the internado and adopt one of the girls who didn't have a family. Maybe I'd even meet someone at school, someone who'd accept me as a divorcée. From there, I documented all the reasons I wanted to leave. They reached back as long as we'd been a couple and covered all issues from the big, "You Have No Ambition," to the small, "You Need to Shave on Weekends." And it was current.

Mama was so concerned by my outburst that she booked Lina on the flight back with me, and then she flew out to join us a few days later. Although their ten-day visit provided a much-needed distraction to ease me back into my life with Hadi, this did not keep me from updating my list throughout their stay. "You Have Poor Time Management Skills," I wrote when Hadi refused to drive Mama, Lina, and me to the beach. After all these years of not studying, now, when my family was visiting, he decided he had to study and would need to drop us off at the bus station instead. "You Are No Comfort to Me," I scribbled when Hadi's open arms were not enough to stop my tears the night after Mama and Lina left. Mama had asked me a number of times if I wanted to go back home with her, and I'd told her that Hadi and I still needed an opportunity to talk. But, reviewing my list, I could not think of any greater proof than this final point that we were not meant to be. Movies and television made it clear that your one true love was supposed to be the salve to your every hurt.

I had no intention of showing this list to Hadi; its purpose was to organize my feelings so that I wouldn't lose my resolve during our breakup conversations. For weeks, after Mama and Lina's visit, I brought up the items on my list, one by one, as if they'd only just occurred to me in the course of us talking after dinner, or before bed, or on weekend mornings, but those conversations wound up being soliloquies rather than dialogues. Because of Hadi's passivity, I could not bring myself to say that I planned to leave, that I'd fallen apart during my last visit home, and that Mama was expecting me.

It was on a Sunday morning when Hadi's quiet presence during these sessions became intolerable. I was sitting up in bed, and he was stretched out by my feet, his head propped up on a hand as he listened. No comments. No arguments. No solutions. And, most importantly, no anger. This both baffled and annoyed me. Hadi took so much abuse from me. Where was his self-esteem, his will to defend himself? I snapped because it was time. Somebody had to break.

"What's the matter with you? Don't you get that I want to leave you? And you're just lying there."

And then suddenly he wasn't. Without a word, Hadi got up and left the room.

Anger rose within me. After all that, Hadi preferred to walk away rather than defend himself, rather than say something, anything, that could save us. Was it any wonder I wanted to leave? I had been so good, so patient for trying so damn hard to get through to someone so thick.

I threw the covers off my lap, and in my nightgown I stormed into the hallway, calling out, "You do get that I want to leave?"

"Yes," he said, turning to face me, his expression serious but dispassionate.

"You realize that if I leave this time, I am never coming back?"

"Yes," he repeated, his tone so even that I wanted to shake him.

"So that's it. I tell you I'm leaving, and you don't care. You don't even want to stop me."

Hadi took the steps down into the foyer, unlocked the sliding glass door to the patio, and walked out, slamming the door behind him. From the other side of the glass, I watched Hadi fill up a watering can from the spigot in the wall and carry it over to the plants.

I opened the door and asked, "You're actually going to water the plants now?"

At this, he put down the watering can, stepped inside, and slammed the door shut again so hard the glass shuddered. I stepped back.

"What do you want me to do? You've been telling me for weeks how you're miserable, how it's all because of me. You want to go, so just go."

I didn't know what to make of Hadi's tone. I'd never heard it before—this mix of insult and surrender. I brought my hand up to my mouth and cried because he was right. I had blamed him for everything that was not working in my life, and he was finally angry enough for me to see that I'd taken the most even-tempered person I knew and broken him.

Hadi stood with his hands on his hips. He was not moved by my tears, and at this point, I didn't expect him to be.

I took a deep breath, wiped my face, and said, "I didn't say that I was leaving tomorrow."

In the weeks that followed, I made a number of different lists: Reasons to Stay. Things to Work on at the Internado. How to Fix Hadi and Me. Possible Places to Go for Weekly Date Nights.

At the top of my list of reasons to stay in Mexico was the internado. I'd missed the girls over the summer, and quite selfishly, I missed the way being around them shrunk my problems down into the realm of the petty.

During my first weeks back at the internado, the girls did not fail to deliver generous doses of perspective. First came Gabriela, asking me, "Joya, why don't you have a baby? You don't want one?"

I had no intention of bringing up my own baby angst, and so I told her I was waiting until I was older so that I could keep coming there to be with them. Gabriela locked eyes with me from the old plastic patio table where we held our reading group and in one breath said, "My mom was sixteen when she had me, and she has four kids, and she is only twenty-eight, and she never got married."

When I proposed the advantages of a different timeline, Gabriela was unfazed. "But the Virgin was only fifteen when she had Jesus."

I tried to convince Gabriela that despite this very special example, teen pregnancy was not ideal, but as I watched Gabriela's attention wander, I realized there was nothing I could say that would undo the reality of a world where women got pregnant at sixteen. Gabriela was eleven years old now. Visible through her T-shirt were the signs of developing breasts. Soon she'd have her first period, and shortly after that, she'd reach the age where she said to herself that it was normal to have sex and babies. As I did this math, something clicked for me. In all these years of blaming Hadi, I hadn't given enough consideration to the sheer power of imitation. When I was in high school, I'd constantly calculated how many years I had left before I reached the age Mama was when she got married and then when she had my brother. After my engagement, I'd thought about those numbers again—married at seventeen, before finishing high school, and three kids by twenty-eight—and felt as if my timing was appropriate. I'd given myself more time to finish school but not too much time that I'd fall behind her in child-rearing.

But the biggest dose of perspective would arrive the following week, when Elena, one of our new arrivals, ran away. After Mass one Sunday, she took off, charging down a highway full of reckless drivers, overloaded trucks, and speeding buses to an aunt's house. Now the internado would not take her back. The director believed it set a dangerous precedent for the other girls, but her aunt had called, concerned. She could not keep Elena.

The director asked me to visit Elena and recommend that she stay with her aunt now that the internado was no longer an option, but as soon as I entered their compound of concrete apartment buildings, I realized how foolish this hope had been. Two small boys opened the door to their ground floor, two-bedroom apartment and pointed me toward the kitchen where their mother—Elena's aunt—who appeared no more than twenty-five years old was spoon-feeding her five-year-old developmentally disabled daughter in a high chair.

Elena's aunt asked me to wait for her in the front room, where I sat on an aging loveseat under a framed glass box crookedly hanging on the wall. Inside the box was a faded wedding picture of a once carefree young woman and her equally hopeful husband. A yellowing headpiece and veil that had once been pinned alongside the photograph now pooled at the bottom of the frame, next to the pieces of two broken toasting glasses.

This was not Mama's manila envelope, tidily resting at the back of a photo album, each picture still crisp from lack of exposure. This was not my poster-size wedding portrait, hanging above the fire-places in both Mama and Mrs. Ridha's home, my dress, headpiece, and veil carefully stored in the closet of my childhood bedroom. The same hopes and dreams had inspired all our attempts at preservation, but our respective memorabilia had met such different ends.

Even though I was surrounded by a tower of evidence as to why Elena could not stay, I still played the role I'd been assigned, asking if Elena could join their family of five and listening to her aunt explain why she could not as if it was not already painfully obvious. The next day, I went to the director, having spent all night rehearsing my plea for Elena to be taken back, only to be told that arrangements had already been made for Elena at an internado for *niñas caidas*, fallen girls.

For weeks, I turned over the images that had been seared into my memory that day in her aunt's apartment, the frame of shattered hopes and dreams on the wall, the bedroom with bunk beds where Elena and her two cousins had slept, the tender way Elena's aunt had fed her daughter, the way she avoided directly saying Elena could not stay but that she'd have to check with her husband.

For so long, my thoughts had traveled down two channels, one for all that was Muslim and Arab, and one for everything I'd pegged American, but there was no geography, no identity that promised any kind of a life. All this time I'd been chasing down an American love story that followed Muslim rules when the idea itself was baseless. American culture was not the sole proprietor of any experience, but I'd given it total ownership over love and romance. The only thing that had ever been wrong with how Hadi and I met, or how he proposed, or even me following him to Mexico, was that it didn't meet my expectations, expectations I'd simply made up from years of hearing a single kind of story about love and success. I questioned whether I'd ever truly wanted to divorce Hadi or if I'd merely wanted to force an ending to the tiresome story I'd crafted about us.

That concrete specific was something I felt as if I could tell Hadi—something I should. On our next date night, I sipped a cold sparkling *limonada* and said, "I don't really think about leaving anymore."

We sat in the courtyard to the side of a grand colonial building that had been recently converted into an upscale Italian restaurant. The tent raised above us was trimmed in white lights. Hadi nodded but did not meet my gaze.

I ran a hand along the starched table linens and said, "I've been thinking that maybe I didn't go to grad school, but coming down here and really seeing what life is like in another country was probably way more important."

Hadi reached across the table and squeezed my hand without saying a word. I added, "I don't say this enough, but I'm really proud of you. I may have pushed you to get here, but I've realized that I'm not the one in the room with you taking your tests or examining your patients. I'm not the one who got a perfect score in surgery. You're doing that all on your own."

Now Hadi touched the tip of my wedding ring with his index finger and said, "But I wouldn't have even come down here if it wasn't for you."

"Maybe, but that's not what I am trying to tell you. What I am trying to say is, yes, I helped you with your applications, and yes, I came down here with you, and yes, it was a kind of support, but it was also a burden. I feel like I blamed you for so long that I didn't leave you with any power to feel good about yourself when, really, the things that matter now you achieved on your own."

Hadi brought a hand up to his chest. "But I don't want you to discount what you've done for me."

"Okay, but I need to feel like I am lucky to be with you too. And I am lucky. Because you love me and this is just the beginning for you. You are going to be an amazing doctor. I know it. Your patients will be so lucky to have you, and I'm not saying that because I'm your wife. I'm saying that because you're smart. You remember stuff in a way I just don't. After three years of college and all those As, I remember nothing. And you went ahead and read what you wanted, and it all stuck."

A waiter in a white dinner jacket slid two steaming platters in front of us, with tiny diced peppers scattered like confetti around their edges, and our conversation was suspended. Hadi and I could've never afforded to dine in a restaurant of this caliber in California. The dessert that arrived shortly after was even more stunning in presentation, three flavors of fruit sorbet nesting in a delicate and delicious sugar cage. I cracked into the shell of my sweet confection and thought about the contradiction I had been to Hadi, both a help and a hurt. How woefully unprepared for the task of marriage I'd been. Nobody ever warned me of the gravity of blending two lives together. Nobody ever told me I'd hold another person's sense of self in my hands, that I'd have the power to both build and destroy the life I now shared.

CHAPTER 35

❀
_____

FICTIONS OF LOVE

It was New Year's Eve, and I was ovulating. Hadi and I were staying at his parents' house with our families—parents, grandparents, siblings, and, now that Jamila had two children, a niece and nephew.

I didn't like having sex at Hadi's parents' house, but I liked it even less when it was this crowded. As a young married couple, we had our own room, but given the sheer number of people staying at the house, staying in one of the four bedrooms guaranteed little privacy. But still it had to be done. Now that I'd made the decision to stay with Hadi, I hadn't been able to get pregnant again. I talked to my doctor about our failure to conceive, but apparently a woman in her twenties had to have been trying for at least a year before anyone would take her fertility problems seriously. Sex was my new homework. I tracked my cycles and then pretended I was interested in sex at the end of every month. I'd have to feign desire while we were getting ready for the New Year's Eve party. It was the only opportunity we had to lock the doors and then shower, and everyone would understand that these were the actions of people who were getting dressed, not having sex.

Hadi regarded my newfound enthusiasm for sex with patient bemusement. As soon as I closed the door behind him, he took a breath, puffed out his chest, and said, "I know. I know. You want my body."

We started out on the bed, but even with the door to the hallway and the door to the shared bathroom locked, I felt too exposed; the bed was too noisy.

"Get in the closet," I said.

"Really?"

"Do you not hear the bed squeaking?"

Stretched out on the floor of the closet, I made the unfortunate discovery that its length was a tad shy of our five-and-a-half-foot average. The door stayed open. Above us, dress shirts, slacks, and coats lined the four walls. Our suitcases were crammed in the corner to the right of our heads.

"Do you want to have a baby or suffocate us?" Hadi asked.

"We're fine. Let's just do this."

Lying there with the carpet pressed against my backside, I felt that this too was another one of life's milestones that had not lived up to its romantic image. Conceiving a baby on Valentine's Day, after our first time trying, would have been a memory to cherish, but no, it was my destiny to go about it like this, in the closet, rushed and hiding. This was not an act of love but of gardening. Hurry up now. Plant your seed.

That night at the party, Ibrahim, Lina, and I settled at one of the folding tables set up in the living room. I watched Hadi from across the room as his mom called him back and forth to bring this, take that, repark this car, and so on. He'd grown a goatee over break, and he wore the kind of three-piece suit that was fashionable at the time. He was handsome, sexy even, but something about being in the Ridhas' living room made me restless. It was in this same living room where, as a six-year-old girl, I'd met Hadi, where I'd watched Jamila get engaged, where I'd sat after my first kiss. In Mexico, Hadi was just the man I was trying to make a life with, but here, in this living room, with our wedding picture hanging above the fireplace, so many memories of my engagement rushed back, all the dread and angst, the day when Dr. Ridha asked me if I wanted to leave. Why was I still here? Why hadn't I run when I had the chance?

When the time for the countdown arrived, Hadi was standing on the other side of the room, talking to his cousin. I motioned him over to the table where I was sitting, but Hadi stopped behind the chair where his mother sat next to her friends. I waved at him again, but Hadi stood his ground, shaking his head. On the large television at the front of the room, the countdown began. At the stroke of midnight, I hugged my mother and father, sister and brother. During each one of their hugs, Mama asked, then Baba asked, and then Lina asked, "What's wrong with Hadi?" Only Ibrahim did not comment, and I could only shrug as an answer because I was confounded and speechless. Something had happened. I just didn't know what.

It took every ounce of strength I had not to march over to Hadi and scream, "What's the matter with you?" For the next two hours, I forced a smile while waiting for our guests to leave and while tidying up with our families, but the entire time my mind shifted between anger, indignation, fear, and sadness. Knowing that I'd pushed Hadi away countless other times made the sting all the more bitter. Who knew that being rebuffed could hurt so much?

When the door to our designated bedroom finally closed behind us at a little past two in the morning, my eyes burned and my body craved sleep, but first I asked, "What happened out there?"

"Nothing," Hadi said. "You were over there with your family, so I thought I'd be over there with mine."

My jaw dropped open. "Are you kidding me? What did you want me to do, get up and cross the room just to make the point that I left my family to come stand next to you?"

Hadi sat down on the bed without comment. Memories of our engagement arguments, of his sulky possessiveness over things like who saw me first on our wedding day and what I wore on our honeymoon flooded over me and made me want to cry. "Why? Why did you have to pick today of all days to do this? It's a new year, a new century on top of that, and we just tried to have a baby. Did you ever think, 'Maybe now's not a good time to hurt my wife's feelings'? 'Maybe I can bring up my concerns to her later rather than make our mothers and sisters and God knows who else wonder if we are having marital troubles'?"

I covered my face with my hands and groaned just imagining the rumors. Newly married couples in our community were minor celebrities. People watched the bride to see how she was holding up, they watched the couple and tried to guess if they were happy with each other, and, most importantly, they waited for news of their first baby. When I came home on break, people regularly asked me if I was expecting, and when I said no, they always asked why. To my stock answer of "It's in God's hands," an aunty once asked me, "Are you using something or not?" I could hear the rumors that would start after tonight, that I'd asked Hadi to stand next to me and he didn't, that our relationship was in trouble and that was why Hadi and I didn't have a baby yet.

"You've got me thinking that we're just too messed up to be having kids," I said.

Hadi took my hands off my face and pulled me next to him on the bed. "You don't have to take it to such an extreme. I just saw you over there, and I felt like you didn't make any effort to be with me. It's always me who has to come over to you."

"Really, Hadi? I know I'm difficult about a lot of things, but you're difficult too. Look how much you read into that moment. I was just sitting there because that's where I was sitting."

Hadi put his arm around me. This was one aspect of our lives that was less complicated in Mexico because we only had each other. There were no sides to retreat to where we could complain about our problems. Maybe we would have had more issues as a couple if we'd stayed here, negotiating our lives around our two families.

"You could have come over to me," I said into the curve of his shoulder where my head now rested. "You could've said something, invited me to come be with you. Anything but just standing there, leaving me hanging."

He kissed the top of my head. "I'm sorry."

"Tell me, how come when I think things are better between us, they're not? When will our problems really be fixed?"

It shook me to think that I'd made the decision to stay with Hadi and start a family, but that my renewed commitment had done so little to spare us conflict.

"I don't know what you mean by 'fixed.' I think we're fine. People argue and get over it, and it doesn't have to mean anything."

The possibility of an argument not having to mean anything about us as a couple had never occurred to me. I analyzed every conversation and fight we had, but I did not question my mind's constant dissection of our daily lives.

That night, in spite of the late hour, it took me a while to fall asleep, my thoughts more troubled than angry. I hadn't realized that I'd replaced one ideal with another. I'd believed that accepting my marriage came with its own version of a happily ever after, a place where all our arguments were a thing of the past, where all our problems as a couple were resolved. I wondered how many other fictions of love still lurked in the corners of my mind. How liberating it would be to finally let them go.

CHAPTER 36

---✿---

AS IF BY MAGIC

Guadalajara was the only place I'd ever lived where it was colder inside during the winter than it was outside. A chill clung to the mud walls and tile floors, but this nippy breeze didn't prevent life from carrying on as usual at the internado. The girls still showered and dressed in stalls with curtains that billowed in the wind. They still combed their wet hair in the courtyard. And I still got off the bus in a T-shirt, only to throw on a sweater after I arrived, to brave the draft.

By April, the cold gave way to warmth. At the orphanage, the girls and I now sat without sweaters, toasty but nowhere near hot. I was making progress not just with the girls' lessons, but I also had finally found the courage to talk to Viviana about trying out different discipline methods. I still was not pregnant, but I was far too distracted to be concerned. Hadi had come home from school the week before and called me to the door, his tone as excited as if he had a dozen roses hidden behind his back. He told me he'd been given permission to do his last year of medical school at the General Hospital in Tijuana. We could move back to San Diego as soon as classes were over in June. In the fall, he'd commute across the border, and I could finally start taking classes again. There wouldn't be enough time for me to start a PhD program before he had to apply for his residency, but maybe I could squeeze in a master's.

I'd listened to him with too-good-to-be-true skepticism. After three years of dealing with the university's inconsistent policies, I didn't believe this was any more likely to be happening now than when Hadi told me he was going to try to apply for it three months ago. But Hadi was not the type to get excited about anything before it was a sure thing, and he responded to my doubt with insistence. "This is happening. I'm not the only one going. Two other guys are doing it too." He dropped his backpack to the floor and added, "You can start packing and selling our stuff tomorrow if you want."

"I'm having a hard time believing you."

"I know."

I stared at him for a second. "If this is true, I have to see if I can still apply to programs."

"You should."

I nodded thoughtfully, doubtfully.

Hadi took my hands in his. "Just think. No more going to the grocery store to pay our bills at the register. No more disappearing electricity. No more roaches. No more diarrhea."

Hadi was finally rescuing me, and the pride that lifted his voice was something new and endearing. He deserved to know he had made me happy. I believed this. I felt this, but when I opened my mouth, I said, "And no more niñas."

I wanted the next thing out of my mouth to be, "We can't go. Let's just stay here for your last year so I can be with the girls," but I couldn't say it.

To my surprise, Hadi offered it. "We could stay if you wanted."

Hadi loved San Diego. He pined for its coastal highways and ocean views. It bothered me that given the chance to go home, Hadi was still so eager to please me that he couldn't see through the game I was playing with myself—this pretending I didn't want to go so I wouldn't have to admit how much I did. I released Hadi's hands after a gentle squeeze and said, "No, we should go."

In the weeks that followed, everything that was once so intolerable became precious. Oh, you funny old bus driver you, passing me up on the street. Oh, you grouchy guy at the bank who never smiles at me when I change money. Oh, medical school that wanted a photocopy of Hadi's grade school report cards and junior high school diploma, you I will not miss, but to you I am most grateful. Thank you for giving my husband this opportunity, and for now finding me a way to go home, and yes, thank you for inviting us to your end-of-the-year dance. Even though your formal parties have always struck me as a bit sophomoric, now we'd be delighted to attend to say goodbye.

The evening of the dance, Hadi and I went out to dinner with a few other couples before heading out to the university campus. As we took the steps up to the hall, I noted how formally dressed the Mexican students were. The women wore long cocktail dresses, and the men wore pressed suits. It reminded me of my prom, with my ostentatious custom-made dress and Hadi's rented tux.

Now Hadi wore black slacks and a white button-up shirt with no tie. I wore a fitted top with a shiny skirt and open-toed heels. My hair was not stacked up on top of my head as it had been at my prom, but blow-dried straight and resting on my shoulders. We were a far cry from any "Lady in Red" fantasy, and this was a relief to me, a point of pride even. We'd finally grown up.

As we walked in through the double doors, the pulsing Latin music blaring from the loudspeakers enveloped us. I spotted a Puerto Rican couple from Hadi's class, on the dance floor. The boyfriend spun his girlfriend around, and they laughed before resting their foreheads together. I felt a tug on my heart. They were so beautiful, their movements perfectly synchronous, but how foolish had I been to think Hadi and I could have danced like them, as if the magic of being young and newlyweds had the power to transform us from two children who'd grown up in households where dancing in public was practically forbidden into people whose bones had rhythm.

We settled in with our group at a table off to the side of the dance floor. Waiters came around with beers and with shots of Tequila. Hadi and I were the only ones at our table who did not reach for a drink. As our friends sipped, I tried to resume our conversation as if nothing had changed, but I felt uneasy. I always felt uneasy around alcohol.

A group of the wives got up to dance. "Come with us," my closest friend among them, Danette, said.

I was about to say no when Hadi said, "Go."

I looked at him and asked, "Really?"

"Just go."

I followed Danette onto the dance floor, but as soon as my feet landed on the waxy, wooden floor, they felt heavy, as awkward and as cumbersome as they would have felt in combat boots. Danette and the women with her formed a circle and started to clap and sway, but my legs wouldn't budge. I felt too exposed. After all this time dreaming about dancing, it finally dawned on me that I didn't want to dance in public spaces as much as I wanted to blame Hadi for not allowing it.

I whispered an excuse to Danette and returned to our table.

"You're back so soon?" Hadi asked.

I shrugged. "I felt silly."

He put an arm around me, and I felt cozy and secure, like I did during our quiet dinners together when we ate at the coffee table and watched movies on the couch. Now I understood what a good feeling that was.

"Let's go," I said.

"Are you sure?"

"Yes," I said, knowing that soon we'd be home to our same couch and our same television, but that tonight would be different.

I spent a week preparing for my last day at the internado. I wrote a letter to each girl, telling her how much I cared about her, everything I hoped for her future. I made cupcakes and goody bags filled with candies and small toys.

On that day, each group had class at its scheduled time. While the rest of the group was busy inside with cupcakes and coloring, I called out the girls one by one to take a seat at one of the two patio chairs I'd set up outside the door. There, I gave each girl a goody bag and read her letter to her. Some of the girls blushed with pride, smiled, and gave me a tight hug. Some cried on my shoulder. And then there was Daniela. It would be too simple to say that she cried. When I started to tell her what a sweet and wonderful girl she was, how proud I was of all the progress she'd made, and how certain I was that she would succeed, her face lit up, and then it fell. She rested her head in her hands and sobbed, her shoulders bobbing up and down. I pulled her into my lap and told her I meant everything I wrote, that she was very special and that I would always remember and love her. And then she looked up at me and said, "Ay, Joya, who will love us like you?"

The urge to stand up and say, "That's it. I've changed my mind. I'm not going," overwhelmed me. The girls would cheer, and I'd finally have a grand, cinematic resolution to at least one chapter of my life. But I knew this ending was not only impossible; it was also inaccurate. I'd never been the hero, saving these girls. They'd always been the ones rescuing me from romantic love's grip.

By the time I finished saying my farewells to each girl, I felt heavy but empty all at the same time. I returned to my small classroom and stacked up all the white patio chairs in a corner. No one would be coming up here for a while. In the closet, I organized all the books, crayons, and notebooks, and then I said a little prayer that it wouldn't be long before they were used again. I gathered my backpack and my cupcake trays, took a deep breath, and walked out the door. No last look. No lingering in the doorway. I couldn't.

As I neared the bottom of the staircase, I heard singing coming from the chapel, and as soon as I stepped into the courtyard, I saw pictures and letters taped to every post. To the background of the girls' voices, I walked the perimeter of the courtyard, pulling down each of their letters. Daniela had drawn me a diamond ring. Above it she wrote,

> Joya, I hope you will return very soon because I want to see your beautiful green eyes and I want to tell you more than anything that finally in my life, I found a heart full of love. I love you. Come back soon.

When I had finally made my way around the courtyard, I was standing at the chapel door. The Madre, in her white linen habit, turned to the girls and said, "Let us raise our voices and thank Joya for all the love she has shared with us."

I had barely made it past the doorway when the girls turned and surrounded me in my last group hug. I knew that I would not remember the words to their song but that the beauty of their voices and the touch of their hands would stay with me always. It was this thought of the girls no longer being in my present but shifting into my memories that unleashed the tears I'd been holding back all day. I looked around at the circle of arms that enveloped me, the mud walls, the small wooden pews, and the large cross standing at the head of the chapel and wondered what I could do with my life that would rival the fullness I knew now. Maybe I wouldn't start the master's program I'd been accepted to in San Diego. Maybe I would go back to school to get the skills to work with kids just like these. Maybe I would become a mother who no longer doubted that was enough of something to be.

When I finally left, Hadi was waiting for me outside the internado gates. We went home and finished selling off our last few items of furniture, our bed, our desks, and our refrigerator. And then I stood back and let Hadi pack our remaining belongings. I watched him lay out everything we wanted to bring in the car, study their shapes, put some things in, and take others down. The process took two days, but now rather than fume over how long Hadi was taking to pack, I saw something in this, a gift for visualizing spaces. Hadi's mind held images—the inside of the car, a human body, a computer. My mind held only words; it made lists and told stories. And for the first time in our lives together, I understood that this was a good thing, that our different minds complemented each other.

Hadi and I left Guadalajara at dawn on a Tuesday morning. He drove, and I read street names off the map because I could never find where we were until we'd already passed it. Somehow Hadi made sense of the clues I dropped him, and we got to where we were going. Together.

ACKNOWLEDGMENTS

I've always believed the best thing about being a writer is the company I get to keep. I am profoundly grateful to my writing community, the mentors and friends who have supported and encouraged me over the years. Susan Muaddi Darraj was my first writing teacher and the proof I needed that Arab women can, indeed, write. Neal Chandler taught me to treat my writing like a profession and founded the workshop that connected me to a wonderful group of early readers and to masterful editor Charles Oberndorf, whose feedback has been my personal master of fine arts. Developmental editor Jane Rosenman offered the definitive diagnosis on what was missing in this book and has been an ongoing source of advice and direction.

My writing soulmates, Laura Maylene Walter and Jennifer Marie Donahue, are behind my every publication. Nothing is good enough until Laura and Jennifer read it, and I see them on every page of everything I write. Deonna Kelli Sayed has been a dear writing-friend and also a tremendous resource on bookselling and literary festivals. John Frank, Nouran Hashimi, Margari Hill, Narjes Misherghi, Tracy Niewenhous, and Lynn Ameen Rollins read early drafts and shared invaluable perspectives. Adrienne Brodeur, Saadia Faruqi, Bayley Freeman, Zareen Jaffery, Honorée Fanonne Jeffers, Soniah Kamal, Molly Nance, Aisha Saeed, Sabaa Tahir, and Jen Waite all offered much-needed encouragement and support at critical moments. Faith Adiele and Jasmin Darznik generously offered not just their time but also their names to my project. Ayesha Mattu and Nura Maznavi, editors of the anthology *Love, InshAllah: The Secret Love Lives of American Muslim Women*, published the first excerpt of this memoir and also created the most supportive community for their writers. I hope this book will carry on the much-needed conversation they started. And, I am so very thankful to Aspen Words and Cuyahoga Arts and Culture, with the Community Partnership for Arts and Culture, for their generous gifts of fellowships.

To the agent who finally chose me, Myrsini Stephanides, thank you for representing this book better than I could have myself. Your confidence in this book and in me as a writer has been nothing short of a dream come true. To Maile Beal and others at the Carol Mann Agency, thank you for all your tireless efforts on my behalf. Suzanne Kingsbury, thank you for teaching me how to articulate and share the message in my own work. Liz Psaltis, thank you for showing me how to navigate my way in the world of book marketing. Christina Morris, thank you for my beautiful new website design, and Missy Chimovitz and Mariana Velez, thank you for making my book cover a love story in itself. And, most importantly, thank you to Steven L. Mitchell and all the wonderful people at Prometheus Books, Bruce Carle, Jeffrey Curry, Hanna Etu, Mark Hall, Jill Maxick, Lisa Michalski, Liz Mills, and Catherine Roberts-Abel, for being the change-makers we need in the world. Whatever I hoped to say with this book would be nothing without the champions, like you, getting my work into readers' hands.

Writing a memoir takes an entirely different kind of a toll on a family, and I would not have had the courage to send this book into the world were it not for the unwavering support of my parents and siblings, my in-laws, my husband, and most recently my children. (When they were younger, their support was only made possible through the assistance of many wonderful babysitters. For sticking with us the longest, I thank Emilie Sandham, Angie Allison, and Maggie Sabolik.) A special thank-you to my sister for cheering me on during our nightly chats and to my brother, the dynamic professor Ibrahim Al-Marashi, for not only marking up my drafts but for also always pushing me to situate my work into its wider historical context. To my dear husband, I owe a completely different kind of gratitude. This book has made him privy to thoughts no spouse should ever have to see let alone share with the world, and I thank him for embracing my purpose and vision for this project with such grace and generosity.

I don't know many writers who were not blessed with wonderful teachers, and in this regard, I have been incredibly fortunate. Most notably, Rosanna Little, Dr. Sita Anantha Raman, and Dr. David Pinault laid the foundation for the work I was able to do here.

Finally, I offer my deepest and most heartfelt thanks to my readers, for allowing my words space in your mind. We live in a busy world, chock-full of entertainment choices, and I am so honored that you chose to spend these hours with me.